SOUTHERN BIOGRAPHY SERIES

Bertram Wyatt-Brown, Editor

Samuel F. B. Morse (American, 1791–1872), *Portrait of Dr. Stephen Duncan,* ca. 1820.
LSU Museum of Art, Gift of the family of William Bull Pringle.

AN AMERICAN PLANTER

Stephen Duncan

of Antebellum Natchez and New York

MARTHA JANE BRAZY

LOUISIANA STATE UNIVERSITY PRESS

BATON ROUGE

Published by Louisiana State University Press
lsupress.org

Louisiana Paperback Edition, 2024

Designer: Melanie O'Quinn Samaha
Typeface: Fournier MT
Typesetter: The Composing Room of Michigan, Inc.

Cover illustrations: (*top*) M. O'Connor, *Merchants' Exchange. Philadelphia*, 1840. Lithograph by
J. T. Bowen. Courtesy of the Library Company of Philadelphia. (*bottom*) Portrait of Dr. Stephen Duncan.
Photographed by Mark Coffey. Courtesy of the Auburn Garden Club.

LIBRARY OF CONGRESS CATALOGING-IN-PUBLICATION DATA

Brazy, Martha Jane, date.
An American planter : Stephen Duncan of antebellum Natchez and New York / Martha Jane Brazy.
p. cm. — (Southern biography series)
Includes bibliographical references and index.
ISBN 978-0-8071-3141-1 (cloth : alk. paper) — ISBN 978-0-8071-8291-8 (paperback) — ISBN 978-0-
8071-4272-1 (pdf) — ISBN 978-0-8071-4275-2 (epub)
  1. Duncan, Stephen, 1787–1867.   2. Plantation owners—Mississippi—Natchez—Biography.
3. Slaveholders—Mississippi—Natchez—Biography.   4. Slavery—Mississippi—Natchez—
History—19th century.   5. Natchez (Miss.)—Social conditions—19th century.   6. Natchez (Miss.)—
Race relations.   7. Natchez (Miss.)—Biography.   I. Title.   II. Series.
F349.N2B75 2006
305.8009762'26—dc22

2006004936

For Mom and Dad

+>-<+

CONTENTS

-+->-<+-

ACKNOWLEDGMENTS

I first began my research on Stephen Duncan while a greenhorn graduate student pursuing my master's degree at the University of Wisconsin–Milwaukee. Little did I know then that twenty years later I would still be thinking and writing about this topic, let alone that someday it would evolve into a book. Over the years, I have incurred the many intellectual and personal debts that come with such an endeavor. Numerous institutions and individuals have helped me. Some have been present from the beginning while others have dropped in along the way, but all have made this oftentimes solitary process more communal and certainly far better. It is not possible in this brief space to mention all those connected with this endeavor, so I extend my apologies to the many people who are not mentioned here, but who gave me help over the years.

The Department of History at the University of Wisconsin–Milwaukee and its excellent faculty provided a great environment to launch this project. The department's Theodore Saloutos Research Fellowship and A. Theodore Brown Award enabled me to make my first trips ever to Mississippi and Louisiana. Reginald Horsman and Glen Jeansonne gave me valuable feedback on the first thesis attempts. My thesis advisor, Walter B. Weare, a first-rate scholar, has left an imprint on this project from its very beginning to its very end. I first met Bud when I was a sophomore pursuing my undergraduate degree, and I knocked on his office door in hopes that he would give me permission to take his upper-level course on the New South. Over the years, Bud has been a brilliant mentor in so many ways: he has not only taught me how to be a better scholar, historian, and teacher, but his deep passion for social justice has resonated with me and has brought me more than he will ever know. He gave generously to his students—we were just as likely to have discussions for hours in the classroom as on his front porch, or while he was restoring one of his beloved "classic" cars. Bud, as well as his wife, Juanita (a committed educator herself), have supported me in countless ways, and I treasure their friendship.

While pursuing this project as my dissertation at Duke University, I had the good fortune of a great faculty and fellow graduate students who pushed me intellectually. Departmental and university financial support and teaching opportunities helped keep me afloat along the way. Larry Goodwyn, Kristen Neuschel, Julius Scott, and Peter Wood helped crystallize my thoughts as this project matured. My committee members, Ed Balleisen, Jan Ewald, and Ray Gavins provided first-rate advice that made me think about my subject in a broader scope. My co-advisors, Nancy Hewitt and Syd Nathans, with their meticulous engagement of my work, challenged me to think to my highest potential, and their insight was invaluable. Since then, Nancy has continued to provide wise counsel on a range of matters for which I am most appreciative.

Without the help of the knowledgeable staff at numerous archives, libraries, and county and parish clerks' offices from the Deep South to the Northeast and a few places in between, I might still be navigating the records. I want to thank the staff at the Louisiana and Lower Mississippi Valley Collections at Louisiana State University; the Adams County, Mississippi Courthouse; the Mississippi Department of Archives and History, especially Ann Lipscomb Webster; the New York Historical Society; and the Historical Society of Pennsylvania and the Library Company of Philadelphia, particularly James Green. The Library Company made it possible for me to conduct crucial research in Philadelphia with their award of an Andrew W. Mellon Foundation Fellowship. Finally, the staff at the Center for American History at the University of Texas provided expert knowledge on the collections, as well as boatloads of official yellow paper upon which researchers had to take their notes (the laptop—about the size of a small microwave then—hadn't yet come into widespread use). I am most grateful to the directors of the Center for American History, Don E. Carleton and Kate Adams, for giving me access to what was then the newly acquired and mostly unprocessed Natchez Trace Collection, which has been invaluable to this project. Also, thank you to Mimi and Ron Miller of the Historic Natchez Foundation, who have shared with me their vast knowledge of Natchez history, and to Dottie McGehee of the Auburn Garden Club for important assistance.

As this enterprise slowly evolved into a book, a number of individuals were instrumental in formulating, critiquing, and contributing to this work. They have been generous with their time and talent. This manuscript has benefited from the advice of Peter Coclanis, Ed Countryman, Richard H. Kilbourne Jr., Mel McKiven, Clarence Mohr, Morton Rothstein, Leslie Rowland, Brenda Stevenson, and Amy Young. Delene Case contributed important last-minute research assistance and did so with her characteristic generosity. Also, I wish to thank Mary Lee Eggart for drawing the map in the book, and Mark Coffey for his photograph of the Duncan portrait at Auburn, and David denBoer for the index.

My departmental colleagues at the University of South Alabama—Betty Brandon, Rich Brown, Marsha Hamilton, Woody Hannum, Bob Houston, Mara Kozelsky, Lenny Macaluso, Howard Mahan, Mel McKiven, Harry Miller, Mike Monheit, Joe Nigota, Dan Rogers, and Mike Thomason—have, in their individual ways, been most supportive of my scholarly and teaching endeavors. They also have been fantastic to work with and have provided great humor and conversation since my arrival late in the last century. I have been extraordinarily lucky to have as my chair Clarence Mohr, the soundest of scholars whose friendship and belief in my work has never wavered; his example has enriched this book and my outlook on education more than he knows. Michelle Cagle and Debbie Thomaston of our department's administrative staff have helped me in countless ways. Also, I express great appreciation to my teaching assistants—F. G. Baldwin, Delene Case, Royal Dumas, Dottie Gill, LaToya Rogers, and Kathy Skipper—who made my life easier, thus enabling me to work on this book. Finally, I want to thank my students, particularly the ones who have stuck with me for their entire undergraduate or graduate careers, for making me a better teacher.

I am extremely grateful for the unfailingly helpful and supportive staff of the Louisiana State University Press, especially Cynthia Williams and Rand Dotson, who have made this book a reality. I greatly benefited from the anonymous reader whose close reading offered extremely helpful suggestions that significantly improved this book. Alisa Plant, my copy editor, did an excellent job in making this a far better read, while pointing out those conceptual potholes that I somehow rode over but hadn't noticed. Bertram Wyatt-Brown went several extra miles as series editor with his solid critique, guidance, and enthusiasm for this project. In the end, all errors and faults in this book are mine.

I cannot thank my family enough for the incredible support and love they have given me over the years. My sister Nikki and my brother Tim have been wonderful in their own ways and have been a constant in my life. Many times they assisted with this project: my sister read, reread, and commented on all the various incarnations of this project and did so with a smile, and my brother always lent a hand with the quantitative parts while providing needed levity with countless games of online Scrabble. Both never ran short in cheering me on. Thanks to my sister-in-law Angela Luchini for her encouragement. I come by my interest in history honestly—my grandmother Marie Froemming was a great archivist who saved and dated everything from photos to political campaign material. Occasionally she offered glimpses into her world as a child laborer in a factory and telephone operator during the 1910s, as well as the first time she was allowed to vote in 1920—I regret not asking her more. Finally, my parents each, in their own way, gave up much so that their children could have much; such opportunities allowed me to follow my heart and become a historian and professor, and for that, I am forever grateful. For most of my youth, I chose playing outside over studying and books; the irony of it all is definitely not lost on my parents. They never once doubted my ability to finish this project with flying colors. For all of this and more, I dedicate this book to them.

A number of friends have been with me a long time, even if it is unfortunate that we are geographically scattered. My longtime friend since high school, Lindsay Hammerer, has always been a source of goodwill over the years. Rena Hemlock, Tamara Kibler, and Mary Janet Shinske of the Wisconsin Northwoods buoyed my spirits (oftentimes with spirits) and gave me new perspectives. Nancy Astrike and Joan Davis gave me much love and allowed me to become part of their family—North Carolina is home too. I am most appreciative of Meg Whitaker, Melissa Starr, and Helen Renner—a triumvirate of wisdom and compassion. I have also found great solace in certain friends of the canine variety.

My graduate school friends made Durham a wonderful and very special time: many cheers to Christina Greene, Ian Lekus, Deborah Montgomerie, Kathy Rudy, Tim Tyson, and Mary Wingerd. I am especially grateful for Alan Bloom, Anthony Cashman, Gretchen Lemke-Santangelo, Anthony Santangelo, Colleen Seguin, and Stephanie Yuhl—their enduring friendship and love have meant much to me.

I have enjoyed the years in Mobile infinitely more thanks to friends I have met here: Nancy Grey, Lynn Kwiatkowski, Susan McCready, Laura Spagnoli, Colette Windish, and Chitralekha Zutshi—a circle of much support and dear friendship. One of the reasons I think Michelle Comstock and I got jobs in Alabama was just so we could meet; though distance now separates us, our friendship is truer than true.

Finally, no one can tell me that serendipity doesn't exist. Deep as the ocean is my thankfulness to Hélène Windish for so very much—"juste toi et moi." With delightful humor, she has pored over this manuscript with unmatched skill, and her astute intellectual engagement on numerous fronts always keeps me sharp. But most of all, thanks for making life de-lovely.

AN AMERICAN PLANTER

‑‑►‑◄‑

PROLOGUE

"An Important Crisis Is at Hand"

O n a fall day in October 1831, United States senator Josiah S. Johnston of Louisiana opened a lengthy letter from a concerned citizen that began with the alarming lines: "I am satisfied, an important crisis is at hand, which it behooves the wise & the good of all parties to be prepared for. There can be no longer any doubt, that the spirit of the age, is opposed to slavery." It was as if the author was foretelling the events that would throw the nation into civil war thirty years later. He warned Johnston that "although this spirit is at present in a quiescent state in the U.S.—the period cannot be far distant, when it will break forth in all its energy & strength."[1] Johnston received this letter as the South was still reeling from one of the most significant slave revolts in the history of the United States, which had taken place that August. Aware of the importance of the Nat Turner rebellion in Virginia, the author outlined a plan for gradual emancipation and the elimination of slavery. Yet Johnston's correspondent was not someone with a specific political agenda within the abolition movement. Instead, it was Stephen Duncan of Natchez, Mississippi, who, by the eve of the Civil War, would be one of the largest and wealthiest slaveowners in the antebellum South.

Duncan's rhetoric and political position restricting the growth of slavery was in sharp contrast to the reality of life on his plantations. This paradox was one of many that characterized the life of northern-born Duncan, who in 1808, at the age of twenty-one, ventured into the economically ripe Mississippi Territory. There he would combine the seemingly opposed worlds of high finance and capitalism with southern agriculture and slavery—all of which he made compatible through his nationalistic economic, political, and social practices.

The career of Stephen Duncan shatters the image of the large, insular planter who solely focused on agriculture and his slaves while assuming the role of the premodern lord of the southern manor. Anything but insular, Duncan's economic and political views were national and international in their scope. The cosmopolitan Duncan was an ultramodern master of capitalism who incorporated slavery as an integral part of his overall economic base.[2] Shortly after his arrival in the Mississippi Territory, planting and slaveowning captured his interests, but he also embarked upon other entrepreneurial pursuits, in particular an involvement in Mississippi's earliest financial institution. As the Mississippi frontier gave way to increasing development, Duncan struggled to balance the interests of the state's only bank with the demands of both the local populace and new settlers who wanted to take advantage of the booming economy. Like a vigilant hawk, he watched the horizon for opportunities to expand his wealth and power. Over the course of several decades, he seemed always to pluck the greatest prizes, which included prudent investments in manufacturing, railroads, and steamboats, as well as promising stocks and bonds. Complementing his vigorous acquisition of land, slaves, and various entrepreneurial ventures, he extended a mixture of cash loans, credit, and endorsements to family members, friends, business associates, and members of the Natchez elite. Such transactions produced a steady stream of income that added to his overall liquidity. Stephen Duncan's identity, then, was not only as a landowner and slaveholder in the Old South, but also as a creditor and investor who operated in a national economy.

Though Duncan constructed a diverse economic foundation, slavery remained one of its strongest underpinnings. Without a large slave labor force generating enormous amounts of cash from agriculture, he would not have been able to prime his other endeavors. Likewise, his entrepreneurial pursuits fostered his plantation economy. All of his ventures worked in dynamic fashion to enlarge his wealth and create his base of power.

Over the years, Duncan masterfully manipulated the various economic, social, political and familial networks of the Natchez elite. These nascent networks intertwined deeply with one another, particularly through marriage. Over time, an inner circle of privilege emerged. Through a variety of social and economic strategies, as well as marriage into prominent Natchez families, Duncan first positioned and then anchored himself at the center of this inner circle. The connections he made early in his career helped propel him into the planter elite. Later, such connections helped him maintain his power.

The bonds Duncan fostered and maintained were clearly vital to his success. But the ultimate base of his power and wealth rested not within the walls of the banking houses and the offices of commission merchants, but in the slave labor camps he called Carlisle, Duncannon, Oakley, Holly Ridge, and L'Argent. Though he held thousands in bondage, he barely acknowledged their presence except on a few occasions, as when disease threatened to wipe out his assets. Rarely did he see his slaves possessing any humanity; for him, they were a means to an economic end. He never exhibited any paternalism, and he managed to keep his distance from those he enslaved. In turn, the slaves kept their distance from him as they carved out their own communities of deeply extended families. Slave networks—equally as rich as the white networks that Duncan relied upon—provided daily strength and solace to those caught in the chains of slavery.

Though Duncan owned one of the largest slave labor forces in the antebellum South, his economic and political vision stretched well beyond Mississippi and Louisiana. This allowed him the freedom and opportunity to define himself in a broader fashion, beyond geographical boundaries. As a result, he did not fully embrace the regional agendas of the day. His identity was not strictly northern or southern. Instead, he developed a more complex and hybrid set of loyalties that allowed him to mesh the distinct worlds of section and region that others had created. His life brings into focus the fluidity of personal, regional, economic, political, and social identities during a period in American history when sectional lines and interests are usually assumed to have been sharply drawn. Though certain aspects of Duncan may be more representative of the planter aristocracy than others, his life sheds new light on the multifaceted and diverse nature of the elite slaveholding class in the South. In the process, it illuminates earlier debates that have framed the history of the antebellum slaveocracy and offers an alternative view of achievement of wealth and mastery in the Old South. Stephen Duncan was a nineteenth-century planter of multiple, fluid, and often conflicting identities—businessman and agriculturalist, large enslaver and banker, northern-born and one of the wealthiest southerners, sectionalist and nationalist, deeply connected to family and elite networks in both North and South. He was an American planter.

I

⤙⤚

"TO SEEK HIS FORTUNES IN THE DISTANT SOUTH"

Stephen Duncan's Migration from Pennsylvania to the Mississippi Territory

T ucked within the gentle rolling hills of Pennsylvania's Cumberland Valley, surrounded by the Blue and Kittatinny Mountains, lies one of the oldest towns in the state west of the Susquehanna River—the borough of Carlisle. Here, in this idyllic setting, Stephen Duncan was born on March 4, 1787. His parents, John Duncan and Sarah Postlethwaite, were descended from prominent local families who played significant roles in the history of early Cumberland County. Duncan's great-grandfather, Thomas Duncan, helped establish this frontier area in the 1740s, while grandfather Stephen Duncan followed in his father's pioneering footsteps and became one of the first to settle in the locale of Carlisle through an indenture given to him by King George III of Great Britain. While grandfather Stephen found success as a merchant and involved himself in local politics as treasurer of the county and member of the Assembly, his wife, Ann Fox, raised nine children. Like their parents and grandparents, the Duncan children lived a life of comfort and eventually all married into the established Callender, Walker, Mahon, and Postlethwaite families.[1]

The intermarriage of these families strengthened and reinforced their social and class standing, and such ties were just as valuable as hard currency. The Duncans' connection with the Postlethwaites began in 1785, when Stephen and Ann Duncan's son, John, married Sarah Eliza Postlethwaite. Like the Duncans, the Postlethwaites also played a role in the early civic affairs of the locale: family members served in such positions as county sheriff and treasurer of the local college. Beyond Carlisle, the Postlethwaites maintained financial ties to the growing business community of Philadelphia, which contributed to their prosperity. After John and Sarah married, they had five children in rapid succession—Matilda Rose, Stephen, Samuel, Mary Ann, and Emily—passing on a privileged legacy to all of their children.[2]

However, the Duncans' marriage ended abruptly in June 1793, when John Duncan received a fatal head wound in a duel with James Lamberton. An arcane political argument between the two gentlemen quickly escalated into a deadly dispute. Though some spectators eventually quieted them, Duncan believed that his honor had been damaged during the argument, and he challenged Lamberton to a duel the following morning. As dawn broke and the seconds measured and marked the battleground at the Carlisle army barracks, Lamberton suggested that if either of them missed on the first shot, they should put the matter to rest. According to witnesses, Duncan vowed that "he would never leave the ground until one of them was killed." With that warning and in dramatic fashion, the two men stood back to back and commenced marching in opposite directions. After several paces, the seconds signaled for them to turn around, move towards one another, and fire their pistols at any point they wished. Neither chose to discharge his weapon, and the duelists ended up back at the center mark, standing face to face. Unflinchingly, Lamberton drew his pistol to Duncan's head and pulled the trigger, killing him instantly. According to legend, those who knew John Duncan carried his body from the ground to his parents' home. At five o'clock in the morning, the "Banshee which shrieked at the proper time" woke the Duncans, "who went out to see what it meant and met the body of their son being brought home." Just barely six years old, the young Stephen Duncan grappled with the shattering loss of his father.[3]

After several years of raising her five children alone, Sarah Duncan married the father of her deceased husband's second in the fatal duel, Colonel Ephraim Blaine, "one of the wealthiest men of interior Pennsylvania at that day," on September 20, 1797. After their marriage, they continued to live in Carlisle and at Blaine's estate in Middlesex, where they reared the Duncan children as well as their own son, Ephraim.[4]

While growing up in the Blaine-Duncan household, the young Stephen Duncan received the standard preparatory schooling for his day. Later, he fulfilled familial roles and expectations by attending Carlisle's institution of higher learning, Dickinson College. The expectations for Duncan were high. His grandfather and namesake helped found the school and served as a trustee of the college as well as its preparatory grammar school. Honoring the family connection with Dickinson, Stephen matriculated there, following a general course of classical education.[5]

While Stephen pursued his education at Dickinson, tragedy again struck his family. In the winter of 1804, the swiftly moving waters of the family mill swept away and drowned the Blaines' young son, Ephraim, at their Middlesex estate. Shortly afterwards, on February 18, 1804, Colonel Blaine died, leaving Sarah Duncan Blaine, at the age of forty-five, widowed once again. Emotionally unable to live in the homes where she and Blaine had resided, Sarah and her daughters—Matilda, Emily, and Mary Ann—moved to Philadelphia. There they settled into a fashionable home that Colonel Blaine had purchased shortly after the Revolution.[6] In the ensuing years, Sarah, Matilda, and Emily formed the Duncan family household at 357 Walnut Street, while Stephen, Samuel, and Mary Ann ventured forth on their separate ways.

Following his graduation from Dickinson in 1805, Stephen moved to Philadelphia to be closer to his mother and sisters. But a desire to be with his family was not the only factor that pulled him to Philadelphia: he also wanted to study medicine at the University of Pennsylvania under the renowned Benjamin Rush. (A friend of Duncan's grandfather, Rush was also a founder and trustee of Dickenson College.) Like most aspiring physicians of that time, Duncan trained mainly by apprenticeship and did not actually graduate from the university.[7]

With his mother and sisters comfortably ensconced in Philadelphia and his childhood homes of Carlisle and Middlesex only a tragic memory, Stephen Duncan left Pennsylvania in 1808, at the age of twenty-one, for the unknown lands of the Natchez District in Mississippi.[8] Many stories circulate as to why he left for the Old Southwest, but none can be substantiated. There were several plausible preconditions for his migration: he had finished his education, his mother and sisters were financially comfortable, and he was unmarried. But a more compelling factor pulled him to the region: family members had already settled and found some measure of success in the Mississippi Territory. Duncan knew from his relatives' experience that this area was a new frontier full of economic opportunities. As one of his contemporaries later wrote, Duncan left a "quiet home in the old commonwealth of Pennsylvania to seek his fortunes in the distant South."[9]

By no means was Duncan unique in wanting to take advantage of the region's economic potential. From the late eighteenth century to the antebellum period, over half a million Americans from New England, the Mid-Atlantic, the

Upper South, and the Southeast ventured into the area known as the Old Southwest, which eventually would be carved into the states of Alabama, Arkansas, Louisiana, Mississippi, and Tennessee. The Mississippi Territory dominated this vast geographic expanse and was marked by a rich history, particularly of its native populations. As white Europeans from Spain, France, and Great Britain invaded, explored, and alternately laid claim to the region, they decimated the indigenous populations, enabling white settlers from both Europe and the mainland American British colonies to stake their ground in the Old Southwest.[10] As the three European empires wrested control of the region from one another over the course of the eighteenth century, the white settlers, particularly the British, carved out markets in the fur, livestock, timber, and indigo trades. Despite the growing economic activity, small frontier villages still dotted the Natchez District. Later, as Spain gained control of the area, these villages grew as generous land grants from the Spanish government attracted larger numbers of settlers.[11]

These vast lands slipped out of Spanish hands a mere sixteen years later, in 1795, when Spain agreed to cede to the newly formed United States the area east of the Mississippi River above the thirty-first parallel, along with navigation rights on the river and the right of deposit at New Orleans. In 1798, Congress created the Territory of Mississippi and officially opened it for settlement under American governance.[12] Even so, unsurveyed government land created intense boundary disputes. Further complicating settlement were people who held British and Spanish land grants. As historian Robert V. Hayes aptly writes, "Land claims overlapped like shingles on a roof." In spite of these political difficulties, settlers poured into the area, lured by new and abundant economic opportunities.[13]

For the most part, early settlers—such as Stephen Duncan—migrated into distinct geographic areas of the Old Southwest, such as the Mississippi and Red River Valley or the Natchez District. Unlike the Old Northwest Territory, where forced Indian removal cleared the way for white settlers, the population of the southern frontier consisted of pockets of white settlements around the established presence of Native American Indians and their villages. (However, forced Indian removal quickly became policy in those geographic areas beginning in the earlier nineteenth century.) Of these settlements, the Natchez District received the greatest influx of migrants.

Around 1800, the city of Natchez enjoyed healthy river traffic and merchant activity. The only significant place of river trade between New Orleans and

Cincinnati, it supplied the Crescent City with such goods as lumber and naval products. Regular steamboat service—the first of its kind on the Mississippi River—connected Natchez and New Orleans, which made Natchez an integral part of the commercial life of the lower Mississippi Valley. Merchants in Natchez boasted annual net returns of $50,000, while planters produced 1.2 million pounds of cotton and nearly the same amount of tobacco. What began as a small frontier town on the river eventually became a critical link between the territory's farms and plantations and a range of commercial markets. But in spite of its economic vitality, the city grew slowly. In 1810, the population of Natchez totaled 1,684 inhabitants; by 1820, it had grown only to 2,184. Meanwhile, other towns along the river, such as Memphis and Louisville, began expanding at a far faster rate. As the antebellum era began to unfold, the significance of Natchez as a commercial center faded. Tensions between planters and merchants as well as debtors and creditors also became evident, which caused strains within the city; but some contemporaries still viewed the city of Natchez as a place of opportunity. Unlike the city of Natchez, the Natchez District exploded with settlers. Between 1800 and 1810, its population quadrupled from 7,412 to 29,000 inhabitants. A similar pattern emerged in the Mississippi Territory. By the end of the eighteenth century, the Natchez District, a chess piece in a century-long game amongst three empires, was populated with whites who depended on an ever-increasing force of black slaves to make the region profitable. Slowly, the Natchez frontier of decades past began to fade.[14]

Before Stephen Duncan left Pennsylvania, he might very well have been aware of the challenges and abundance that lay in Mississippi, where family members had already staked their claim. One family connection to the area was through his aunt, Martha "Patty" Callender Duncan. Her father, Captain Robert Callender of Carlisle, had received from King George III a land grant near Natchez in 1768, comprised of two thousand acres sixty miles below "the Natchez at the great Cliffs and fifteen Miles above the River Rouge on the River Mississippi." Commenting upon the condition of the tract, one of Callender's sons-in-law, General William Irvine, wrote, "I have enquired at [sic] officers and other intelligent men who have seen it all agree it is very valuable."[15]

Like many other citizens who received eighteenth-century land grants, legal and political obstacles prevented the Callenders from developing their land. The Louisiana Purchase of 1803 fully cleared the way for settlement and development.[16] With a more hopeful outlook, the Duncan family's interest in settling the tract grew. It was suggested to another of Callender's sons-in-law,

Thomas Duncan, that cousin Jesse Duncan, who also lived in Pennsylvania, settle the land and "seek his fortune in this Country," though it appears that this plan never materialized. The Callender land tract might have influenced Stephen Duncan to migrate to the South, but it is unclear whether or not he originally settled there. A second family connection to the region was through another cousin, also named Stephen Duncan, who migrated to Louisiana and operated a plantation on Bayou Teche in St. Mary's Parish until a decade before the Civil War.[17]

However, Stephen Duncan's most valuable family ties to the region were through his maternal uncle, Samuel Postlethwaite. It was Samuel who provided Stephen with priceless introductions to the nascent economic and social networks of Natchez. Postlethwaite's journey to the region was circuitous: he left Carlisle in 1800 and traveled downriver on his own flatboat to Lexington, Kentucky, where he became a merchant. After exploring the Natchez District in 1802, he decided to remain in the town of Natchez, where he eventually opened a store. Taking advantage of his Pennsylvania connections, Postlethwaite soon engaged in commerce with the very well-known Philadelphia merchants Thomas and John Clifford, who handled trade between their city and New Orleans. With Postlethwaite's business beginning to flourish, his brother Henry joined him in his venture around 1810.[18]

Off to a prosperous start, Samuel Postlethwaite became a fixture in the Natchez community. He cinched his place among the local elite in 1805 when he married Ann Dunbar, daughter of the prominent Sir William Dunbar, one of the earliest settlers and wealthiest planters of the Natchez region. Dunbar's extensive business connections stretched beyond Natchez to the East Coast and across the Atlantic to Liverpool, England, where he forged relationships with George Green of Green, Wainwright, & Company, and George Salkeld of Barclay, Salkeld, & Company. Samuel Postlethwaite's propitious marriage boosted him financially, and he soon began to invest in plantations and slaves. At the same time, it placed him at the nexus of Natchez's social and economic networks. His success reached its pinnacle when he helped found the Bank of the Mississippi in 1809.[19]

Thus, Stephen Duncan had family already successfully in place in southwestern Mississippi when he set out for the Natchez District in 1808. Reaching the city by boat, he saw what had captured the attention of others before him— the town of Natchez perched high on a hill overlooking the Mississippi River, which gently hugged the bluff and riverfront landing. Below the cliff lay

Natchez-under-the-Hill, one of the most vibrant pockets of gambling and prostitution along the river. Upon Duncan's arrival, locals immediately cautioned him about this area and particularly the Kentucky Tavern, which newcomers frequented in spite of its reputation. Before he had even disembarked, his boat's captain "hailed [him] in a stentorian voice" and warned, "Duncan don't go to that Kentucky Tavern; it is a damned rascally place."[20]

With the help of Samuel Postlethwaite, Duncan quickly began to integrate himself into Natchez society. He filled his days by practicing medicine; in the evenings, he involved himself in the local social scene, where he found enjoyment in the Natchez Dancing Assemblies, an elite club. Eventually he became manager of the club, which proved to be fertile ground for forging some of his most significant social and economic relationships.[21]

Within a few years, Duncan secured his place within the nascent power structure of Natchez through his courtship of Margaret Ellis, whose grandfather, Richard Ellis, had pulled up the family's Virginia roots when lured with a Spanish land grant to Louisiana's Pointe Coupee Parish in the 1760s. Serious flooding three years in a row devastated Ellis's agricultural pursuits, prompting him to secure a new land grant farther north, in an area which became known as Ellis Cliffs. Here, just prior to the outbreak of the Revolution, he built the family homestead, Laurel Hill, and reared three children—all of whom eventually married into prominent local families. It was near Ellis Cliffs that son Abram Ellis and his wife, Margaret Gaillard, built their plantation and raised their two children, Nancy and Margaret. Over the years, young Margaret had a number of suitors; as her sister scrawled on one of Laurel Hill's walls, "Sister Peggy have had Mister Hunt for a sweetheart and Mister Elliot and Mr. Simson." In the end, she cast her fate with Stephen Duncan, and the couple married on September 19, 1811.[22]

To what extent the Duncan's marriage could be characterized as companionate is not known, but it was undeniably a lucrative economic contract that benefited Stephen Duncan, as well as the Ellis family, both socially and financially. Duncan was instantly linked to a plethora of the local elite: his father-in-law's sister, Mary Ellis, married Captain Benjamin Farar, whose family helped settle the area. Their daughter, Anna Farar, eventually married Dr. William Newton Mercer, who became an integral part of Duncan's social and economic network. Another aunt-in-law, Martha Ellis, married Stephen Minor, president of the Bank of the Mississippi, whose family also helped to settle Natchez. In 1813, Duncan's sister-in-law, Nancy, married Thomas Butler, an enslaver, Federal judge, and U.S. congressman. Butler had migrated from Carlisle around the same time as Duncan and had also been befriended by Samuel Postlethwaite. Indeed, it may have been through Thomas Butler that Stephen Duncan first met Margaret Ellis. Duncan and Butler might even have known each other in their childhood home of Carlisle, where they might have discussed their impending journeys to the Old Southwest. Until Butler's death in 1847, he and Duncan remained the best of friends and confidantes as well as economic associates.[23]

Shortly after Duncan's marriage, his medical practice gave way to agricultural and slaveowning concerns. Some of the first seeds Duncan sowed were on Margaret Ellis's dowry lands, located on the Homochitto River. With no prior experience as a planter, Duncan learned about agriculture and slave management when both he and brother-in-law Thomas Butler assisted with affairs on the Ellis family plantations. The strong bond between the two men was tested when Butler and his family moved sixty miles south of Ellis Cliffs, near St. Francisville, Louisiana. There Butler built the Cottage plantation, leaving Duncan to look after his 2,000-acre Homochitto plantation in Mississippi. A typical example of Duncan's role in Butler's affairs can be seen in 1814, when he advised Butler to hire a certain overseer and "his Negro boy (a good plough boy and an excellent cotton picker)" for a salary of $500 per year; he also advised Butler to buy "good wholesome meat 25 lbs coffee & 50 lbs sugar—bed & bedding," but only if cotton commanded twelve cents per bale. In fact, Duncan handled Butler's business so frequently that some members of the white community thought he was Butler's agent—a claim that he had to deny in writing on various occasions.[24]

Though his newly acquired land and managerial roles required great attention, Duncan also gave consideration to his family. He and his wife continued to nurture familial bonds both near and far. Meanwhile their own family took on a new shape with the birth of their first child, John Ellis, on August 3, 1812. Two years later, Margaret became pregnant with their second child. With great anticipation of the birth, Thomas Butler predicted that "John's expected Sister may be as beautiful as John himself." On July 14, 1814, Sarah Jane Duncan arrived. Butler was soon able to judge the infant's beauty for himself; as they had done regularly prior to their children's birth, the Duncans undertook the two-day trip to St. Francisville to visit the Butlers, with whom they remained extremely close.[25]

Stephen and Margaret also made an effort to stay connected with relatives in the North, frequently traveling to the Duncan-Blaine homestead in Philadelphia. Wanting to see her brother, sister-in-law, and nephew but unable to do so because of the War of 1812, Emily Duncan declared to Margaret, "Brother and you have so often disappointed us that we should give up all hopes of seeing you." She remained optimistic, however, that the "prospect of *Peace* will revive every hope" of a family visit. Meanwhile, Stephen's brother Samuel relocated to Natchez during the mid- to late 1810s. Samuel, a graduate of Dickinson College and a physician, quickly purchased "a most desirable tract of land . . . [that] had [produced] the finest crop in the county." Because both of her sons had moved to Natchez, Sarah Blaine considered migrating to Mississippi herself, which as Stephen recalled, would "only be with a view of being near us."[26]

Due to the proximity of relatives in the South on both sides of the family, the Duncans enjoyed the comforts of close family ties, which broke the isolation that so often characterized plantation life. To help alleviate her seclusion, and perhaps to hold on to her own identity and independence, Margaret visited friends or relatives in Natchez, sometimes going to town without her husband. On one such occasion, Duncan remarked, "Margaret is still in the neighbourhood of Natches. . . . I am at home honourable [*sic*] . . . playing overseer." Though living some distance away, Margaret Ellis remained close to her sister Nancy. She also forged friendships with Stephen's sisters, creating a meaningful long-distance bond with them. Matilda Duncan deeply regretted her inability to see her sister-in-law due to her mother's illness, lamenting, "I never had my heart fixed so much on anything as visiting you." But just as Matilda, Emily, and Mary Ann Duncan began to nurture their relationships with their sister-in-law, sadness struck the family when Margaret Ellis died during a yellow fever outbreak in 1815.[27]

Faced with caring for his young son and infant daughter alone, Duncan turned to his relatives, who subsequently raised John and Sarah Jane to adulthood. At first, the children lived with the Butlers in St. Francisville as Duncan traveled and developed his lands. Eventually, his sister Emily reared the two children at the family homestead in Philadelphia.[28]

Duncan placed an extraordinarily high value on his family and remarked on many occasions how miserable he was without them. "I wish I could see my dear little children," he bemoaned in a note to Butler. "I am really more anxious than I can describe to you . . . a thousand kisses for my dear little children." Yet Duncan failed to make any arrangements so that his children could live with him. Compounding his anguish even more was his inability to come to terms with the death of his wife. Though he busied himself with getting his planting operations underway, he was never quite able to escape his past; as he finally conceded, "In truth, I am heartily tired of the life I have led the last two years. I enjoyed nothing like rest, solid happiness and the more I reflect on the subject the more dissatisfied I am." Wanting desperately to alter his circumstances, he nonetheless avoided making a hasty decision, as he believed in the "necessity of extreme caution . . . [when] making a change."[29]

While adjusting to life without his wife and children, Duncan pursued his cotton and sugar plantation interests; in addition, he regularly oversaw Butler's Homochitto operations. With Margaret's death, he received more land through the legacy bequeathed to her from her maternal grandfather, Isaac Gaillard. Duncan slowly continued to build his Homochitto and Walnut Grove planta-tions. With relative Benjamin Farar, he also owned a half interest in nearby Chapitoulas plantation.[30]

Though Duncan had a growing agricultural domain, the early years pre-sented challenges. In 1817, he predicted that his plantation would be able to pro-duce 250 hogsheads of sugar the following year, but the cane died in the fields and his crop prospects were accordingly bleak. With ninety more arpents un-der cultivation than the previous year, Duncan noted that even the "most favourable season . . . cannot make us more than 200 hhds." In spite of such difficulties—as well as a smallpox epidemic which swept through the slave quarters—he continued to plan for internal improvements to be made on his plantation. He wrote Butler that he hoped to "extend [his] canal to the Lake, or to the Bayou emptying into the Lake," so that the following year "we can make brick & build a sugar house, negro cabbins—and the year after, a dwelling house."[31] While conveying in detail the grand plans for his plantation, Duncan was not loquacious about the virulent smallpox epidemic that decimated the lives of his slaves. To remain silent on such subjects was typical of Duncan, re-vealing a chilling indifference to the humanity of those he enslaved.

In contrast, Duncan frequently talked about the men he hired to manage his slave force; at times, he was obsessed with his overseers. In his estimation, they did not always come up to his standards. "My overseer is about the poorest Devil you ever saw," Duncan noted with exasperation, continuing, "He is not actually worth his hominy & Salt. . . . I would be just as well without him for I now have the whole weight on my own shoulders."[32] The fact that Duncan felt that he had to work the land was not a new concept to him; during the early years of his agricultural pursuits, he worked the plantations along with his slaves. As his friend William J. Minor recalled, "The first crop of cotton [Duncan] ever grew, he ginned with his own hands . . . the first crop of sugar he ever made, [he] worked as a hand every night at his own kettles." As Duncan himself once stated after a rainstorm, "I shall work like a Turk now, to stir the ground while it is in order."[33] Like many who did not inherit a situation that automatically exempted them from such labors, Duncan appears to have been initially a hands-on planter and slave manager, working side by side with those he enslaved. As his holdings became larger, so did his slave force, and Duncan's presence in the fields faded.[34]

The racial context in which Duncan lived during his first decade in Natchez was not totally unfamiliar to him, for he had witnessed slavery in Pennsylvania. In spite of the gradual northern emancipation that followed the American Revolution and the Pennsylvania abolition act of 1789, slavery remained a fixture in Pennsylvania, albeit a declining one. During the years of Duncan's childhood, whites enslaved almost four thousand Africans and African Americans in the Keystone State. By the time Duncan headed for the Mississippi Territory in 1808, however, the number of slaves had dwindled to 795. As an institution within Pennsylvania, slavery was most firmly rooted in the area of Duncan's childhood home, including Cumberland and the other counties that bordered the southern slaveholding states of Maryland and Virginia. By 1810, Cumberland and its two neighboring counties held half of the state's slave population. Indeed, Duncan's own stepfather, Ephraim Blaine, owned or traded slaves in Pennsylvania. Thus the institution of slavery was not foreign to him, although the magnitude of its southern incarnation dwarfed what he had seen in Pennsylvania.[35]

As the 1810s drew to a close, Duncan held over seventy-three slaves on his plantation along the Homochitto River, which firmly established him within the higher echelons of the white southern aristocracy. Also part of this growing elite was his brother-in-law, Thomas Butler, who owned seventy-nine slaves on a nearby plantation. Because the Butler and Duncan plantations shared a common denominator—land inherited from their father-in-law—and were in close proximity to one another, slaves frequently moved of their own accord between the two plantations. This demonstrates some level of slave agency, of which their white enslavers remained acutely aware. Shortly before her death, Margaret Ellis Duncan received a letter from her sister Nancy, asking, "I wish if you could ascertain which of the Negroes belong to us[,] you would let me know."[36] The slaves' fluid movements between the plantations almost certainly allowed them to maintain their kinship and friendship bonds across plantation lines, visiting one another as they took advantage of Duncan and Butler's over-lapping management of these properties.

The movement that characterized slave life on these plantations could be banned or broadened in an instant by either Nancy or Margaret, reflecting that fact that power over slaves was not exclusively masculine. In one case, Nancy instructed Margaret to inform a Butler slave named Diana, who was visiting on the Duncan place, that "her master says she may stay at Papa [*sic*] till she is better." At the same time, she requested that Diana's daughter, Hester, be brought back to the Butler plantation. Surprisingly, however, Nancy asked her sister to inquire whether Diana "would have any objections to hesters coming down here I don't wish to send for her [unless] she is willing. . . . H. is her only child."[37] The sisters' correspondence suggests their flexible mastery over slaves. It may also be reflective of Stephen Duncan's own style of slave management and philosophy at this time, as he used a more flexible system of control to extract greater work from his slaves.

Within a decade of his arrival in Natchez and with the help of family connections and a propitious marriage, Stephen Duncan had achieved planter status.[38] While comfortable within this niche, he did not tie himself solely to agriculture; instead, he sought to diversify his economic base. To this end, he quickly took advantage of other financial opportunities that presented themselves. In 1818, along with forty-one area planters and merchants, he chartered the Natchez Steamboat Company. This company existed "for the exclusive purpose of purchasing, or building and equipping one or more Steam Boats *at Natchez*." Duncan invested two thousand dollars in the company—a considerable sum at this time—and received twenty shares in it, becoming one of nine investors who owned a controlling interest on the day of its inception.[39] With the subscription of stock completed, the Natchez Steamboat Company prepared to engage in commerce between the two port cities of New Orleans and Natchez. At the company's command were the steamboats *Vesuvius* and *New Orleans*, both built under Robert L. Livingston and Robert Fulton. However, by the time the company purchased these vessels, both were in extremely poor shape; one eventually sank a year later.[40]

Though Duncan's shipping venture turned out to be a near-total loss, his other investments at this juncture were almost literally golden, as he had strong connections to the Territory's only banking institution. At the helm of the Bank of the Mississippi sat Samuel Postlethwaite, who served as its president from 1815 to 1825. This vital familial tie provided Duncan with a perfect entrée into the state's only financial institution, and he purchased his first shares of its stock in 1816.[41]

For Stephen Duncan, the early years of the nineteenth century were ones of hope and promise, at times overshadowed by grievous personal losses. Yet he forged ahead, not seeming to dwell on the past or his misfortune to any great extent—a characteristic pattern that would be evident over the coming years. Even as he grappled with his wife's death and the subsequent distance between himself and his children, he chose to remain in Natchez, carefully laying the foundation upon which he would realize his base of power.

2

---><-<-

LAYING THE FOUNDATIONS OF MASTERY

Land, Slaves, Capital, and the Network of Elites

As the dawn of the antebellum era crept over the ever-changing land-scape of the nation, hints of monumental economic and social change could be glimpsed on the horizon. Slavery, race relations, the expanding economy, and growing sectionalism all loomed as pressing issues. Nonetheless, the future seemed to hold much promise for Stephen Duncan. During the 1820s, he continued to pursue his agricultural endeavors, dramatically increasing the number he enslaved and building the family fortune even as he explored other entrepreneurial avenues. It soon became evident that he would not depend solely on agriculture and slaves to produce the family's wealth, but rather on a variety of revenue-producing activities. Perhaps Duncan's greatest assets in the 1820s were related to the banking industry. His involvement in the Bank of the State of Mississippi provided him, at the very least, with a power structure from which he operated. This created new bonds while reinforcing already existing ones with the economic, social, and familial networks of Natchez. These connections were priceless, helping to catapult Duncan to a position of power and prominence by the close of the decade.

Though his business interests were diverse, Duncan structured his yearly calendar around agricultural concerns, gradually settling into an annual plantation routine. Following each spring planting, he gravitated toward the cooler climate of the North. From the spring through early fall, he stayed in Philadelphia, Carlisle, and Saratoga to escape the detested Mississippi heat. These extended visits also maintained his familial and financial ties to the North. Though deeply connected to the Pennsylvania–New York region, he remained equally committed to his new life in the lower Mississippi Valley. After the death of his wife, he considered returning to Pennsylvania but ultimately decided to remain in Natchez. As he remarked on one occasion, "I can answer, that whether married or single, *there* shall be my residence for the remainder of my days."[1]

Stephen Duncan's vacillation over where to reside was but one part of the restlessness he experienced in the wake of his wife's death. As the last weeks of the summer of 1816 drew to a close, he spent time with family and friends at Middlesex, Pennsylvania, while his children remained in the care of the Butlers in Louisiana. Disconsolate over Margaret's death as well as his own life, Duncan confided in brother-in-law Thomas Butler that he wished he could find "a woman who would not only be a good wife to me, but a good mother to my dear little children. Should it be my good fortune to meet with such a woman, I should not long remain in my present situation."[2]

Three years later he realized his hopes, marrying Catharine A. Bingaman of Natchez on May 25, 1819. Like the Ellises, the Bingaman family helped constitute the core of the Natchez elite. They counted among their relations the Lintot, Minor, and Surget families, who were among the most economically powerful in the area. Catharine Bingaman's siblings also married into well-established families. Her sister wed merchant James C. Wilkins, who would eventually become Duncan's cotton factor and business associate; her flamboyant brother, Colonel Adam Bingaman, married Julia Murray of Massachusetts, the niece of Winthrop Sargent, who was Mississippi's first territorial governor. Duncan's marriage into the Bingaman family—coupled with his preexisting links to the Ellises and his uncle, Samuel Postlethwaite—helped him solidify and entrench his position within the small but growing Natchez inner circle.[3]

Following their marriage, the Duncans resided on Stephen's plantation in Adams County. Though now wed, Duncan never sent for John and Sarah Jane to come live with them, even when he and Catharine had their own children. Why Duncan's children from his previous marriage remained with relatives is not known; nevertheless, it created a dynamic characterized by an odd mixture of abandonment, love, and loyalty. This strange emotional bond would be illuminated in a variety of ways over the years, although Duncan remained nearly silent on the subject. Nonetheless, as Duncan went about his business building his new life with Catharine, he also went about building the family business. He positioned himself to reap the benefits of a profitable cotton market fueled by an expanding economy and the need for American cotton overseas. In order to meet the demand for cotton in the late 1810s, farmers and speculators had grabbed land at a dizzying pace, while the Federal government and banks fed the frenzy by granting loose credit. The future looked promising for white farmers who wanted to move beyond mere subsistence farming. Meanwhile, planters took advantage of the favorable economic market to increase their profits. Yet the foundation was being laid for financial failure.

Mississippi's growing economic dependence on cotton production proved to be rewarding when prices skyrocketed, but financially devastating when they tumbled during the depression of the early 1820s. For those who cast their fate with cotton, the volatility of the market was not a new occurrence. As hostilities between the United States and Britain increased in the early 1800s, prices plummeted; but as trade with Europe resumed after the War of 1812, the Natchez cotton market tripled in value. For the next four years, the delta economy boomed. By August 1818, New Orleans cotton prices reached a high of thirty-five cents per pound. The Natchez market was nearly as high: the average price per pound was over twenty-seven cents. In 1819, Mississippi's cotton production almost doubled from the previous year, totaling 49,500 bales valued at almost $3 million.[4]

The financial rewards that came with the intense economic activity of these years reverberated throughout Mississippi, but such rewards were reserved for a select group. For blacks, increased economic gains translated into the further entrenchment of the slave system and its brutal oppression. For whites, the distribution of wealth depended upon class status and geography; cotton proceeds fell to the wealthy landed slaveowners of the Mississippi River counties more than to settlers in the central and eastern portion of the state. The economic success garnered from cultivating Mississippi's rich soil could also be seen in the soundness of the Bank of the State of Mississippi. By the eve of the antebellum era, its paid-in capital had tripled, which induced the bank to extend more credit through the increased circulation of bank notes.[5]

But this meteoric success did not last. By 1819, the price of cotton fell to fifteen cents per pound as Britain's demand for the staple and other cash crops waned. Creditors called in debts on individuals as well as banks. The Second Bank of the United States began to redeem its notes from state banks and, in turn, state banks began to call in their loans, regardless of a borrower's financial status. In 1819, borrowers owed $22 millions to the Federal government, with Mississippi and Alabama responsible for over half of this debt.[6]

When the Second Bank of the United States began to demand specie payments, officials at the Bank of the State of Mississippi, led by Samuel Postlethwaite, constricted its credit and started to call in its loans. Those who bought high-priced land and slaves on credit during the boom years quickly found themselves in grave economic trouble. The short cotton crop of 1819–1820 further exacerbated the situation. The bountiful harvest of the previous year, which commanded an average price of twenty-four cents per pound in New Orleans and twenty-one cents in Natchez, failed to be reproduced, and prices fell below twenty cents a pound in both markets. From the perspective of the Bank of the State of Mississippi, its tightened credit policies paid off; its financial strength grew by late 1820. The economic rebound resulted in a resumption of somewhat looser credit and the granting of some new loans. Meanwhile, cotton production increased and surpassed the previous year's crop by five thousand bales.[7]

Despite this brief economic respite, Stephen Duncan predicted that the economy of the 1820s would be deeply troubled. "I fear we are going to have d—d hard times," he wrote, resigning himself to the fact that "there is great confusion in monied affairs all over the world." Duncan's prediction came true. Following a short peak in 1824 and 1825, cotton prices tumbled for the remainder of the decade. They bottomed out in late 1829 at ten cents per pound in New Orleans and nine cents in the Natchez market.[8]

When the panic of 1819 hit, the Duncans found themselves in excellent economic health, due to the family's seventy-three slaves and land on the Homochitto River (as well as other properties). One of Duncan's most important acquisitions of prime assets came in 1817, when he purchased one hundred shares in the Bank of the Mississippi. As a major stockholder in the bank, he could obtain credit at bargain rates—a potentially significant economic tool.[9]

In spite of Duncan's strong economic standing, the depression still affected him. At one point, he beseeched his brother-in-law "to loan me . . . for 60 days—the sum of 500 doll[ars]. My funds are entirely exhausted—and I have several debts to pay—and wd. be glad to borrow 500 doll. for a couple of months." It was unusual for Duncan to be in the situation of having to "beg the favor of" others.[10] Rather, it was commonplace for others to borrow from him—a frequent occurrence, which may have helped to contribute to this particular financial predicament. Though he had easy access to cash as a stockholder in the Bank of the State of Mississippi, perhaps he had momentarily exhausted these connections. It also might have been more expedient for Duncan to borrow money from his brother-in-law interest-free or at low interest to pay off his immediate debts.

Despite occasional difficulties and Duncan's warped perception that his eco-
nomic position remained fragile, he still loaned substantial amounts of money
to friends and family. A stark example of this was a cash and land exchange between him and his brother-in-law, Adam L. Bingaman. When the executors of
Catharine Bingaman Duncan's late father divided and liquidated the estate,
Stephen and Catharine received a parcel of property, ironically named Poverty
Hill, which consisted of 690 acres located on St. Catharine's Creek in Adams
County. After the executors settled the inheritance, Catharine's brother Adam
wished to have the land. The Duncans were willing to sell it to him, but in the
wake of the panic of 1819, Bingaman lacked the resources to make the purchase.
Duncan thus executed a series of legal instruments whereby Bingaman borrowed $46,671 from him to pay for the land. The indenture stipulated for the
loan to be paid off in five years. If Bingaman defaulted, Duncan would receive
Poverty Hill and the nine slaves who labored on the plantation.[11] In addition to
cash loans, Duncan continued to build his assets during the 1820s by purchasing property on the cheap in a depressed economy. Acquisitions such as
Saragossa, a 1,000-arpent plantation located five miles south of Natchez, for
which he paid $20,000 in cash, had enormous potential for appreciating, and
Duncan was able to seize such opportunities because of his liquidity.[12]

Given Duncan's positive cash flow, the loans that he provided for friends and
acquaintances were not a financial drain; on the contrary, they were quite remunerative. As a stockholder in the Bank of the State of Mississippi, he secured
cash loans from the bank at below-market interest rates. He could also borrow
anywhere from half to the full value of his shares in the bank, receiving bargain interest rates of 6 percent. (Without a bank connection, he would have
paid double that rate on the local money market.)[13] These unsecured loans were
renewable every sixty-three days, with most borrowers extinguishing the loans
in two to three years. Shareholders like Duncan used the loans to purchase additional properties or more shares of bank stock. Restrictions on purchase limits of new bank shares were legally limited to ten shares every ten days for each
individual buyer. However, those who already owned bank stock routinely purchased shares from one another, which allowed for any one stockholder to
amass a large number of shares without being constricted by the legal accumulation limit.

The regulations intended to restrict the purchase of bank stock by those outside the inner circle effectively prohibited them from accumulating economic
power. For the moneyed elite, however, such regulations failed as stockholders

found a way around such protections. They could borrow off of their shares, or obtain cheap loans and extend them to others at a higher rate, but one that was attractively lower than the rate on the general market. An example of this is Duncan's loan to Theodore Stark at 10 percent, which was a lower rate than Stark would have received on the local money market. The dynamics of this system of privileges enabled those who held its keys to unlock the doors of unprecedented advantages.[14]

Given Duncan's liquidity and access to venture capital, the economic foundation of the Duncan family was multifaceted. In spite of this, much of the economic framework that comprised not only Duncan's financial security, but also of the South at large, can be seen clearly in black and white—slaves and cotton.

Prior to the nineteenth century, Mississippians cultivated long-staple cotton imported from Siam. This variety produced one of the highest quality lints, but a fungus, referred to as "the rot," attacked and destroyed the state's crop year after year. In search of a variety immune from such natural scourges, Mississippians imported the short-staple, Georgian green seed, which eventually succumbed to rot as well. Finally, in the late 1810s, planters in Rodney, Mississippi, experimented and cross-pollinated three different varieties of seed that remained heartier. What they produced changed the South forever and catapulted the region's crop to one of the finest cottons available on world markets. Petit Gulf cotton, as it came to be called, defied the rot fairly well and adapted to different climates, which made it easy to cultivate across the entire South. Its good quality fiber and large bolls made it relatively easy to pick. As a result, slaves could gather up to two or three hundred pounds per day, as opposed to seventy-five pounds per day of the small boll variety. With the Petit Gulf strain, Mississippi and the lower South became ever more dependent both on cotton as a cash crop and on those they enslaved to cultivate it.[15]

Duncan invested much in cotton's success and remained ever vigilant of its production and prices. Not only did his own coffers depend on a steady market, but he also saw it as a critical component for the economic success of the region and nation. However, he also remained conscious of its limits. Faced with poor cotton crops afflicted by the rot, he became very disturbed at the downturn in the Liverpool cotton market in the mid-1820s. He predicted "that we can hardly calculate on more than 15 or 16 [cents] this year" and went on to note that British imports of United States cotton had fallen over the course of the year from 105,000 bales to 77,000 bales. Duncan correctly foresaw the trouble in Liverpool. Heavy speculation in the Liverpool market in March 1824 shot cotton prices upward. As a result of increased production in response to this speculation, a surplus of cotton accumulated and prices plummeted to six cents per pound in 1825.[16]

Worrying Duncan even more was the presence of foreign cotton, particularly cotton from Egypt and South America, which he believed flooded the market and drove prices down. "Last year . . . we heard nothing of Egyptian cotton," he noted with consternation, continuing, "I fear the British Manufacturers—may take it . . . to exclude our cotten as much as possible."[17] Over the next few years, he became increasingly apprehensive and obsessive over this situation. Though the cultivation of cotton seemed infinite, he opined that the South curtail its production or it would exceed consumption and drive prices even lower.

In October 1827, as cotton prices headed toward their nadir, Duncan voiced his concerns to Senator Josiah S. Johnston of Louisiana.[18] In hopes of pumping up the market and lifting prices, he suggested that bagging, rope, and other items should be manufactured in the United States from homegrown cotton. This would not only reduce the United States' dependence on foreign finished goods, but it would also reduce the amount of cotton on the market due to overproduction. As he informed Johnston, "I have taken great pains to bring this subject before the people, and have determined to spare neither labor nor expense in endeavoring to have *bagging, coarse shirtings, & cloth yard wide* for pants & petticoats, made for our consumption in the South." He ended emphatically, "Much may be done, to increase the consumption of our staple;—and I will do all in my power to further that object."[19]

To this end, Duncan went as far as having blanket samples made that were half cotton and half wool. "I have offered premiums for the best samples of [blankets] made in this way, and have offered to contract for a quantity, if made equal to the sample," he told the senator. He estimated that the United States would consume one thousand bales of cotton from the manufacturing of bags and twenty-five thousand bales each for cordage and blankets.[20]

As Duncan tried to solve the puzzle of overproduction, foreign markets, and a regional economy based on a single agricultural staple, his own fields suffered from the uncontrollable forces of nature. In 1825, the rot struck his crops. Two years later, they struggled under the longest drought that Duncan had ever experienced—seventy-one days without a single drop of rain. These natural calamities put great pressure upon Duncan, a man who tried to plan for even the most minute risks.[21] In spite of these difficulties, he remained composed and in control as he focused on strengthening what was becoming a family fortune. During the second half of the decade, he expanded his family's assets exponentially. Though a number of elements contributed to this growth of income, the sharp escalation of Duncan's wealth and power was triggered by a single event in 1825. On October 18, the news of Samuel Postlethwaite's death from yellow fever spread through Natchez.[22]

Postlethwaite's death led to a vacuum at the helm of the financial institution that he had helped found in 1809, but his seat would not remain vacant for long. Shortly after his uncle's demise, Stephen Duncan assumed the presidency of the Bank of the State of Mississippi. Since 1816 he had been closely involved with the bank and had participated in managerial decisions as one of its directors. He clearly possessed the capability to administer and guide the bank. But soon he became embroiled in the miasmic politics of banking.[23]

As a result of the institution's credit-tightening policies during the 1820s, the bank produced prosperity for those who controlled it. After Duncan took the helm, the bank continued to pay its shareholders generous dividends of ten and eighteen dollars per share over the next five years.[24] The circle of beneficiaries remained a tight one. With the bank's success for a select few, it became a target of intense political axe-grinding among a variety of factions both within and outside Natchez.

Until the antebellum era, Natchez was home to Mississippi's largest and most powerful institutions: the state capital and the state's banking monopoly. In 1821, however, the prestige of Natchez began to sink. The state legislature moved the capital to Jackson, and Governor George Poindexter attacked the bank's monopoly status. As small farmers began to populate Mississippi's backwoods in the central and northern sections of the state, they slowly chipped away at the power held by the more established western river counties. As the eastern region of the Pearl River Valley became more settled, the east-west split became stronger. Further contributing to this divide was the steady growth of counties and cities north of Natchez, such as Vicksburg, which would eventually rival it. Soon the Bank of the State of Mississippi was caught in the middle of these tensions. In many ways, it helped foster them.[25]

Settlers in the newly populated areas of the state desperately needed greater access to credit—something that the Bank of the State of Mississippi resisted, which generated fervent opposition. Complicating the situation even more, on three occasions in the mid-1820s state legislators brought forth a bill to authorize the establishment of a branch of the Bank of the United States in Natchez, only to meet with failure. During the entirety of Duncan's tenure as president of the state bank, those who lived in Mississippi's interior fought to have branches of the bank extended to their areas. This was a particularly contentious issue for the settlers in the Pearl River region because the bank was obligated in its 1818 charter to establish a branch in that area. Instead, the bank established branches in the wealthier Mississippi River towns of Port Gibson and Woodville. It even refused a branch in the prosperous river port of Vicksburg. Duncan and his directors argued that the Pearl River region was not populated or wealthy enough for the bank to flourish there, and that it lacked sufficient capital to fund a branch. It was not lost on poorer Mississippians that the men who controlled the bank ranked among the wealthiest individuals in the state and that they used their positions to maintain their power as well as control the flow of capital in the region. Any threat to the bank was a potential threat to them personally. As Duncan and his cohorts steered the financial flagship through the rough waters of public discontent, anti-Natchez sentiment bubbled up in its wake and eventually helped to weaken the political influence of Natchez.[26]

Though the bank issue caused some dilution of political power in Natchez, the elite maintained their social and economic hegemony. The patriarchs of these families—such as Samuel Davis, Alvarez Fisk, William Mercer, John Minor, and Francis Surget—all served on the bank's board in 1829. Through an intricate web of business deals and personal loans, coupled with friendship and familial ties, they personified the overlapping economic, social, and familial networks of Natchez. Historians have dubbed the most elite men within this group (including Stephen Duncan) the "Natchez Nabobs." Marriage tightened this circle further and was as valuable as capital itself. Among the Duncan family, Catharine Bingaman's mother was a Surget, Duncan's first wife was related to William Mercer, and Stephen and Catharine's daughter Charlotte would marry Samuel Davis's son.[27]

Though seemingly solidified in the 1820s, these networks were still in the process of developing and coming into their own. This can be seen in the leadership of the Bank of the State of Mississippi. In 1829, the bank's board of directors was comprised of both original settlers of the region and men of the second generation (like Duncan). As the original settlers died, a second generation took their place and oversaw the maturation of the networks. Over time, a few leaders emerged whose power practically went unchallenged. In particular, Duncan's appointment as president of the Bank of the State of Mississippi cinched his position as leader of Natchez's economic network. Being chosen by his peers symbolized their confidence in his leadership and his ability to represent their group within the Mississippi aristocracy.

One of the keys to Duncan's mastery of capital was economic diversification, which he engaged in almost from the beginning of his career. Some of his ventures were totally separate from his agricultural pursuits; others remained more interconnected. Yet he never relied solely on agricultural endeavors to generate income. A master of timing, he usually knew when to strike or retreat, when to sink in capital or liquefy it. Even so, he sometimes made miscalculations and mistakes. One such example was his investment in a steamboat, *Walk in the Water.* Wanting to ship their cotton more cheaply, Duncan, Butler, and other Natchez planters purchased the steamboat to streamline their operations. As it began to traverse the waters of the Mississippi River in early 1826, it seemed to hold much promise. John Ellis Duncan, who was fourteen at the time, excitedly wrote his younger sister, Sarah Jane, that "the new steamboat 'Walk in the Water,' in which Father has a share, has commenced running; and it is very highly spoken of by the Editor of this paper."[28]

Though *Walk in the Water* enjoyed a most favorable reception by the community, it soon ran into financial difficulties. Shortly before Christmas 1827, Duncan reported to the other owners of the vessel that "Capt. Vail of the Steam Boat 'Walk in the Water' has made no deposites to credit of the Boat since he has been in command." The owners' initial agreement, however, stipulated that "the Captn. shall deposite with the Treasurer of the Boat on the morning of his departure for N. Orleans—the nett profits of the voyage previous." Duncan's continued frustration with the financial state of the venture became apparent the following year. Almost $6,000 in acceptances for the boat were due, and he believed that there was "no hope that the Boat will contribute any thing (from her earnings) to meet these acceptances." As treasurer and part owner of the boat, Duncan suggested that the owners divest themselves of the floating albatross. "I am clearly of the opinion," he explained to Butler, that "the interests of the owners will be best promoted—by an immediate sale of the boat, at public auction in N. Orleans at 6, 12, & 18 months credit. She is running now, for the sole benefit of the *Captn., crew, & grocers.*"[29]

Duncan's business associates usually followed his lead, especially in financial matters; in this case, however, they outvoted him, and the steamboat continued to operate. Duncan thus inadvertently avoided a major error in economic judgment. Under a new captain, *Walk in the Water* became profitable and eventually paid large dividends to its shareholders. Over the years, Duncan and others within his social and economic circles, such as Frank Surget and Adam Bingaman, utilized the steamboat extensively. Their commission merchants, Wilkins and Linton, constantly used *Walk in the Water* to ship their cotton and to carry other goods, as well as messages.[30]

Nevertheless, the greatest increase in Duncan's wealth came not from his participation in such ventures, but from his aggressive acquisition of property between 1825 and 1830. During this time, Duncan spent more than $112,000 in cash and purchased over 3,500 acres and seventy-eight slaves in Adams and Wilkinson counties.[31]

One of the properties Duncan procured was a suburban Natchez homestead, Auburn, where he and Catharine—and eventually the children from their marriage, Charlotte, Maria, Henry, Samuel, and Stephen—had lived since 1820 under a lease agreement. In December 1827, Duncan acquired the property for $20,000 in cash. The estate consisted of 410 arpents and lay next to the lands of Adam Bingaman and Job Routh (one of the area's original settlers).[32] Auburn was designed and built by Levi Weeks, a promising architect who fled New York in the early 1800s after being accused of murdering his lover by throwing her down a Manhattan well. After being defended by the equivalent of the nineteenth-century legal "dream team" of Aaron Burr and Alexander Hamilton, Weeks was acquitted. He migrated to Natchez and designed Auburn for Lyman Harding, a Massachusetts-born jurist and friend of Winthrop Sargent, the territorial governor. Weeks found his niche as a prominent architect and builder and constructed numerous Natchez buildings, including the Bank of the State of Mississippi, but Auburn remained his greatest achievement.[33]

Auburn was the "first academically correct building in the Anglo-American classical revival style" built in Natchez. Graced with ornamental woodwork, doorways, and a freestanding spiral staircase, it was a great architectural specimen. "The brick house I am now building is just without the city lines and is designed for the Most Magnificent building in the territory," Weeks wrote to a friend, noting, "The body [of] this house is 60 by 45, with a portico of 31 feet, projecting 12 feet, supported by four Ionic Columns with Corinthian entablature, the ceiling vaulted, the house two stories, with a geometrical staircase." Auburn became the Duncan family's southern homestead.[34]

Duncan made several other significant land transactions in the late 1820s.

Built in 1812, Auburn was the Duncan family's Natchez residence.

Photograph by James Butters for the Historic American Buildings Survey, 1936. Courtesy of the Library of Congress.

Following the purchase of a city lot near the center of town from the widow of his uncle, Henry Postlethwaite, he considered expanding his plantation lands. One of his options was five hundred acres parceled out from Thomas Butler's Homochitto lands, for which he was willing to pay $35,000. After he made the offer to Butler, the cotton market dropped, and he lowered his price dramatically to twenty dollars per acre, or $10,000. In respect to these economic forces, Duncan carefully weighed the prospect. After six months of vacillation over the purchase, he informed Butler, "I can only say to you, I am very indift. [indifferent] about it, at present—and at this *moment* would rather decline the purchase." Backing away from the deal, he cited the failure of his current cotton crops. "My cotton at Homochitto has rotted—continues to rot so much that I shall not make ⅔d of a crop," he wrote, noting, "This rather disheartens me . . . and my desire to extend the culture of it."[35]

Though disgruntled about his crops and the Butler deal, he still considered purchasing land from B. F. Conner under the same terms he had offered Butler. But given the fact that on Duncan's plantation they had "*four* times as much rotten, as . . . anywhere else," he was again inclined to decline the Conner offer, even though it would have been a bargain. After these crop failures, Duncan considered placing some of his resources where they might make him more money. To this end, he weighed the "very favourable reports from a cotton factory in which I am interested," and concluded that they "almost determine me to . . . invest all of my surplus means in another factory."[36]

Duncan's interest in the processing of raw cotton was clearly connected with his advocation of the manufacture of bagging and slave clothing with home-grown cotton. Unlike many southerners, he preached the gospel of economic diversification, as it promoted self-sufficiency, which he believed would lessen the South's reliance on foreign imports and help alleviate the overproduction of cotton. Diversification would integrate the increasingly distinct regional economies, thus fostering the growth of a national economy. "I can only aprise you from present appearances that it is more profitable than either cotton or sugar planting," he told Butler regarding the manufacture of raw cotton into finished goods. Yet he did not disregard cotton planting as a profit-maker. In fact, a few months later he considered the purchase of a plantation that would enable him to grow Sea Island or long-staple cotton. Duncan's interest in this variety was due to his belief that "if the British govt imposes a high duty on short staple cotton (in which class our cottons rank) and admit sea Islands free of duty," the cultivation of it would be very remunerative.[37]

Duncan always painstakingly measured how risky, profitable, or deleterious any financial prospect would be for him and his family. His deliberations about purchasing the Butler lands stretched out to over eight months, as he calculated the costs of the investment. During this time, the possibility of purchasing Conner's tract and the opportunity of acquiring brother-in-law Richard Ellis's plantation, Ellislie, were also thrown into the mix. Duncan carefully weighed each option. For the Conner land, he feared that he would have to purchase "12 or 15 Negroes that would nearly exhaust my funds," although he intended to purchase slaves anyway. He waited until the last possible moment to make his decision, but he was pressured nonetheless by the fact that he wanted to avail himself of the opportunity to choose from a "large gang of Negroes" that were being brought to town, "out of which I would expect to purchase 20 or 30 and I am promised the first choice."[38]

Ultimately, Duncan declined both the Butler and Conner tracts, but in 1828 he succeeded in procuring Ellislie—along with two other tracts of land—from William Shipp, a fellow bank director and former business partner of Samuel Postlethwaite. The Shipp tracts consisted of 1,000 arpents along the Mississippi River in Adams County and included sixty-eight slaves, for which Duncan paid over $66,000 in cash. One month later, he purchased Ellislie for $25,000. This 2,000-plus-acre plantation, originally owned by Richard Ellis's uncle, Isaac Gaillard, lay nestled along Second Creek to the south. The Homochitto River cut a north-south path through the middle of the property, which left half of the plantation in Adams County and the other half in Wilkinson County. The slow acquisition of these properties—which, as a unit, constituted his largest expenditure of funds to date—only emphasizes the meticulous way in which Duncan built the family assets.[39]

Along with acreage, Duncan also directed his resources toward the purchase of slaves. He searched prudently for slaves who met his needs, and, as with his other property decisions, he refused to purchase any slaves who did not fit into his labor designs or financial plans. "I find it utterly impossible to procure women of the description I want at any price in this place," he wrote John Ker, emphatically adding, "unless I would buy Kenty. [Kentucky] negroes; and this, I will not do." Duncan preferred slaves from Virginia, particularly women, whom the Natchez market valued up to fifteen dollars more than slaves from Maryland and twenty dollars more than slaves from Kentucky. In December 1828, however, the Natchez market was too high for his liking. "I should not *gamble* at 500# each—for 5—if they are very likely & not exceeding 18 or 19.

nor under 16 or 17—that is, if they are suited—in *age & appearance* for the purposes for which I want them," Duncan wrote Ker. In light of this, he instructed Ker, who was in New Orleans at the time, to "purchase 4 that would suit my purposes at present," adding that he would wait until he "could buy others on better terms here in the spring."[40] Duncan failed to specify exactly how he desired his human property to "appear"; yet his directives to Ker exemplify his desire to be in control, literally, over the slave body. For someone who so rarely discussed slave procurement, and who maintained an image of disdainful disinterest toward those he enslaved, such instructions speak loudly.

Though the cotton market bottomed out in the 1820s, Stephen Duncan took advantage of this downturn—something that he would do often in subsequent years—and utilized the resources available to him to expand his land and slave holdings. He also continued to extend personal loans to acquaintances, family, and friends. According to Adams County records for the period 1820 to 1830, Duncan issued ten loans totaling $49,000. Though he legally recorded these loans, it is likely that he informally loaned money as well. All his formal loans were secured with property, which totaled 3,700 acres, three city lots, and forty-three slaves. Most of these loans ranged between two and three thousand dollars, though Duncan did grant larger amounts.[41]

The schematic Duncan used to loan money was in the form of promissory notes, which contained fairly liberal terms. Most were renewable, and many remained interest-free until the final note was due. For instance, Duncan's loan of $1,875 to Woodson Wren was in the form of four promissory notes due over the course of four years from the original date of issue. Interest would not accrue until after the last note was due, after which Duncan charged 10 percent per annum on any outstanding balance. Similarly, John T. Scott borrowed $1,800 in the form of three notes due over the course of three years, all interest-free. However, unlike Wren, Scott never had to pay interest when the note expired. In contrast, Duncan loaned $6,500 to William C. Conner, and Conner owed 10 percent interest on the balance of every note when it came due. The evidence suggests that in the 1820s, Duncan did not acquire any of the property related to the secured loans. More significantly, such loans solidified Duncan's ever-growing web of patron-client relationships and testified to notions of white reciprocity that undergirded many of his relationships.[42]

Even at this early stage of Duncan's career as planter, enslaver, and entrepreneur, patterns of economic and social behavior started to emerge. In terms of strictly economic behavior, Duncan carefully controlled the flow of his monetary resources. He was a cautious investor who took calculated risks and scrupulously weighed the possible outcomes. He clearly integrated his economic activities with his social, political, and familial networks. For example, six of the ten loans that Duncan granted during the 1820s were to extended family members or men whom he knew through business.

Vital to the operation of Natchez's economic infrastructure were commission merchants, who connected the town's inner circle and its larger economic network to the financial world outside it. Throughout the 1820s, Duncan utilized the services of John Linton Jr. and James C. Wilkins, who became partners "for the purpose of doing Commission business & Carrying on trade" in January 1816. Linton moved to the Crescent City to conduct business there, while Wilkins remained in their Natchez office. They soon became one of the most successful firms in Natchez.[43] Both men were well known in the area, and their business was built on familial relationships. Wilkins was the widower of Fannie Minor, whose father, Stephen Minor, was the former Spanish governor of the Natchez District and first president of the Bank of the Mississippi. Her mother was Catherine Lintot, whose family had helped settle the territory. After Fannie Minor died, which was around the same time that Wilkins and Linton formed their partnership, Wilkins married the sister of Catharine Bingaman Duncan. He was related to the Duncan family in another way as well: Fannie Minor Wilkins's father had previously been married to Margaret Ellis Duncan's sister, Martha.[44]

Wilkins not only provided the Duncans with another connection in the Natchez networks of power, but his firm also provided the necessary services of marketing the family crop—a key source of Stephen Duncan's liquid income. Until the early 1830s, Duncan and his associates retained Wilkins and Linton to sell their cotton, and the firm eagerly accepted Duncan's business. Duncan's cotton was considered to be of a superior quality, and it usually sold at the highest prices the market could command. Even with the cotton market greatly depressed in February 1827 and with a ruined crop (the result of a serious drought), Duncan still received top dollar as Wilkins and Linton snared higher prices for it. As Linton informed Wilkins, he was able to sell "21 or 27 Bales Duncans @ 13 [cents]" when the going price was a few cents less. The additional one- or two-cent difference in this particular transaction translated into a gain of almost two hundred dollars.[45] It also translated into a higher commission for Wilkins and Linton, which averaged 2.5 percent of the gross price of a cotton sale.[46]

Like most relationships between planters and their factors, Duncan's relationship with Wilkins and Linton operated on a variety of levels. Many times Duncan gave the commission merchants complete freedom to do what they wanted in regard to the marketing of his crop. At other times, Linton refrained from making any decision on his own, noting in one instance, "I would not sell it without his [Duncan's] authority."[47] Conversely, occasions arose when Wilkins and Linton asserted their own authority regardless of what Duncan desired. For example, in December 1817 Linton informed Wilkins that "I made Duncans proposition for his Cotton @ 30 [cents]—he asks 31 [cents]. . . . I will not give him 31 for the Crop in the way he wants—unless you could dispose of at Natchez to advantage."[48] In addition to selling Duncan's crops and purchasing plantation supplies, Wilkins and Linton handled other financial and personal matters. These affairs ranged from issuing notes of discount to the receipt of a menagerie of personal goods.[49]

Wilkins and Linton's connection with Stephen Duncan went beyond a purely economic one—or, for that matter, simply a familial connection. Their relationship was composed of a set of social links that was based in part on the notion of reciprocity. It encompassed mutual obligation, loyalty, and the duty toward and roles of friendship and family. According to Duncan, "our duty here [was] to assist each other" in friendship and with reciprocity. As much as Duncan relied on Wilkins and Linton to build his assets, they relied on him to help them. In one instance, for example, Wilkins and Linton wanted to use their connection to Duncan as a bank shareholder so that they could help some friends of theirs. To this end, Linton wrote, "When Stephen Duncan returns I will go again into [the] Bank for what we may want—& I hope we shall [have] no great difficulty in providing means to assist our friends." It is not clear whether things worked out the way Wilkins and Linton wished, but it is clear that they were depending upon Duncan to help them.[50]

Any sign of failure to hold up one's end of a relationship could be seen by those in the inner circle of the Natchez elite as extremely deleterious. For example, in 1827 Linton expressed concern to Wilkins that Duncan's "intentions so friendly and considerate cannot be carr[ie]d into effect," concluding that this was a "very Serious inconvenience to us."[51] Anything affecting the balance of power was seen as jeopardizing the way in which these interconnected relationships were structured, as well as the relationships themselves. As a result, seemingly straightforward relationships were, in reality, deeply complex.

These overlapping and interconnected economic, social, and familial networks clearly helped propel Stephen Duncan to a position of power by the end of the 1820s. Duncan devoted the first half of the decade to building his plantation base and undertaking other entrepreneurial ventures. During the second half of the decade, he turned to expanding his hegemony, not only through his own personal financial base, but through institutional power as well. By the end of the decade, he had amassed over 4,000 acres of land and his labor force had increased 416 percent, as he now enslaved 377 men, women, and children. Stephen Duncan had finally arrived at the highest echelons of the southern slaveholding aristocracy.

3

⇥⋌

SLAVES, POLITICS, AND FAMILY

Stephen Duncan and the Challenges to Mastery

Throughout the 1820s, Stephen Duncan exhibited mastery over his land, slaves, and money, as well as the familial, social, and economic connections he forged through marriage, friendship, and business. Yet such intertwined relationships could also be fragile. In spite of his wealth and status, Duncan still lived in a world vulnerable to forces beyond his control. The 1820s thus were also a time when his mastery was challenged, both as a slaveowner and as a key figure within the powerful networks of Natchez. One of the most tangible challenges to his mastery came from the growing number of blacks—most of them enslaved—who would eventually become a majority in Natchez. For white Mississippians, anxiety over this situation dated back at least to the turn of the century and the 1800 Gabriel Prosser rebellion in Richmond, Virginia, when Winthrop Sargent, then the territorial governor, informed slaveholders about the events in Virginia. Later, alarmed by the increasing number of slaves and free blacks in the territory, he ordered the militia that they should "not necessarily harass the Men [slaves], but more strongly to impress the Negroes that we are never off our Guard."[1] During the War of 1812, Governor David Holmes requested that the Federal government send more arms, as he feared the ultimate and most threatening of rebellions—the joining of Choctaws and slaves. "Scarcely a day passes without my receiving some information relative to the designs of these people to insurrect," he anxiously noted. "For my own part I am impressed with the belief that real danger exists." A decade later, white panic surfaced even more intensely with news of the Denmark Vesey slave conspiracy in Charleston, as well as significant slave insurrections on several Caribbean islands.[2]

One year after the Vesey plot unfolded in the summer of 1822, Stephen Duncan's immediate and extended family faced slave resistance on their own plantations. In the summer of 1823, Thomas Butler's overseer, Silas Wilson, requested that Duncan, who still effectively managed Butler's plantation, come to the property to handle a serious altercation between himself and a slave. The slave, Old Gloster, had created an autonomous community of runaway slaves (known as a maroon) on the bayou. Wanting to investigate the maroon, Wilson and another white acquaintance, Mr. Lewis, went in search of Old Gloster. When they eventually found him, they discovered that he possessed a gun belonging to Duncan's brother-in-law, Richard Ellis. After a verbal altercation, Old Gloster fired at Wilson and Lewis, but missed. Instead of punishing Old Gloster on the spot, Wilson desired "to act in a manner becoming a good citizen." In his mind, this meant taking Old Gloster into Natchez to have him prosecuted. When Duncan arrived at the plantation, Old Gloster continued to threaten to kill any whites who disturbed the autonomy of the maroon. Eventually, however, the slave turned to flee. As he did, Wilson "took hold of Gloster as he ran, Gloster faced about, and Wilson caught the gun as he presented it, and Gloster fired, without injuring him in the least." Not sure what to do in this situation, Duncan informed Butler that, "I have done for you, what I wd. have done for myself. Sanctioned his taking him to jail & having him tried."[3]

Under Mississippi law and the state constitution of 1817, slaves accused of felonies could receive a jury trial. The jury pool would be comprised of twenty-four white men, half of whom had to be slaveowners. Slaves found guilty of noncapital crimes received physical punishment; those found guilty of capital crimes, such as intent to kill, were often hanged.[4] Although Duncan did not always approve of immediate summary punishment, in regard to Old Gloster's case, he reflected to Butler, "I think that you wd. be benefitted no little, if he were hung," adding, "I cannot avoid, *again* urging you to get clear of him, in the event of his acquittal." Duncan was especially emphatic about selling Old Gloster because he believed that Richard Ellis's slaves gave Old Gloster the gun to kill Wilson and/or Duncan's overseer. Since executing slaves who fought for their freedom would only cause more resistance in the quarters, it was more beneficial, in Duncan's mind, simply to get rid of any troublesome slaves.[5]

In spite of Duncan's, Ellis's, and Butler's attempts at control, their slaves resisted their authority in a variety of overt and covert ways. For example, one of Butler's slaves, Nancy, took bread and salt to Old Gloster's maroon, while other slaves killed "a great many" hogs. Yet another slave, John, swore that he would "never come in till he kills every overseer." Duncan noted that Butler's slaves sheltered others from neighboring plantations, including slaves from Duncan's quarters. In response to these incidents, Duncan claimed, somewhat disingenuously, "I know not why these people shd. be dissatisfied with Wilson. He is certainly a humane man. . . . He is not too severe—on the contrary he is too amiable & mild." Duncan did acknowledge, however, that Wilson's treatment of slaves helped to foment resistance. In the end, he blamed the whole situation on Richard Ellis's slaves, who, he believed, had persuaded Butler's slaves that Wilson was too harsh. Duncan also surmised that Ellis's slaves informed their counterparts on the Butler plantation that Nancy Ellis Butler disliked Wilson because he was "too severe." Clearly, communication among the various slave networks was efficient and active. To gain some sort of control over this situation, both Duncan and Butler forbid any Ellis slave to visit their slave quarters.[6]

Notwithstanding their masters' efforts at control, the slaves on these proximate plantations found ways to defy their enslavement through absconding, forming maroons, stealing food, harboring and assisting other slaves, and threatening violence. From the existing evidence, it seems that the situation on these plantations never went beyond individual or small, collective acts of resistance, but the threat of larger and more organized efforts caused the Butler, Duncan, and Ellis families to be increasingly fearful and watchful.

Though enslavement was the most visible and tangible form of Stephen Duncan's authority, he also exhibited class mastery over the various white networks of Natchez. However, threats to Duncan's sway, at least within Natchez politics, became more evident during the late 1820s. Like the economic, social, and familial relationships that existed in Natchez, political relationships were deeply interconnected and complex. For Duncan, navigating the political world and negotiating power within it created a variety of challenges.

The sophistication of Natchez political networks is aptly illuminated by an examination of what J. F. H. Claiborne called the "Natchez junto"—a powerful Mississippi political machine in the 1820s. On the state level, the junto was associated with five of Mississippi's attorney generals, all of whom were lawyers from Natchez.[7] The junto also backed David Holmes and Gerard C. Brandon, two of the state's earliest governors. On the national level, the junto secured Mississippi's only seat in the House of Representatives in the earliest congressional races, as well as four of Mississippi's first five United States senators.[8]

The leadership of the Natchez junto consisted of Robert H. Adams, James C. Wilkins, and two brothers, Duncan Walker and Robert Walker, who were cousins of Stephen Duncan. The junto supported the administration of Andrew Jackson and Jacksonian ideas nationally; on local and state issues, it rallied behind the anti-Jacksonian camp. According to historian D. Clayton James, the "junto's aim was to maintain the political supremacy of Natchez by de-emphasizing its aristocratic reputation, stressing the Jacksonian Democratic sympathies of its majority, and thereby winning support from the ever-growing eastern populace." Yet the junto's financial backers included Stephen Duncan and Adam Bingaman, both of whom were vehement anti-Jacksonians. J. F. H. Claiborne, a Jacksonian Democrat, despised the duplicity of anti-Jacksonians like Duncan. As he concluded, "They oppose the 'Natchez Junto' upon the Presidential question, but *unite* with them in everything else, as the members of the two parties are mostly connected with one another. In conjunction they form a powerful Aristocracy of wealth and official power."[9]

How could a pro-Jackson faction be financially backed by individuals who detested Jackson? The answer lay in shared economic, social, and familial bonds. Indeed, it might have been those very bonds that blurred the lines of political ideology. At the end of the day, Natchez's elites had to depend upon and interact with one another in intimate realms outside of politics. For instance, Stephen Duncan was consistently solicitous of his cousin Duncan S. Walker, who was an ardent Jacksonian. Upon Walker's arrival in Mississippi in the early 1820s and his subsequent engagement as an attorney, Duncan wrote Thomas Butler, "I feel a great desire to see him prosper," and directed Butler to "aid him all that you can." Though Duncan detested the law and jurists—as he remarked on one occasion, "I have a great horror of the law, and no confidence in the decisions of our courts, and still less in the random or law knowledge of our Atts. [Attorneys]"—he nevertheless fully supported his cousin, characterizing him as a "man of undoubted integrity, honor, & Mentality; zeal & industry in the discharge of his professional duties—and [he] is unquestionably a sound lawyer." Duncan grandly concluded, "I wd. guarantee his integrity & punctuality with my name and fortune."[10]

As connected as Natchez's leaders were, it was difficult to keep political fights from becoming bitter personal quarrels. In part, this was due to the overlapping interests and connections of the involved parties. Mississippi politics also divided sharply along geographical and economic lines, leading to fractious political struggles statewide. The highly partisan nature of local and state politics is starkly revealed in the presidential contests of the 1820s.[11]

Andrew Jackson's defeat in the presidential election of 1824 ignited fierce political battles within Mississippi as the fight over the national prize played out on state and local levels. Both Jackson's supporters and opponents fired up almost immediately for what would become the bitter contest of 1828. Duncan stood in the vanguard of the anti-Jacksonians along with other leading businessmen of Natchez, such as Adam Bingaman, Alvarez Fisk, and Francis Surget. Duncan's opinion of Jackson was not always negative; at one point, he wrote that he "believed [Jackson] to be a man of great purity & spotless integrity." However, as the three-year campaign for the 1828 presidency evolved and the mudslinging between Jackson and his opponent, John Quincy Adams, intensified, Duncan's opinion of Jackson plummeted. "His recent conduct (indeed his *whole* conduct for the last year)," he wrote in a stinging 1827 letter to Senator Josiah S. Johnston of Louisiana, "affords a striking example of the evil effects of inordinate ambition on *weak minds.*" He felt hopeful that Jackson would not carry the majority vote in Mississippi. If Jackson did prevail, he assured Johnston that the pro-Adams forces would put up a struggle, for "in the city of Natchez we can count *noses,* & we find that we have a majority."[12] Two months later, in a typically frank tone tinged with a bit of humor, Duncan exclaimed to Johnston, "I never *can* think and never *will* believe that Gen. Andrew Jackson will be Presd. of these U.S.—It is so gross an absurdity that I cannot, by any reasoning, reconcile it to my mind."[13]

On January 7, 1828, partisan politics took center stage in two dueling political gatherings. At the Mississippi state capital, Duncan's brother-in-law and business associate, James C. Wilkins, presided over a pro-Jackson delegate convention; one hundred miles away, Duncan led the anti-Jackson forces in firing off their first political salvo of the year. He and his cohorts issued a political circular informing the public that as a result of a previous "meeting of persons 'opposed to the election of general Jackson,'" the anti-Jackson committee invited the citizens of Adams County to a public meeting to be held on January 23, 1828. The purpose of the gathering was to whip up support for Adams and to choose candidates for electors. The circular stated that Adams was more qualified and fit to be president than Jackson, and it contained a half-hearted endorsement of Adams accompanied by a burning denunciation of Jackson. "The *partizans of Mr. Adams,* we are not," the authors of the broadside stated, continuing, "yet it would be doing him great injustice, not to accord to him *pre-eminent talents; great experience; extensive political information, both foreign and domestic; the purest patriotism;* and (when compared with his only competitor,) *superior* fitness for the chief magistracy of our union."[14]

Wanting to ensure a Jackson defeat, especially in light of the close race of 1824, the Adams County committee focused on ways to turn public sentiment against Jackson. Their strategy encompassed both political ideology and character. With regard to the former, they honed in on Jackson's sectionalized support. Fearing that politics was becoming too based on regional interests and identities, Duncan and his fellow committee members, all strong nationalists, drove home a central point: by electing Adams, Mississippians would be electing a "*President of the nation,* and not of a *faction.*" Perhaps inadvertently, this assertion cut to the heart of the ideological issues at stake in the presidential election. For Jacksonians, Adams's nationalism affirmed the rights of economic privilege, which threatened republican virtue and liberty. On the flip side of the political coin, Duncan and his fellow "National Republicans" argued that Jackson and the "Democratic-Republicans" endangered the republican notion of politics for the common good. Duncan and his cohorts, who practiced their own brand of National Republicanism, believed that nationalism was a feature of republican virtue. According to them, one's failure to think in nationalist terms was simply serving one's own private interests and not operating for the common good. As the Adams County circular emphatically stated, "We believe *our union* to be the ark of our political safety."[15] Many of Adams's supporters were northerners who had moved South, and who remained more nationalist in outlook than native-born southerners.

The Adams County committee viewed the majority of Jackson supporters as uncontrollable, uneducated yeoman who represented the dregs of society, although they made exceptions for Jackson supporters of strong economic means (particularly those to whom they were related). As their circular stated, they "*dread* the election of general Jackson, as much (if possible) on account of the *violence of many of his adherents*" as because "of *his own peculiar unfitness for the station.*"[16] Duncan believed that republican ideals, specifically citizen virtue, would prevail and prevent Jackson from becoming leader of the nation. In a letter to an ardent Jackson supporter, Mississippi senator Powhatan Ellis, he asserted that "there is too much virtue, too much intelligence in the people of this country: the people are too wise & too good to place a man who has not a solitary qualification for the station."[17]

At noon on Wednesday, January 23, 1828, Adams supporters met at the Natchez courthouse to elect a committee of correspondence to designate "suitable candidates for electors." Duncan heralded the committee as "comprised of nearly all the *wealth—talent* & *respectability* of the county." Though Adams's chances were slim, Duncan remained hopeful, proclaiming that "we are much stronger than our opponents think us." Further distancing himself from Jackson supporters by insinuating that those who supported the general lacked moral character, Duncan affirmed that "we have all the *sober,* reflecting people with us.—and in respectability . . . [and] character we will outnumber them." In regard to Jackson's electoral viability in other regions, he noted, "I *never* shall believe that he can obtain a single electoral vote in the N. England States."[18]

Eight months before the general election, and despite the fact that "the Jackson party have been very sanguine," Duncan refused to give up his expectations that Adams would be elected. "The cause of the administration is gaining ground throughout the whole country," he confidently asserted, "and we have yet hopes that Mr. Adams may succeed."[19] However, Adams lost ground as election day approached, and those who supported him began to face reality. As Duncan admitted to Josiah Johnston, "I feel, in common with you and every other good man, a deep solicitude on the subject of the approaching Election; and I frankly confess, I have great apprehensions for the result." He forcefully suggested to Johnston that their only hope was somehow to spotlight Jackson's shortcomings and failures. They must publicly discredit the general. Duncan suggested that they focus on Jackson's involvement in slave trading. Fearing that Adams would not win Pennsylvania, Duncan wrote that "if any thing can give the vote of the state [Pennsylvania] to Mr. A.—It will be the charge of negro trading proven against Genl. J."[20]

And on that point, Duncan had hard evidence. "I have a distinct recollection myself of a conversation I had with a gentln. there residing in Natchez," he recalled, "who had been a resident of Nashville and well acquainted with Genl. J's movements at that period." While talking about slave prices, the unidentified man noted that slave prices were low in Natchez but higher in Tennessee and Kentucky. As Duncan remembered their conversation, his acquaintance stated that "Gen. Jackson, who sent a large gang here for sale, [was] . . . (about to remove) the greate part of them to Tennessee where he will be able to realize a handsome profit on them—than he can by a sale here." Duncan noted that this conversation took place in 1812 and added that others could corroborate his memory. He hoped that northerners would be appalled at Jackson's lack of morality—not as a slaveowner, which he believed would not cause an outcry, but as a slave trader. "If this does not deprive him of the vote of Penn. nothing will," he exclaimed. "What a curse, what a disgrace it would be to have the country . . . with such a Tyrant."[21]

As the election results came in, Adams's supporters held little hope. Duncan's son John, an undergraduate at Yale University who shared his father's abhorrence of Jackson, wrote his father that "by the papers . . . I fear the old general will get the 'port of Honour' (which certainly he does not deserve) after all."[22] By December 1828, Duncan believed that only "luck" would carry Adams to victory, even in New England. Despondently, he wrote a confidante, John Ker, that "God have mercy on us," concluding that as a people and a nation "we have, I fear, . . . been guilty of great sins." Otherwise he could offer no explanation for Jackson's election.[23]

Yet Duncan resigned himself to a Jackson presidency. As he told Ker, "If Gen. Jackson is to be the instrument in the hands of a wise providence—we must submit with fortitude." Regardless of who won the election, he believed, economic issues remained of supreme importance. "It is folly to comment on what cannot be avoided or redefined," Duncan said of Jackson's impending success, but also added that "we may say—'While Bank Stock' flourishes & cotten grows *d—n* the odds who is elected."[24]

In the final results, Adams secured victories only in the New England states and some areas of the Mid-Atlantic. In the South, Jackson received almost all of the region's electoral votes; in Mississippi, he captured over 80 percent of the ballots cast. Weary over the "drawn *battle*" for the presidency and its unpalatable outcome, Duncan confessed to Ker, "I will try & forget that two such individuals as A. Jackson & J. Q. Adams exist—or ever have existed," and disgustedly quipped, "I am *done* with politics, & I hope forever."[25]

Still smarting from the loss and in spite of his grandiose proclamations, Duncan found himself back in the political arena a mere few months later. Commenting upon Jackson's one-month-old administration, he gleefully exclaimed to Josiah Johnston, "Well! our Genl. has proved himself what his worst enemies predicted of him. *A most vindictive—hollow hearted—weak—& ignorant old man.*" He reiterated his belief that Jackson defiled the purity and morality of the nation. As he looked to the future, he pinned his hopes on Henry Clay to lead the nation. The statesman from Kentucky possessed "a manly frankness, & boldness in his character,—which must attract all reasonable & high minded men to him."[26]

In Duncan's worldview, a Clay presidency would return the leadership of the United States to an enlightened visionary, who would guide the nation back to its virtuous roots. Clay's ideology, put forth in his American System, fit well with Duncan's own agenda. Duncan's economic and political interests were so closely intertwined and mutually reinforcing that they resulted in a very complex ideology. He believed that the foundation for the nation should be a virtuous citizenry, thus harkening back to a Jeffersonian republican ideology; yet he also embraced a very nationalistic political and economic outlook. On the surface, Duncan's ideology appears to be in conflict with itself. However, he defies the ideological labels of this period. Duncan based his political ideology on a set of moral values and a notion of the way an enlightened society should operate—excepting, of course, the moral issue of slavery. These beliefs, coupled with an economic agenda which benefited him, translated into an ideology where economics was thought profitable for the whole nation instead of just one region.

But if Duncan hailed Clay as a savior of order and authority in America, that salvation was in the uncertain future. The immediate reality at the end of 1828 was that economic mastery no longer translated into political dominance, at least in Mississippi. The drastic transformation of presidential and state politics during this period eroded the authority that Duncan and his cohorts commanded in the political arena. As a result, Duncan focused on the more tangible manifestations of his power—his money, land, slaves, and intimate relationships.

Indeed, the intersection of politics and family presented Duncan with unparalleled challenges. This connection brought together the critical networks of economic, familial, political, and social relations. How did relationships in one network affect relationships in the others? In early 1830, Duncan found himself struggling with this very question. That year, Mississippi's representative in the U.S. Congress, Thomas Hinds, decided not to seek reelection. Taking advantage of this opportunity to run without having to face an incumbent, six individuals declared their candidacy. Among those who threw their hat in the ring was Duncan's brother-in-law, friend, and business associate, James C. Wilkins. No stranger to politics, Wilkins actively participated in political affairs on the state and local levels, but he had never held any public office.[27]

Though Hinds threw his support behind Wilkins, the premier commission merchant of Natchez remained a clear target for his opponents. Wilkins had presided over Mississippi's pro-Jackson delegate convention in 1828 and claimed to be a Jackson supporter, yet some of his contemporaries saw him as the antithesis of who Jacksonian Democrats were supposed to represent. His earlier association with the Federalists, coupled with the support he received from anti-Jacksonians in the Mississippi River counties, made him unpopular, particularly in the heavily yeoman and newly settled areas outside of the old Natchez District. Fellow candidate Franklin E. Plummer asserted duplicity in Wilkins's political behavior and focused on his economic status. On the campaign trail, Plummer exclaimed, "I base my prospect of success not on wealth, for riches I have none . . . but on the character I have formed during a residence of many years among you." Further hammering home the point about Wilkins's privilege, Plummer declared, "We are taught that the highway to office, distinction and honor, is as free to the *meritorious poor* man, as to the *rich;* to the man who has risen from obscurity by his own individual exertions, as to him who has inherited a high and elevated standing in society, founded on the patrimony of his ancestors."[28]

Plummer and other "politicians seeking power, especially those from areas outside the plantation districts, could not always resist the opportunity to tap nonslaveholder resentment as a means of getting votes." Plummer held out promises to poor whites and pointed out the class differences between them and the Mississippi River planters. This tactic spoke volumes to those who resided outside the old Natchez District. But, as historian Charles C. Bolton notes, "Plummer . . . proved to be more opportunistic politician than poor white savior."[29]

As the summer of 1830 came to an end, Mississippians cast their fate with Plummer, who won 35 percent of the vote. Wilkins came in third. His supporters charged in the *Woodville Republican* that Plummer used the issue of Wilkins's wealth to divide the public into "artificial and invidious orders, of rich and poor" and thus accounted for his loss.[30]

Counted very reluctantly among Wilkins's supporters was Stephen Duncan. Though Wilkins could have run under the banner of the National Republicans, he chose to throw his support behind the Jackson administration. Even so, he represented the interests of the larger planters in the Mississippi River counties, many of whom would eventually become Whigs. Though Duncan fervently detested Jacksonian Democrats, he looked beyond Wilkins's political label, knowing that his economic interests would be well served and protected by his brother-in-law. After all, Wilkins's interests intertwined with his own. Still, Duncan wished Wilkins out of the race for reasons beyond politics and wealth.

His opinion was based not on his relationship with Wilkins in the economic network, but rather on familial and social ties. "I am informed, that you are before
the public—a candidate for Congress—at the ensuing August Election," Duncan wrote in 1830 to Wilkins, bluntly stating, "I must confess, I do feel some regret that your name has been announced."[31] These words were perhaps the least
difficult for Wilkins to read. Duncan's entire letter was nothing short of a plea
for Wilkins to reconsider his candidacy for a variety of reasons, most of which
were intensely personal.

Duncan knew that Wilkins would face criticism because of his economic
stance, but he also knew that Wilkins was vulnerable on another level: he was
an alcoholic. Wanting to spare his friend and relative from either an open attack
on his problem or from the stress of a bitter campaign which might cause him
to drink, Duncan warned him to be careful. "My object now particularly, is,—
to beg—(and I hope you will believe me when I say, that it is a warm & interested regard, that in dears me to make the request) that you will, during the canvass, keep cool & collected, and entirely aloof from . . . the least excitement of
feeling," he wrote. Cautioning Wilkins against others who may lead him to
drink, Duncan continued, "My great apprehension is, that you will be thrown
among people, whose society you ought, on many accts. avoid; and that you
will be led into excesses, which your own sense of propriety must condemn;—
and your *best* friends will regret." Lamenting how alcohol had affected
Wilkins's life, Duncan sadly noted, "I have for some time past, looked on your
career, with feelings of deep & poignant regret." He declared, "I would stop at
no sacrifice—either pecuniary or personal, however great, to assist in restoring you to what you once were."[32]

Although conscious of the fact that his advice might hurt Wilkins and their
friendship, Duncan was convinced that his friend failed to realize the "dangers"
that surrounded him. To this end, he told Wilkins that he would be foolish "to
console yourself with the hope, that you may indulge in excess a little longer,
and then return to habits of prudence & temperance. Do not, I beseach you—
thus deceive yourself." Duncan apologized for his unsolicited advice, asking
Wilkins "whether an old friend—in whose heart the pulse of friendship still
beats with freshness—may not be excused for wanting to express his feelings
& his advice."[33]

In navigating the waters of their relationship, Duncan did not waver from
his position as friend and relative. Though aware that Wilkins's election to
Congress would be beneficial to those in their economic and social circle, Dun-

can also acknowledged that Wilkins's own best interests should outweigh any such considerations. "I am fully sensible of my own incompetency to advise you on any subject," he wrote, "and now especially on one, in which your own interests & happiness; and the happiness of those men immediately connected with you are also concerned. . . . *Do you think your happiness will be promoted by your election to Congress?*"[34]

On several levels, Wilkins's candidacy for a seat in the U.S. Congress is illustrative. It illuminates how Duncan's various networks overlapped. Moreover, it demonstrates how a person's activities in one area could affect his other kinds of relationships. Though a challenge for Stephen Duncan, usually family and friendship—and the sense of duty and honor that accompanied them— ultimately triumphed over economic interests or other material concerns.

Indeed, even as Duncan tacked between the competing demands of family and electoral politics, he was confronted with the politics of family and friendship. The Duncan family was a close-knit group, but various individuals' desire to assert authority over other family members led to moments of disharmony and contributed to the creation of a family system based on control, ownership, and subordination. A family facade of superiority and invincibility only heightened hidden family tensions. Although Duncan strived for perfection in his business and plantation worlds, his seemingly perfect family was marked by dissension and flaws. In spite of Duncan's desire to have full authority, his power was often illusory; family members challenged him, and he sometimes found himself faced with situations beyond his control.

As master of his family, Duncan was a typical nineteenth-century patriarch—the protector of his wife and children. When plantation or other business affairs took him away from Auburn, he felt great uneasiness about the safety of his family. "I do often reflect, & seriously too," he anxiously expressed to John Ker, "on the misfortune of being called off—leaving a young family— to the *wiles* of this world."[35] As a father and husband, his protectiveness was certainly an ordinary response for his time. However, Duncan also was anxious and mistrustful of people beyond his immediate familial, social, and economic circles, which manifested itself in his desire to shelter his children from the outside world. He was particularly concerned that the habits and ways of "southern society" would negatively affect his children. On one rare occasion when he drew a geographical or sectional distinction, he told Thomas Butler that the South was "a sad country to bring up boys," and proclaimed that "New England is the only place, where steady habits are to be acquired. I wish most truly, on my childrens acct., I was there. Indeed, I would be there were it not for the rascally climate."[36]

Perhaps this attitude helps to explain why Duncan's children from his first marriage spent part of each year with their Philadelphia relatives, where their aunt, Emily Duncan, eventually became their full-time caretaker. Duncan had great gratitude for Emily's willingness to take on this responsibility. Shortly before Sarah Jane's ninth birthday, he proclaimed, "I am much indebted, to her [Emily] for her kind and motherly attention to John and Sarah."[37] His children came to think of Emily as their mother. In a letter to Sarah, John referred to Emily as "your more than Mother—Aunt Emily." They cherished their aunt's opinion and guidance. After John left the family homestead at the age of fourteen to study at Yale University, he advised his younger sister to "always abide by the advice of your most excellent Aunt Emily, *never* slight it—no not even in the slightest instances. Be ever guided by her counsel: for be assured that while you act according to it, you will always do well." He warned his sister that if she ignored her aunt's advice, she would soon "find that 'all is wrong,'" and he added with a reflective tone that was perhaps beyond his years, "I feel confident you (as well as myself) have discovered by experience, that never failing guide."[38]

As Stephen Duncan went about building the family assets, he held out high expectations, standards, and hopes for all of his children. Perhaps most strongly fixed in his mind was the hope that one day John would succeed him as master over all that the family owned. Throughout John's childhood, Duncan mapped out this role for his first-born son. Yet John failed to perform to the level of his father's exacting standards. Just before John's eleventh birthday, Duncan lamented to Thomas Butler, "I have lately had letters from Emily Duncan, who speaks of Sarah in the most flattering manner . . . of John, I am sorry to say, she does not speak so favourably. He has lost much of his ambition—in fact has become [*sic*] with inattention and has been whip'd at school."[39] Under the surface, a profound conflict existed between father and son. John did not meet—and sometimes even defied—his father's expectations, rebelling against them even as he lived with his Aunt Emily. John's behavior may well have reflected the deep losses he suffered at a young age, when his mother died and he was effectively abandoned by his father.

Over time, Stephen Duncan became distraught over what he judged to be his son's poor academic performance. He attributed it to John's cousin, William Postlethwaite, whom he saw as a bad influence on the boy. Anxious about his son's behavior, Duncan moved him to a different school and informed the head-master, "I want my son made a good scholar, . . . I wish him to have anything that a gentlemen's son ought to have." As he declared, "I will spare no pains or expense to make him a good scholar & an accomplished gent[leman]!!"[40] The change seems to have worked. By the time John celebrated his fifteenth birth-day, he had matriculated at Yale University—certainly a big step on the road to fulfilling his father's wishes. As Duncan's forty-second birthday approached, he confided to Ker, "We are getting old, or at least *I* am—and infirm, too." Feel-ing these changes, he wrote that "if I could be spared to see my son John set-tled—I think—(if his character does not materially change)—he will be able to supply my place to some degree."[41]

In spite of Stephen's plans for his son, John Duncan yearned to carve his own path. In the summer of his junior year, he told his sister, "I expect to be a Botanist myself and a Chemist—And a Mineralogist."[42] Wishing to break free of his controlling father, John felt himself caught between being the dutiful son and his own destiny.

Both John and Sarah's relationship with their father was often undergirded by fear, particularly the fear of disappointing him. Further exacerbating this impossible and manipulative dynamic was Duncan's own exaggerated sense of self, which appeared from time to time. Often he believed that the behavior of those with whom he associated reflected back upon himself. This situation pro-duced an even greater desire in him to control the behaviors of others. "I care what others may think or say," Duncan admitted to his friend Ker. "I have, un-fortunately, the character of extreme selfishness."[43]

Consequently, John and Sarah felt the constant desire to win their father's approval. When Sarah was twelve, John cautioned her, "I hope dear Sister, that you devote yourself to your studies. . . . You know the expectations your Fa-ther has formed." Influenced perhaps by his own experiences, John continued, "You have proved that by diligent study you can be one of the best in your class; it then lies entirely with yourself, whether you will gratify your parent or not." And with an admonition, he flatly stated, "Depend on it that you will dis-appoint him unless you study constantly, perseveringly, and attentively." Sev-eral months later and after Sarah's thirteenth birthday, John placed even more pressure on his sister, telling her that "writing to *me* is not, by *far*, so important a duty as pleasing your *Father* . . . [and] when you receive *less* (than 3 good marks) you for one displease your *Father*, your *Aunt* [Emily], and your *Brother*."[44] The following year, John encouraged his sister to "enter with re-

doubled vigour and renewed escertions upon the prosecution of your studies . . . never lay aside your books until you have your recitation perfectly committed." This implies that Sarah, too, became entangled and began to falter in
her father's—and brother's—web of extremely high expectations. Even so,
she received superior grades and comments in such subjects as English, geography, history, and philosophy, which were incorporated into the classical
education program at her school, the Philadelphia High School for Young
Ladies.[45]

John's advice to Sarah stemmed from his own fraught relationship with his
father. Expressing mixed emotions about an upcoming visit with his father, he
wrote her, "I shall feel a pleasure in meeting him doubly enhanced—by the
fears and dreads which I have been subject to—and the horror of falling into
'disappointment which I have experienced.'"[46] Though Duncan placed pressure on both his children, John doubtless felt it more keenly because of the expectations for him as eldest son. Even though Sarah was not burdened with such
exalted expectations, her father held the same exacting standards for her in regard to schooling as he did for her brother, the heir apparent.

Geographical distance compounded the difficulties of family relations between John, Sarah, and their father. Wanting very much to visit his children,
Duncan told Butler that if he was able to leave Natchez, he would do so—"this
I have promised them, and they have a right to expect it of me, for they are dear
to me & deservedly so." There is no question as to Duncan's feelings for his
children, but words are not actions, and Duncan's inaction in regard to his children led them to feel, at times, abandoned. Distance, compounded by the fact
that Duncan prioritized his business affairs over his family, profoundly affected
his children. On Christmas 1828, John sadly wrote his sister that it had been four
weeks since he had received a letter from his father and that he had had only a
few letters before then. "I can only ascribe my Father's silence to the number
and variety of his avocations," he told Sarah, plaintively adding, "for I am sure
he wd. not neglect me."[47]

In spite of their father's controlling behavior, the "horror of falling into disappointment," and their intense feelings of loss, both John and Sarah respected—or at least felt forced to honor—the family patriarch. "I received a
letter from Father on Friday last," John wrote to Sarah, which "was as usual
filled with good advice. I am *sincerely* obliged to him for it."[48] The family dynamic was both one of mutual love and affection, and one of great dysfunction
and coldness. Underneath it lay the Duncan family quest for unreasonable and

unobtainable perfection. Stephen Duncan's desire for this faultless state—not only for himself, but for others—fostered familial relations that were built on fear and intimidation. Indeed, the Duncan family dynamic eerily mirrored the system upon which Stephen Duncan had built his wealth—slavery. The Duncan children were enslaved to their father's desires. In order to escape the icy emotional alienation that faced them if they did not meet their father's excessive expectations, the children subordinated their own desires and lives.

After struggling for much of his life to win his father's approval, John Duncan finally did so. Yet it came, sadly, in the last days of his life. On September 13, 1829, John, barely seventeen years old, died from dysentery culminating in typhoid. "It has pleased the almighty to visit me with new affliction by taking from me my dear,—darling son John," Stephen Duncan wrote to John Ker. "He expired on the evening of the 13th at New Haven, where I had been in attendance for 3 weeks."[49] Perhaps shaken into a deeper realization of John by his son's last weeks, Duncan's eulogy was of the highest order. In it he revealed his thoughts regarding his son, as well as his own philosophy of life and his role as father, physician, and friend:

> He was a youth of high promise—gifted with talents of the first order; a mind highly mature for one his age, and with application & emulation sufficient to insure him the highest honor in all he undertook; and with a disposition so kind & affectionate; a temper so mild & amiable—and manner so soft & engaging—as to make him universally beloved by his classmates. It cost me much to part with him,—for he was most dear to me;—and rendered still more dear in his last moments,—by the manly firmness & patience with which he bore his long suffering;—and the saint-like calmness & composure with which he resigned his life.[50]

The disease rendered Stephen Duncan, the physician, powerless, while Stephen Duncan, the father, was forced to shoulder the emotional weight of his inability to intervene as a doctor and as a parent:

> For 18 days & 18 nights I nursed him with all a parents tender care; I anxiously *watched*, & not infrequently *wept* over his pillow—; and seriously & fervently prayed that he might be spared to me—but all—all in vain. The will of the almighty is more powerful, then the vain efforts of man; and I must learn to bow in submission to his decrees. He was, I trust, fully prepared to go, and left this world confidently relying on more permanent happiness in the world to come.[51]

As difficult as it was, Duncan surrendered himself to providence. Equally as difficult was his acknowledgment that he had wanted his son one day to walk in his footsteps. As he confided to Ker, "I had found high hopes for this youth, and too frequently indulged in the most delightful anticipations—that in him, I would leave a faithful representative, and an able & kind protector . . . to those most dear to me, when I was no more."[52]

As a tribute and memorial to John, his friends at Yale commissioned a nine-foot monument in memory of him. The inscription proclaimed that "Duncan was a youth of great promise. Powers naturally strong he cultivated with un-wearied diligence & attained to high destination as a scholar." A newspaper obituary noted that "his high attainments in his colegiate studies had excited the most pleasing anticipations."[53] As Stephen Duncan read the homages to his son, he must have realized his own blindness before John's achievements. He opened his eyes too late for both father and son.

Four months after John's death, the carefully managed world of Stephen Duncan shattered again with the death of his only brother, Samuel Postle-thwaite Duncan. The brothers claimed to know each other's every feeling and had built an extremely close relationship. Angry over his losses, Duncan bit-terly exclaimed to Ker, "It has pleased an all-win god to try [me] now once more with affliction,—by taking from me, my dear & only brother." After some re-flection, Duncan retreated to a Job-like position, acknowledging that "these visitations of his providence are ordered for some purpose. I can no more doubt—this [than] I can doubt my own existence. His ways are mysterious, though just; and we must submit with resignation to his will, in all things." De-spite this realization, he was hard-pressed to find some measure of solace. "I am at time[s] my friend almost heartbroken," he wrote Ker, "and did not I hope to meet my son & my brother again—I should be a miserable man." Even though distraught, Duncan believed that his mourning was divinely sanctioned, and that if the "Saviour could weep over the dead body of his friend Lazarus . . . [then so could] imperfect [human] beings."[54] After ten years of seemingly in-vincible prosperity, he and his family had to confront the destruction of what meant the most to them—those they loved. Despite being protected by such tangible fortresses as money, land, slaves, institutions, and mammoth homes, they remained vulnerable to a variety of forces that lay beyond the scope of Stephen Duncan's mastery.

4

✦

"WE WILL ONE DAY HAVE OUR THROATS CUT
IN THIS COUNTY"

Stephen Duncan and the Challenges of Slavery

I n the 1820s, Stephen Duncan slowly and meticulously built his family's
wealth and anchored its position of power within the inner circle of the region's most important social and economic networks. As the 1830s opened,
he held a variety of valuable assets: expansive tracts of land, hundreds of slaves,
and valuable family and business connections. Yet maintaining the value of
those assets required constant vigilance, since frequently Duncan had to con-
tend with larger forces that he could not personally control.

Among these forces was the value of land and crops, which declined significantly in the summer of 1831. Having suffered through a drought in June,
Duncan's crops fell two-thirds short of what he expected, and his fields produced half of the previous year's yield. Meanwhile, at the close of the crop year
that August, the average price of cotton dipped to 9.92 cents per pound in New
Orleans—its lowest price in that city since 1812. Markets elsewhere, especially
in New York and Liverpool, mirrored this drop.[1] For Duncan, the year's serious crop difficulties gave way to potentially even graver dangers in the fields.
As the summer sun of late August seared the Mississippi landscape, events in
faraway Virginia unfolded that would, in the coming months, burn indelible
images in the minds of black and white Mississippians.

In the Virginia Tidewater county of Southampton, August 21, 1831, began
as ordinarily as the thousands of days that came before it. By the time sunset
fell over the Old Dominion, cataclysmic events had ripped through Virginia's
master class. Nat Turner and several fellow bondsmen received what they believed to be signs from God indicating that it was the propitious moment to

forge ahead with their plot to bring freedom to the enslaved, and they rose up in rebellion.[2]

After killing Turner's enslavers, the self-emancipated group enlisted nearly seventy followers, who methodically proceeded to execute white slaveowning families as they moved through the county. By the morning of August 24, the rebels had cut a swath of freedom encompassing more than twenty square miles. Trying to get control of the rebellion, armed white vigilante groups gathered by the hundreds and enlisted the help of military troops. The ensuing bloody clashes resulted in the slaughter of hundreds of slaves, including slaves who were not participants in the uprising. Turner initially eluded authorities but was eventually captured at the end of October. Within a few days, a Virginia court sentenced Turner to hang.[3]

For Stephen Duncan and other white southerners, the Turner revolt struck at the heart of their strength—and their vulnerability. Though open acts of slave resistance occurred from the time that slave ships first brought Africans to colonial America, the Turner revolt and its outcome brought forth white fears of black rebellion that were unmatched.[4] Whites rushed to enact tighter and more rigid methods of control over slaves. Symbolic of this reaction was the intersection of two roads in Southampton County, where whites impaled on a stake the severed head of a black man. Blackhead Signpost, as the crossroads came to be known, stood as a grim reminder that slaves who sought freedom would be met by certain and brutal death.[5]

As news of the rebellion spread across the South, panic spread through white society, profoundly affecting slaveholders' consciousness. A captured runaway slave from Mississippi claimed that the scars that marked his body were from a "severe whipping with a cow-skin, at the time of the South-Hampton insurrection."[6] The distress created by the Virginia revolt eventually found its way to Auburn. Duncan initially dismissed the event, proclaiming in a letter to Thomas Butler, "I don't credit the story of the extension of the Virginia insurrection." Yet his very next sentence revealed his deep alarm: "I have great apprehension that we will one day have our throats cut in this county." The existence of a majority black population fueled Duncan's fears. "We now have 5 blacks to one white; and within 4 hours march of Natches there are 2200 able bodied male slaves. . . . It behooves us to be vigilant—but *silent*."[7]

As the days and weeks passed, Duncan was increasingly anxious as he focused on the reality of a black majority in Natchez. In Adams County, slaves and free blacks numbered over 11,000, while the white population totaled slightly less than 4,000. Exacerbating his fears was the general belief, with which he concurred, that nervous slaveowners in Virginia and the eastern seaboard would begin selling slaves to the lower South in order to reduce their black populations. "There cannot be a doubt the recent occurrences in Virginia & N. Carolina will have the effect of increasing to a great degree the exports from those states," Duncan declared, adding, "We must expect to receive, *four fifths of all that are for sale in Virginia & Maryland.*" Even without these additional slave imports, he believed, the area's black population was already too large. "It is certain our numbers are at present, sufficiently large, to excite serious apprehensions for our *safety,*" he exclaimed to Louisiana senator Josiah Johnston. The racial imbalance was, he believed, a "disproportion sufficiently great to make every mother 'bring her infant more closely to her bosom.'"[8]

With a black majority in Natchez, Duncan feared the possibility of organized black mass resistance. "I confess, I am not myself, entirely free from apprehension," he noted as he pondered the mixture of black slaves and free whites in Natchez. "The day is fast approaching when we will have increased cause for our fears."[9] Yet he did not allow his anxiety to govern his behavior as well as to control him outwardly. Instead, he devised concrete solutions to assuage his own fears, while refusing to acknowledge the potential power of those whom he enslaved.

Inevitably, the Nat Turner revolt caused Duncan to sharpen his views on the institution and management of slaves. Though he expressed anxiety about slave resistance, he did not radically alter his style of slave management in the wake of the Turner revolt, but rather reinforced already well-honed practices. Prior to the Turner uprising, Duncan advocated selling troublesome slaves instead of severely punishing them. He reasoned that the harsh discipline of one slave might cause resistance among the others and that the occasional sale of a slave was therefore a more effective form of social control.[10] This philosophy was unaltered in the wake of the Turner rebellion. In September 1831, Duncan offered advice to Thomas Butler, who had noticed an increased agitation among his slaves. Aware of the slave resistance that had taken place on Butler's plantation before and after the Turner revolt, Duncan warned his brother-in-law that his new overseer, Mr. Ford, carried a reputation for harshness. "From what Mr. U told me of the conduct of the Negroes—I am sure Mr. F will not get along with them," Duncan informed Butler, urging him to tell Ford to "observe great laxity with your people. They will not fear contrary treatment." Believing at this time that restraint was more effective than the lash, he forthrightly wrote, "I think that it is important that they should not be dealt harshly with otherwise they will run off," and warned that once "the habit of absconding is fixed," it would be most difficult to reverse.[11] With this advice dispensed, he assured Butler shortly thereafter that Ford would work out, "especially if you impose rigid restrictions on him in regard to severity."[12]

Part of Duncan's overall style of management was driven by his belief that if he paid high wages to overseers, they would help to ensure optimum slave management practices. Accordingly, he counseled that Butler pay Ford a salary of $600 for the first year of service. If satisfactory, Ford would earn $650 in his second year, with raises of $50 per annum until the yearly salary of $800 was reached.[13] In effect, Duncan employed a similar policy of relatively lenient control for both slaves and overseers. In the latter case, he used wages to control a group of white employees who occupied a low status in the southern social hierarchy, even though their work was critical to the functioning of the slave system. As he bluntly stated, "I find this the only way to manage this class of men."[14]

Duncan's use of wages to control lower-class white employees may have represented his belief that overseers, like slaves, reflected back upon the master. He frequently felt that the actions of his associates cast judgment directly on him and signified what kind of man he was. Paying an overseer a high wage would help to ensure, so Duncan might have thought, that the overseer would be of a superior quality, which would throw a positive light back upon him.

Two years after the Nat Turner rebellion, Duncan's principles of slave management were tested when he found himself again in the position of advising Butler, this time with regard to a plantation manager. In weighing the merits of two candidates, Dr. Calhoun and R. T. Dunbar, Duncan centered his analysis on who would provide the best style of slave management. On the one hand, Calhoun's lack of experience, poor decision-making skills, and harshness caused Duncan to conclude, "At present, I don't think [Calhoun's] management is the best. I infer this, from his many many runaways—& many deaths." On the other hand, a drinking problem impaired R. T. Dunbar's judgment. In Duncan's opinion, however, by hiring Dunbar, Butler would be "assured [his] Negroes wd. be treated with great humanity for he [Dunbar] is indulgent to his own, to a fault."[15]

Though both candidates possessed negatives, in the end Duncan advised Butler to choose the more brutal Calhoun, believing that "when he has more experience[,] will probably make a good manager" and that "a few years will make a great change in his management." Although Duncan's pick was at odds with his own philosophy of slave management, he rationalized his preference by noting that Calhoun's lack of judgment and tendency towards harsh treatment was common. "All young planters err in this particular," he wrote, offering, "at best, I find, the older I grow, the less disposed I am to [have] ordinary security precautions." Referring to his own management problems, Duncan acknowledged that "I am compelled to discharge an overseer for this fault now," and admitted, "I was much distressed at the wretched appearance of some of my Homochitto Negs."[16]

Though Duncan did not admit—and perhaps did not recognize—that his advice was often contradictory, he was conscious of the fact that his own style of slave management had changed over time. This was not necessarily a result of his deep anxiety over slave rebellions, such as Nat Turner's, but rather, as Duncan argued, the development of emotional maturity over time, which informed his approach to slave management and punishment. He had become more lenient in terms of discipline, especially the use of threatening physical punishment as a form of control. Like the well-known slaveholder from South Carolina, James Henry Hammond, Duncan practiced more psychological than physical control in order to foster outcomes and behaviors, such as greater production and less resistance, which he desired in his slaves. Hammond's movement away from harsh physical treatment was intended to elicit the slaves' conformity to his brand of paternalism. As Hammond's biographer, Drew Gilpin Faust, points out, Hammond's slaves were aware of their owner's strategy and used it to their advantage to carve out some autonomy in their lives.[17]

Duncan did not consciously practice an overarching form of paternalism, nor did he discuss paternalist philosophy or goals in any significant way. Yet he cared a great deal about how others—either black or white—perceived him, and whether their behavior was a reflection upon him. It is thus not that far of a stretch to suggest that some form of paternalism, albeit a low-level one, existed in his master-slave relationships. Nonetheless, Duncan did not engage in a Hammondesque quest to gain his slaves' acceptance and cooperation. In all of his writings, revelations about his relationships with his slaves are tellingly and chillingly absent. Unlike Hammond, he did not reveal in tortured detail, or even broad strokes, his feelings about his slaves; nor did he record what he believed they thought about him. He was consistently silent on the subject of whether or not he considered his slaves as an extension of himself.

Though Stephen Duncan's style of slave management remained virtually unchanged in the wake of the Nat Turner rebellion, the revolt deeply affected his views on the politics of slavery. For the first time, he explicitly asked potentially disruptive questions. What would be the future of slavery and the economic life of the South? More importantly, how would white and black society live together, with or without the peculiar institution? The Turner rebellion catapulted these issues to a position of significance that had not been present since the Missouri Compromise debates. In his quest to find answers to these vexing questions, Duncan philosophically dissected the very system he helped foster and from which he benefited. His response encompassed a multifaceted approach that he melded into a single master plan to relieve white fear, strengthen the South's economy, and preserve slavery in the present. At the same time, his long-term goal would streamline slavery and plant the seeds of its ultimate dissolution.

Duncan believed that a crisis of slavery was at hand, a crisis rooted in a variety of interconnected elements. In his view, the Turner rebellion and other forms of collective resistance in North Carolina and Virginia would cause an increase in the number of slaves sold and exported out of these states, as anxious whites sought to reduce the slave population and alter racial imbalances in certain areas. Slaveowners in neighboring geographic regions, who would normally purchase a good number of these slaves, would balk at buying them because of the economic constraints placed upon them by the tariff of 1828, which added extra costs to a variety of goods. "In the Carolinas & Georgia (if their public men are to be believed)," he wrote Josiah Johnston, "the 'oppression' from the tariff has, & will, deprive them of the means & the disposition to purchase to any extent." Furthermore, the reality of organized slave resistance "will increase the desire to sell; while the planters of Louisiana & Mississi. will be the only purchasers." He noted that the increased number of banks in these states would provide capital for greater investment in slaves. "These states have been exempt from all suffering from the Tariff, and are in a state of prosperity which will encourage larger investment of this kind," he concluded. This increase in slave imports would only magnify the already existing racial imbalance in Louisiana and Mississippi.[18]

For Duncan, now was the time to ward off future catastrophe. He believed that the crisis of slavery lay in a quiet state and was "only kept at rest now, by the predominant & all-absorbing influence of the *anti-masonic spirit*." Hoping to act before "the spirit of the age" unleashed "all its energy and strength" against slavery, Duncan devised a program that encompassed internal improvements, tariff increases and reductions, and checks upon the institution of slavery.[19] First and foremost, Duncan believed that slavery's growth needed to be controlled. This was particularly important as slavery spread into newly acquired territories in Mississippi from lands gained through the removal of the Choctaw Indians in 1830—the result of official government policy, which sanctioned the forcible removal of Native Americans through the Indian Removal Act of 1830. On September 27, 1830, leaders of the Choctaw Nation and the Federal government signed the Treaty of Dancing Rabbit Creek. With an ultimatum in hand, the Federal government and the State of Mississippi left the Choctaws with no choice. They ceded the remainder of their lands in north and east-central Mississippi, opening the area to new settlement.[20]

Duncan remained wary about the imminent opening of this Indian territory. Fearing the influx of new settlers who wanted to reap the benefits of Mississippi's prime soil, he complained, "I confess I have my fears that our newly acquired Territory will be filled—not with proprietors—but with more *negro quarters.*" He went on to lament that "those who are able to remain—will continue in Virginia & establish their quarters with their *overseers* in the Mississi[ppi]." He predicted that "our Legislature will do nothing to prevent this—and nothing to stay the importation of slaves for sale."[21]

Even as he expounded the need to restrict the growth of slavery, Duncan proposed that the South diversify its economy and enter the arena of cloth manufacturing. This idea spun directly out of his belief that the southern economy would be healthier if it was not dependent on single-crop export agriculture. It was also tied to his fear that British manufacturers would shun U.S. cotton because of its availability from elsewhere, such as Egypt. If that happened, cotton grown overseas and its overproduction in the United States might lead to reduced prices. In order to avoid this danger, Duncan advocated that the South undertake the production of finished cotton goods in order to increase consumption, raise the price of cotton, and foster the diversification of the South's economy.[22] Such a plan, however, would not necessarily retard slavery's growth. In fact, for all Duncan's fear about a burgeoning slave workforce, his ideas for economic diversification had the potential to expand slavery to even greater proportions. "I am myself interested in a factory at Louisville conducted all together by slave labor," he stated in the winter of 1832. Noting that the Kentucky factory produced cloth equal in quality to any in the North, Duncan believed that "if the South would but turn their attention to the subject they could soon manufacture all the coarse fabrics required for . . . consumption." Aware that manufacturers in the North might find this objectionable, he sug-

gested that manufacturers in the northern and middle states "would then confine their operations to the fine goods & all would be satisfied." Furthermore,
he believed that the use of slave labor in manufacturing could be extended into
the North. Astonished by his northern colleagues' lack of imagination, he exclaimed, "It is a capital error of New York That slave labor is not adapted to
manufacturers."[23]

In light of Duncan's position on the expansion of slavery, did his advocacy
of slave labor in manufacturing contradict his stance on the restriction of the
institution? As he saw it, if factories used slave labor, slaves would then be si-
phoned away from the fields, which would lessen the danger of agricultural
overproduction. Yet the increased demand for finished goods produced by slave
industrial labor would then cause an increased need for more slave field labor.
Duncan's suggestion that northern factory owners utilize slave labor directly
opposed his call for restrictions on bondage. His contradictory stance might
have been rooted in pure economics: he was always in search of the greatest opportunity that would yield the most profit. As he exclaimed, "I have no hesita-
tion in believing—that I could manufacture *here* 500 bales of cotton per
an[num],—and would draw a greater revenue from the capital thus employed—
that I would from my cotton estates in the most productive years."[24]

Unlike many of his fellow southerners, Duncan was not encumbered by personal debt. Likewise, his financial vision was not dictated by the single pursuit
of agriculture. This, in turn, gave him more freedom to define himself economically and politically; it also freed him from having to form—or at least to
claim—any regional loyalty. He could operate unfettered in what was slowly
becoming the distinct worlds of North and South.

In Duncan's complex quest to resolve the slavery question, he also confronted the question of tariffs. Over the previous years, vitriolic debates had
surrounded this issue. The passage of the tariff of 1828, which protected duck,
flax, hemp, iron, molasses, sailcloth, and raw wool, had sparked intense regional
controversy.[25] Except for Louisiana sugar planters and Kentucky hemp growers, the tariff of 1828 enraged southern planters and farmers, as it forced them
to pay higher prices for goods they needed to sustain their agricultural operations. Public outcry against the tariff found its way to the local papers. In 1830,
the *Natchez Gazette* estimated that the tariff cost Mississippians $6 million per
year.[26]

South Carolinians led the attack on the tariff, declaring it unconstitutional.
Mississippi's response was negative but less intense, in part because it did not

suffer from soil exhaustion and population loss, which served to exacerbate the issue in South Carolina. Duncan claimed that South Carolinians wrongly blamed the tariff for their economic problems. In a letter to Senator Josiah S. Johnston, he noted with surprise that Johnston's Senate colleague from South Carolina, Robert V. Hayne, would "reiterate the state tale of 'oppression'. . . attributed to the Tariff." Duncan implored Hayne to examine South Carolina's economic condition and its "causes with an eye of candor." By doing so, he believed, Hayne would find that the "barren hills of Georgia, & sand hills of Carolina, have been abandoned by all professional agricultural skill & enterprise, for the settlement of new & fertile lands [in Mississippi and Alabama] which yield 6 bales when 3 were raised before."[27]

Despite the improved economic outlook for Mississippi planters, in January 1829, Mississippi governor Gerard C. Brandon asked the state's General Assembly to lodge a formal complaint against the tariff as "impolitic and oppressive in its operation on the Southern States." The assembly advocated fighting but not nullifying the tariff. For Mississippians, rejection or nullification of the tariff was not a statement about the Magnolia State's allegiance to the South and states' rights, as South Carolina claimed; rather, it "revealed instead widespread preoccupation with local, individual political and economic concerns."[28]

With nullification in the air, Duncan predicted that Congress would have to address the tariff issue. "It is very evident, a vigorous effort will be made at the approaching session of congress, to effect a modification of the Tariff," he informed Johnston in 1831, quipping, "so as to adopt it, to the whims & caprices of our 'high minded Southerners.'"[29] Though this was one of the first times Duncan aligned himself along sectional divides, he still distanced himself from the label of "southerner." He realized, and maybe even regretted, that regional identity was becoming more sharply defined. The days of building a frontier community comprised of migrants from all over the nation who were spurred on by a common quest for economic advancement had faded, to be replaced by a way of life that was coming to be defined as "southern."[30]

A supporter of protectionism and other measures to create a national economy, Duncan found himself caught between identities: that of northerner and southerner, national and regional. Though his connections and roots in the North remained strong and vibrant, he reaped the benefits of the southern economic system, as well as its class, racial, and gender structures. In light of this, the question arises: to what extent was Duncan a southerner, a northerner, or a hybrid combination of the two, which might be defined as "American"? Much of his political and economic philosophy marginalized him from his neighbors, and he found himself in the minority on a variety of issues, like the tariff.[31] With a much broader economic vision than most white Mississippians, Duncan grounded his support of the tariff in nationalistic economic policies. Nor did he allow regional issues to circumscribe his political ideology. He believed that the political economies of both regions worked together in a dynamic fashion. After all, slavery and race were American issues, not just southern and northern ones: the entire nation, including the Federal government, benefited from enslaving blacks.[32]

Duncan reached across regional boundaries, suggesting that a compromise be sought between antitariff southerners and antislavery advocates in the East, West, and middle states. His compromise rested on two premises. First, the tariff would be used to eliminate the national debt. Second, any surplus revenue generated by the tariff would be used to dismantle slavery gradually through colonization. Arguing for this concept, Duncan asked, "Would not the South consent to the most ample protection to the eastern western & middle interests, by an *increase* of duties, provided the revenue was thus applied?" With such a compromise, northern and eastern manufacturers would receive permanent protection from the tariff, while "the Southern interests would be promoted by the enhanced value of their staple from diminished productions." Additionally, the value of the South's slaves would increase due to the reduction in the total slave population. Fewer slaves would also slow down cotton production—a significant point for Duncan, who believed that the South had an unlimited capacity to grow cotton. Unless southerners checked the increase of slavery, he warned, "the production will soon so far exceed the consumption, that the price will scarcely pay for the labour employed in growing it." With this in mind, he fervently believed that his compromise would ultimately prove that the "advantages would be altogether in favor of the South."[33]

For his fellow white southerners who argued that they would have to pay more for essential finished goods, Duncan had a simple answer—tariffs provided economic stability and protection. He argued that overproduction, not the tariff, reduced the price of American cotton. "No man in his senses can believe that the reduced price of cotton, can in the scantest degree be attributed to the Tariff," he exclaimed to Senator Johnston. In a direct attack on the logic of antitariffites, Duncan bluntly asserted that "all men of sense & truth must admit, that oppression cannot be felt from the tax paid on the clothing of slaves. . . . We all know, that the woollen goods consumed by each laboring negro does not . . . near [such an amount, and thereby] surely no oppression can be felt from this."[34]

For antitariffites not convinced by economic reasoning, Duncan employed a racial argument. In order to quell the disquiet whites felt about the increasing numbers of slaves, he argued, a tariff, in combination with measures to slow the expansion of slavery, would impede the growth of the South's black population. He proclaimed that "above all, they [white Southerners] would, in my view, be amply compensated for the high duties they pay, whether as consumers or (as according to the absurd writers as '*producers*') by the sense of *security* they would feel. This is of vastly more importance than the increased value of their products, or their property."[35]

Duncan tried to find a common ground that would bridge the wide gap of economic and political differences between him and his fellow southerners. In doing so, he claimed that it was the duty of a man, and in particular that of a southern man, to do all that he could to protect those who were deemed helpless in the face of any potential black retaliation—white wives and children. "I am sure, no southern man, who is the father of a family & also reflects at all, can feel indifferent on the subject, or views it without *feeling* its awful and dreadful importance," he concluded.[36] In a masterful maneuver that played upon people's fears and beliefs, he manipulated notions of gender, race, and regional identity to bolster his case, providing the perfect rationale for why white southerners should adopt a course of action that seemingly went against their own economic interests.

In order to achieve economic stability for the South and security for whites, Duncan proposed the following four-point plan: 1) protection in the form of high duties on all commodities that could be grown or produced in the United States; 2) a lowering of duties on all items that could not be produced at home; 3) the application of 75 percent of the surplus revenue generated from the duties "to the purchase & transportation of slaves [outside of the United States], commencing in those states which have the smallest number"; 4) the remaining 25 percent of the surplus revenue to be distributed among the states in proportion to their Congressional representation for internal improvements.[37]

If his plan was adopted, Duncan projected that slavery would eventually be phased out of existence. "A century or more would be required for the extinguishment of slavery," he wrote, "and the states of Louisiana & Mississi[ppi] would be the last to become *free* states." In the short term, however, the plan would serve to prevent slavery's growth. It is not clear whether Duncan's plan was intentionally to eliminate slavery or whether he assumed that restrictions upon slavery's growth would eventually dismantle the system naturally. In any event, the chances for the success of Duncan's compromise seemed remote. As he admitted, "If the philanthropic feelings of the Eastern, western & Northern people, was not thrown into the scale I should have no hope of its accomplishment."[38]

Despite the odds, Duncan reflected that "a pursuance in this course would, in time, make us an independent, happy, united and *free* people." This conclusion was ladened with murky, multiple meanings. Duncan's vision failed to include an America where those who had been once enslaved lived out the remainder of their lives free in the United States, which they had helped to put on the map economically. Instead, Duncan firmly believed in the "transportation beyond the limits of the U.S. of the surplus slave population."[39] His vision of a "happy, united and *free* people" referred to whites only, who, with the absence of former black slaves, would be free from all the burdens borne by a society constructed on racial bondage. With racial cleansing through colonization came psychological freedom for the oppressors: they would not have to face those they once had enslaved. The compromise was a grand plan to appeal to individuals who refused to live with blacks—or, for that matter, who refused to live with the world they had created. Stephen Duncan was such an individual.

Duncan's position on slavery and his complex solution to the interconnected problems of cotton overproduction and the spread of slavery were not temporary, emotional responses to the fears that followed the Nat Turner rebellion and other insurrectionary scares. His convictions remained vividly on display a decade later. As he revealed to William J. Minor in 1842, "What I consider the most alarming feature—is—the prospect—that ere long—the price of our staple will be so effected by overproduction—that slave labor will be no longer profitable." He again suggested that "when this labor isn't remunerating—To the master,—it be the interest of the master to get clear of the *superanuated* & the *young*—& this will become the acting wedge of a general emancipation."[40]

Anxious over how the growth of the very institution from which he benefited could begin adversely to affect him, Duncan continued to advocate not only for tighter control over the increase and use of slavery, but also for its gradual elimination. Since he believed that the phasing out of slavery would take a century or more to affect Mississippi and Louisiana, he could afford to champion these ideas, which would only occur beyond his lifespan. As a result of his diversified financial foundation, he could also afford to advocate such opinions. Unlike those who depended solely on slave agriculture, he had the capital and freedom to extricate himself from slavery's economic web. Nevertheless, he continued to increase his slave force and argue for its use in other realms besides agriculture.

Deeply connected to Duncan's economic beliefs were those related to race. Though he rarely spoke about such issues even privately, he threw himself very publicly into the fray when it came to the subject of colonization. On June 22, 1831, some of the largest planters and leading citizens of Mississippi, many of whom resided in the old Natchez District, gathered to organize the Mississippi Colonization Society. At this meeting, the society clarified its goals in a constitution, stating, "The object to which its attention [is] to be exclusively directed is the colonization (with their own consent) of the free people of color in Mississippi."[41] For Duncan, colonization was an integral part of the solution to the multifaceted question of slavery. As early as 1830, he labeled it an issue "of vital importance to the southern states."[42] It is unclear whether his agenda at this time included not only the deportation of free blacks but also slaves emancipated with the sole intent of expulsion from the United States, or whether the latter half of his argument came about in the wake of Nat Turner's revolt. Clearly, though, by 1832, Duncan advocated for gradual slave emancipation with colonization. Whether or not the society's other members were aware of his beliefs, the efforts of the Mississippi Colonization Society meshed with aspects of Duncan's larger program.

Participants at the June meeting elected Duncan their first president, a position he held until the late 1840s. The other officers of the society were a roll call of the area's most prominent planters: William C. Conner, William St. John Elliott, Alvarez Fisk, Beverly Grayson, David Hunt, John Ker, Ayres P. Merrill, and Rush Nutt. The society immediately began to organize efforts to resettle the state's free black population outside the South. Less than a year later, Duncan informed Josiah Johnston of the society's progress: "We have raised funds for the transmission of free blacks residing in this state to Liberia. One gent. has raised on his subscription paper, upward of $6000 in less than a fortnight." By the following year, the Mississippi Colonization Society loaned its parent organization $3,000 with the stipulation that the money be used exclusively for colonizing free blacks from Mississippi.[43]

Meanwhile, Duncan continued to believe in his own colonization agenda. While the aims of the Mississippi and American Colonization Societies focused on colonizing free blacks while leaving slavery intact, Duncan thought that colonization could be a tool to control and streamline the growth of slavery. In a vigorous attempt to gain more widespread support for his ideas, he suggested to Johnston that they anonymously publish Duncan's tariff plan, complete with his colonization scheme and ideas about emancipation, in the *National Intelligencer*. In terms of local support for his ideas, Duncan informed the senator, "I have suggested the outlines of my plan to several gent. here who now heartily concur in the propriety of applying the *whole* of the surplus revenue to this object." He believed that some "*anti* tariff gent., would consent to a continuance of their '*burdens*' from this source, to create a fund for the purchase of slaves & transmission of them with the free blacks to Liberia." Duncan declared that the moment had come for such events to take place. As he wrote, "I am inclined to think, *now* is the time to put the ball in motion here." In March 1835, the first colonization from Mississippi took place, as sixty-nine free blacks set sail on the *Rover* for Liberia.[44]

As the Mississippi Colonization Society entered its most intense period of activity, tension between the state society and the parent society steadily mounted. The state society charged the national officers with lack of support and mismanagement, and internal divisions within the parent organization reverberated back to the state organization. Furthermore, the Mississippi Colonization Society was a creditor of the parent organization, and hostility was exacerbated when its members discovered that the American Colonization Society did not utilize the borrowed money for the exclusive colonization of free blacks from Mississippi—a condition of the loan. By the late 1830s, support among Mississippians for colonization reached its peak, but so did strains with the national office. Leaders of the state society walked a fine line. In order to capitalize on the support of Mississippians, state leaders distanced themselves from the parent institution as much as possible, and the state society became quasi-independent.[45]

A significant factor motivating the Mississippi Colonization Society to break away from the American Colonization Society was its desire to establish its own colony in Africa. In January 1837, the state leadership secured land 130 miles south of Liberia's capital, Monrovia, at the mouth of the Sinou River. The society named the new colony "Mississippi in Africa" and designated its capital as "Greenville," after Adams County planter and judge James Green, who had sent twenty-six of his former slaves to Liberia on the *Rover*. Due to financial difficulties sparked in part by the panic of 1837 and the lack of former Mississippi slaves going to the independent colony (only thirty-seven between 1837 and 1839), the Mississippi Colonization Society eventually turned control of Mississippi in Africa over to the parent society.[46]

By 1840, support for colonization began to dwindle in Mississippi, even though the state society transported 350 free blacks and ex-slaves to Africa over the course of the next ten years. Contributing to the society's difficulties during the 1840s was a widely known legal battle, the Ross case, which drew both Duncan and his close friend and associate Dr. John Ker into the fray. In 1837, Jefferson County planter Isaac Ross died, leaving to his daughter, Margaret Reed, 170 slaves. Ross, a supporter of colonization, stipulated in his will that his slaves had either the choice of emigrating to Liberia or being sold as slaves. If the latter occurred, the proceeds of any sales would go to the American Colonization Society to be invested and used to finance a school in Liberia. Though Margaret Reed supported colonization, other Ross heirs, led by grandson Isaac Ross Wade, challenged the will. Wade claimed that slaves could not be emancipated unless the state legislature allowed it, citing an old 1822 state law. The legal battles over the Ross slaves dragged on even beyond Margaret Reed's death in 1838. Anticipating the legal fight while also wanting to see the desires of her father carried out, Reed willed her father's slaves and estate to Duncan, Ker, and the Reverend Zebulon Butler.[47]

As the intense drama which surrounded the case unfolded, the Mississippi High Court of Errors and Appeals ruled against the Ross heirs in 1840.[48] In spite of this ruling, attempts to stop the transportation of the Ross slaves to Africa drew the battle lines even sharper. In 1841, the Mississippi House of Representatives stated that allowing the Ross slaves to go free to Africa would set a dangerous precedent. In response, the following year, the Mississippi legislature passed a law that prohibited manumissions by will. Finally, Isaac Ross Wade openly threatened the Mississippi legislature, claiming that he had under his command five hundred armed men who would use force if the Ross slaves were colonized. The attempts to block the slaves' transport failed, and in June 1843, the *Renown* set sail for Liberia with a group of newly emancipated slaves aboard. Meanwhile, opposition to their colonization mounted in Natchez. It became so intense that Duncan allegedly hid a large contingent of Ross slaves in a remote spot on the banks of the Mississippi while they awaited a boat to take them to New Orleans en route to Africa.[49]

In 1848, after several shiploads, the last of the Ross slaves crossed the Atlantic. With its funds exhausted from fighting the case and personal animosity running high between the state and parent organizations, the Mississippi Colonization Society slowly dissolved over the course of the next decade. Along with the local society's gradual demise came Duncan's growing disenchantment with the American Colonization Society. His generous funding to the parent society, believed to be $50,000 by 1840, ceased with the American Colonization Society's overzealous efforts to collect funds in the aftermath of the Ross case. This angered Duncan to such an extent that he resigned his presidency of the state society and struck from his will a bequest to the American Colonization Society. In spite of this falling out with the parent organization, Duncan still remained a vice president as well as a life director of the American Colonization Society—positions he held until his death.[50] Ironically, given his deep involvement with the colonization movement for three decades, not a single piece of evidence suggests that he himself manumitted any slaves with the intent of colonization.

5

+>=<+

POWER AND POSITION

Redefining Economic Self in Boom and Bust Times

In spite of his myriad apprehensions about the growth of slavery, in the early 1830s Stephen Duncan embarked on a path that perpetuated those very fears: a systematic expansion of his family's wealth and power through plantation profits. Like other wealthy Mississippians, he had been affected by the economic slump of the late 1820s and the beginning of the 1830s, as the cotton market hit bottom; in 1832 and 1833, however, the price and output of cotton began to climb upward. Prices hovered between 10.21 cents per pound in Natchez and 12.32 cents in New York. Compared to 1831–1832, the value of Mississippi's cotton crop increased 35.4 percent.[1] The good fortune that Mississippi planters experienced in the 1832–1833 crop year was felt across the South, as economic activity increased along with the demand for cotton. Between 1831 and 1836, the value of American cotton tripled, from $25 million to $75 million. Mississippi cotton growers saw their crop production and value rise exponentially. Cotton prices reached their peak in 1835–1836, blazing a profit trail from New Orleans to New York. Indeed, at 17.58 cents per pound of cotton, the Crescent City market saw higher values than New York; even Natchez cotton captured over 15 cents per pound. Mississippi's white gold had reached its highest value in thirty-six years and was worth a grand total of $14.6 million.[2]

As the South crowned cotton as king, Mississippians caught the wild economic ride to what Joseph Glover Baldwin, an antebellum Mississippi attorney and humorist, called "Flush Times." Observing the skyrocketing situation, Baldwin, with characteristic wit, concluded that flush times was "a period constituting an episode in the commercial history of the world—the reign of hum-bug, and wholesale insanity." He further proclaimed that it was "the era of the second great experiment of independence: the experiment, namely, of credit without capital, and enterprise without honesty."[3] Stephen Duncan would soon find himself in the vanguard of such economic experiments, though he had plenty of capital behind his credit. The availability of cheap land made possible by Indian Removal and the overly accessible credit granted after the demise of the Bank of the State of Mississippi, coupled with booming cotton prices and an insatiable demand for the staple, helped to create an aura of prosperity. "The people here are run mad with speculation," observed James D. Davidson as he passed through the state in 1836. "They do business in . . . a kind of phrenzy. Money is scarce, but credit plenty."[4]

The origins of flush times can be most clearly seen as it played out in the monetary theater, the Bank of the State of Mississippi, where Duncan took center stage of the financial drama. As the calls to dissolve his conservative bank grew louder, he attempted a last-ditch effort to save it—and also, perhaps, to save the white people of Mississippi from what he believed were unsound monetary habits resulting from cheap and fast credit. In spite of the bank's superior financial health, it received much criticism, particularly from those outside the Natchez District, about its historically tight credit and lending policies. As planting and commercial interests in the Natchez District looked to expand their operations elsewhere, they desperately needed credit in order to catch the rising economic wave. By law, the Bank of the State of Mississippi was the only institution that could make such loans. But in spite of its 1818 charter, which required the bank to extend services to areas outside of the Natchez District, Duncan and his board refused to make credit widely available. Credit-starved residents of fast-growing locales, such as the Pearl River region, hoped for a bank branch in Vicksburg, Columbia, or Columbus. Rejecting their request, Duncan and the board claimed that those towns were not large enough and lacked the potential capital to warrant a branch. Such arguments had deep historical roots that stretched back prior to the advent of flush times. Even by the mid-1820s, talk of the need for additional banking facilities could be heard in Mississippi.

In 1825, the state legislature considered the possibility of breaking the Bank of the State of Mississippi's monopoly by allowing the establishment of either a new state bank or a branch of the Bank of the United States. Public reaction to these schemes varied widely. Elites in the old Natchez District stood firmly behind the old banking monopoly, but they reluctantly supported a branch of the Bank of the United States if additional banking facilities were inevitable. Residents of the ever-growing western river counties outside the Natchez District also supported the Bank of the United States idea. Small farmers, many of whom had migrated to the newly opened lands east of the Natchez District, favored no bank at all. Because the Bank of the State of Mississippi refused to provide services to this piney woods region, they remained suspicious of all banks, seeing them as too powerful. The battle to gain a branch of the Bank of the United States eventually exploded into a bitter fight. In 1828, a resolution in the Mississippi legislature to establish such a branch failed three successive times.[5]

Though Duncan's banking monopoly remained intact, the demand for additional banks did not go unnoticed by him or his board of directors; they reluctantly opened a branch of the Bank of the State of Mississippi in Vicksburg in March 1830. In spite of this, new settlers and established landowners needed still more capital and credit to purchase slaves and recently opened land. Commercial interests—ranging from small merchants to large railroads—became increasingly anxious to tap the economic vein of the region. It soon became apparent that the needs of the emerging society far exceeded that which an additional branch bank at Vicksburg could provide. Recognizing this, the state legislature renewed its efforts to secure a branch of the Bank of the United States, but it again met with strong opposition. In a January 1830 address to the General Assembly, Governor Gerard C. Brandon urged legislators from the piney woods to reject the Bank of the United States and warned them not to invite into "our state an institution over which we can exercise no control, and which we cannot remove, no matter what be its mischievous consequences."[6]

The issue broke wide open in February, when the General Assembly approved a charter for a new state bank. Nine months later, the legislature agreed to establish a branch of the Bank of the United States in Natchez. The long fight for increased banking rights had finally been won. The Bank of the State of Mississippi, which had operated unchallenged for decades, soon found itself in competition with two other banks. Now, significant questions about the bank's future loomed on the horizon. The extent to which Duncan would be able to maintain control over the region's economic capital was yet to be determined. The exclusive power that he and his cohorts held began to crack on a crisp fall day in November 1831, when Planters Bank opened its doors for business. Under its agreement with the state, the new bank's notes could not exceed its capitalization, its stock was not taxable, and it could establish branches in places that were in dire need of banking facilities. Seven of the bank's thirteen directors would be appointed by the governor, thus allowing the state to have majority control of the institution. The state provided $2 million towards the $3 million necessary to capitalize the new bank. In order to complete this transaction, the state pulled $1 million in cash from the Bank of the State of Mississippi and infused it into Planters Bank, thus draining the flagship of the state's banking system in order to support its new venture. Planters Bank was run by none other than Duncan's brother-in-law, Samuel Gustine, as well as another brother-in-law, business associate, friend, and political rival, James C. Wilkins. A third brother-in-law of Duncan's, Adam Bingaman, sat on the new bank's board of directors.[7]

Planters Bank enjoyed some support in the old Natchez District, but most of its boosters hailed from the credit-starved Pearl River counties. Opposition to the new bank ran high in southeastern Mississippi, where the population opposed any banking facilities at all, and also among Mississippians who supported the Bank of the United States. Forced to accept the legislature's support of other banks, Duncan found himself caught in a quintessential power struggle. He and his cohorts supported the Bank of the United States but vigorously opposed Planters Bank, which had dealt a direct blow to their organization. The Bank of the State of Mississippi contested Planters Bank's right to exist, but lost its case in the state legislature. After last-minute efforts to have the legislature look more favorably upon their institution and reinstate it as a monopoly, Duncan and his board of directors called a stockholders' meeting for November 16, 1831, to consider closing the books.[8]

In the wake of the meeting, Duncan and his board drafted a variety of proposals that would complete the transfer of money and power to the new state bank but that also would be favorable to their bank. In the end, the two organizations agreed that the regular commercial banking business of the Bank of the State of the Mississippi would be transferred to Planters Bank, but that the Bank of the State of Mississippi would continue to hold its constantly renewable (or accommodation) loans, which totaled $1.5 million, through the year 1837. This compromise prevented a quick and sharp contraction of loans, while permitting the Bank of the State of Mississippi to continue to reap profits. Additionally, the Bank of the State of Mississippi was given the privilege of complete tax exemption through 1837. Though the compromise stipulated that Duncan's bank could operate until the last day of 1837, at which time its corporate powers would end, the legislature later granted the bank several extensions, which allowed it to carry on its business until 1844. In return for this favor, Duncan offered to cancel a $20,000 loan the bank had issued the state years before.[9]

Between 1831 and 1838, Duncan and the board liquidated 99 percent of the Bank of the State of Mississippi. Though Duncan had charted a favorable course for the bank, its demise dealt him several blows. No longer would he reap financial rewards as president of the state's only bank. He and the bank's other stockholders could not borrow their shares' value at discounted rates. Nor would they have access to the separate lines of credit that made it possible for directors and stockholders to offer personal loans for handsome profits and to fund their own enterprises. In short, much of Duncan's power base disappeared, and as a consequence he lost vital connections to the social, familial, and economic networks associated with the bank.

Cognizant of the usefulness of being intimately connected to a bank, Duncan did not accept the closure of his institution as the final chapter of his banking career. Ever vigilant, he always tried to turn his losses to his advantage, and he regrouped with considerable speed. Even as Mississippi's two fledgling banks began their operations, Duncan and some of his colleagues sought a charter for another bank, snaring public monies to fund what was essentially a private venture. In April 1833, the state fulfilled their wishes and capitalized the new bank at $2 million. Using funds from the liquidated Bank of the State of Mississippi, the Agricultural Bank opened in Natchez. Duncan again sat at the bank's helm, while William J. Minor—Duncan's friend and associate, as well as the husband of his niece—served as the other principal.[10]

Fierce opposition to the Agricultural Bank flared in Natchez. Leading the fight against Duncan were Planters Bank officials James Wilkins and Adam Bingaman. The simultaneous existence of two banks in Natchez drove a wedge into the town's economic network, splitting it into Duncan and Wilkins factions. As Felix Huston, a member of the Planters Bank board of directors and an attorney, stated:

> When I first took an active part in behalf of this Bank [Planters], I knew I would create many and violent enemies, I knew that men who had the entire & complete control of all the money transactions of a whole state, *would die hard* and would never forgive those who had contributed to drive them from their triumphant ascendancy. . . . You can hardly conceive how the whole aristocratic

pack ridiculed the notion of any body but Dr. Duncan and Gab. Tichenor [cashier of the Bank of the State of Mississippi] knowing anything about Banking, or even being able to put their feet in a Bank except as petitioners, until we rejoiced to declare dividends nearly as high as they ever had.[11]

In spite of the many public barbs exchanged between the two factions, their members shared much common ground, since they formed the core of the Natchez elite and were interconnected through marriage alliances. Nevertheless, the unfolding public drama brought to light complicated perceptions of class. Huston, defiant of Duncan and the "whole aristocratic pack" who comprised the Natchez Nabobs, ignored his own privileged position within the local community, refusing to recognize that Wilkins or even himself were part of the elite. Though Huston vigorously attempted to portray Wilkins as not one of the nabobs, others held a different perspective. One observer noted that Wilkins and "his connections controlled, virtually, the whole banking capital of the State, and at that era of expansion and speculation, this was a prodigious power, especially when exerted by men of ability and of high social position."[12] Jealousy and infighting only fueled the factions.

Yet in spite of the intertwining nature of the various Natchez networks, the power plays and piercing hostility that characterized the economic sphere did not necessarily affect relations in familial, social, or political spheres. As hostile as Huston was towards Duncan, they remained staunch Whig allies in the political realm. The intense opposition between Wilkins and Bingaman, on the one hand, and Duncan, on the other, did not seem to color the loyalties of the three men in familial and social arenas; nor did Wilkins's pro-Jackson activities affect his relationship with Duncan and Bingaman in other spheres.

As the bank wars intensified, interesting alliances formed. While Wilkins avidly backed President Jackson, he also supported Jackson's bitter enemy, Nicholas Biddle, and Biddle's Bank of the United States. In 1832, Planters Bank passed a resolution that advocated renewing the charter of the Bank of the United States. As Jackson vowed to put an end to the bank that was "trying to kill" him, Wilkins claimed that the Bank of the United States had "invigorated and extended the agricultural and commercial prosperity of our fellow citizens, and will accelerate the development of the varied resources of our state."[13] Duncan and the board members of the Bank of the State of Mississippi sounded a similar note in 1832. Their resolution stated, "That so far as this board has had dealing with the U.S. Bank, and its offices, and opportunity of knowing its operations, its affairs have been conducted with the utmost liberality and fairness." It went on to proclaim that "we consider said Bank of great advantage to the pecuniary transactions of the Country at large and particularly to the planting interest in this State, which would suffer incalculable inconvenience from the withdrawal of the loans of the Office of this City."[14]

Though both Duncan and Wilkins found the Bank of the United States economically beneficial, their efforts towards the renewal of its charter were for naught: Jackson vetoed Congress's renewal of it. As the president's policy to dismantle the bank took effect, Duncan and Wilkins reaped its benefits. The Federal government designated both Planters and Agricultural banks among the "pet banks" that received Federal deposits. Given Duncan's intense hatred of and opposition to Jackson, such a coup was deeply ironic. Ultimately, Mississippi's banking landscape was transformed in the early 1830s. The closure of the Bank of the State of Mississippi created an avalanche of banking and credit options. Between 1832 and 1837, twenty-seven banks opened in Mississippi, as well as countless numbers of private banks, branches, and savings institutions.[15]

The increased availability of cheap land only helped foster this momentum. Newly opened territories attracted settlers from afar, as well as established planters and investors who resided in the older towns of Mississippi. The abundant credit made available by the fledgling financial institutions created not only a land boom but also an explosion in population and agricultural production. At the beginning of the 1830s, Mississippi's white population numbered slightly over 70,000 inhabitants and 65,000 black slaves. By the end of the decade, the white population of Mississippi had more than doubled, while the slave population had tripled and had become a majority.[16]

With this massive population increase, communities formed quickly, particularly in the northern and central regions of the state. One traveler remarked that the newly created Holly Springs was "one of those towns in the vast West, which seems to have sprung into existence as if by magic."[17] The brisk sale of public lands made possible through the forced removal of Native American Indians transformed Mississippi's land offices into the busiest in the nation. Between 1833 and 1837, the Federal government sold seven million acres in Mississippi; it sold three million acres in 1835 alone. What was once home to abundant wildlife, dense forests, and the area's native populations now became an object of frenzied capitalism and mass accumulation, obtained through bargain rates of $1.25 per acre with a minimum purchase of eighty acres. Within the first two weeks of the Choctaw land sales in October 1833, the land offices at Mount Salus, Chocchuma, and Columbus netted $150,000 through public auction—a figure that would more than double by year's end.[18]

Landless and poor whites who came to the area in search of property saw Mississippi's rich soil, cheap land, and plentiful credit as a potential utopia. However, as Charles Bolton notes, few ever got the chance to own land. The power that speculators and land companies wielded enabled them to acquire property through private sales before the lands ever went on the public market.[19] Wealthy planters in the old Natchez District saw the newly opened lands as an opportunity to expand their larger planting operations, thereby squeezing out potential new yeoman owners.

The availability of cheap public land did not go unnoticed by Stephen Duncan. Like a vigilant hawk, he seized every opportunity to maximize the era's financial prizes. On December 13, 1830, he first took advantage of the public land sales from the Choctaw cession of 1820, paying $188.50 for 150 acres located in the Mississippi Delta. Less than a week later, he bought an additional 420 acres in the same vicinity, in what would become Issaquena County. Over the course of the next four years, Duncan, either alone or with partners Elijah Atchison and Robert McCullough, purchased 2,185 acres from the U.S. government for less than $3,000.[20] In subsequent years, he added additional portions, which eventually totaled more than 11,000 acres. His original investment of $2,700 was worth more than $1.4 million thirty years later.[21]

Out of these tracts of land, Duncan established a group of several adjacent cotton plantations that stretched for over ten miles along the eastern bank of the Mississippi River. This area became known among locals as "Duncan's Reach," or simply "the Reach." Dense forests of pecan, oak, ash, hackberry, and cypress trees originally covered Duncan's property, but they were quickly destroyed for his plantations. The once tranquil land that served as home to the area's Native American population was now carved into black slave labor camps that carried the names of Duncan's childhood homes (Carlisle and Middlesex), honored his first wife (Ellislie) or himself (Duncannon and Duncansby), or simply reflected the landscape (Holly Ridge).[22]

Following his original purchases from the U.S. Land Office, Duncan continued to make additional acquisitions of nearby and adjacent property from private landowners. In Washington County, which would become part of Issaquena County in 1844, he paid private sellers $5,376 for 6,840 acres, 8 lots, and 134 slaves—all of which he acquired between 1831 and 1838. For Duncan, flush times not only signaled property acquisition, but also land sales for profit.

Between 1831 and 1836, he sold some 7,000 acres in the delta for $636,500, all to be paid in the form of promissory notes.[23]

Duncan also engineered a series of complex land transactions through planting co-partnerships. One of the best examples of this can been seen through a series of transactions he conducted with Zenas Preston, who had purchased land in close proximity to his own. In early 1833, Duncan proposed that he would pay off the remainder of Preston's loan in return for a five year co-partnership. Under the terms of this agreement, Preston's debt on his original land purchase was relieved. He did not have to pay into the partnership, as his portion of the debt was advanced by Duncan and would be paid off by the proceeds of Preston's share of the crops. Not only did Duncan pay Preston's debt up front, but Duncan arranged that he himself would pay for expenses and make any cash advances (at 8 percent interest) for or to the partnership, which would be refunded back to him out of the proceeds from crop sales. In return, Preston was to "superintend & conduct the management of said plantation and negroes to the best possible advantage with the greatest advantage and the least expence possible and without any charge for his services for the same."[24] The co-partnership extinguished Preston's original land loan, but it also kept him perpetually in debt to Duncan. Meanwhile, Duncan received interest as well as a superintendent for the plantation free of charge.

Two years later, Duncan offered to sell Preston his half-interest in the land. Because Preston lacked the cash to make such a purchase, Duncan sold his portion for $85,500, payable in ten roughly equal annual installments. Preston pledged his own half-interest in the land as security in case of default. The deal gave Duncan $8,500 per year in income for ten years. Moreover, if Preston defaulted on the payments, Duncan would get his own property back plus Preston's half, thus enabling him to gain the whole tract for himself.[25]

Did Duncan orchestrate this agreement to generate cash income or to acquire Preston's land, which was located near his property? Did he simply want to help out a neighbor who might have been in danger of losing his land? It is possible that Preston was somehow indebted to Duncan, influencing the objective of the entire deal. Alternatively, Duncan might have suggested the partnership in order to acquire better management of the plantation, rationalizing that those in charge would do a better job if they had an equity interest in the plantation rather than a salary. Most likely, he himself wanted to acquire the property. Duncan often made such questionable land deals, which enabled him to capture prime tracts of land that were located near or adjoining his plantations. He exploited the economic weaknesses of his opponents or those he deemed inferior in order to strengthen his own power, with the blessings of "respectable" institutions and networks.

By 1840, Preston found himself already $29,400 in arrears, so Duncan combined all the outstanding debt into a new note on January 21. Yet three years later, Preston found himself still in a financial quagmire, and Duncan essentially foreclosed on the loans and received all of the property. Because of Preston's inability to pay back the loans consistently dating back to 1833, Duncan could have foreclosed years earlier and acquired the land he so badly desired, but he chose not to do so. By stringing Preston along for a decade, Duncan was able to extract free labor from him as a plantation supervisor. By not foreclosing earlier, Duncan's position was never weakened. Indeed, his leverage over Preston increased as Preston's financial condition deteriorated. Duncan entered into a similar agreement with Preston's brother-in-law, Robert McCullough, with the same end result, even though McCullough was in better economic shape than Preston.[26]

During flush times, Duncan's land transactions were not limited to the Mississippi Delta. In 1830, he made a $4,000 purchase of 270 acres of prime land along Second Creek in Adams County, which adjoined property he already owned; he also sold over 1,000 acres along the Homochitto River in Wilkinson County, located south of Natchez and Adams County, for $13,500. One year later, he purchased another 360 acres in Adams County along Second Creek that adjoined the property he had bought the previous year. In a meticulous fashion, he acquired land that surrounded his existing holdings, and parcel by parcel he built expansive plantations. Over the course of the 1830s, Duncan purchased at least 3,800 acres, one city lot, and sixty-one slaves in Mississippi.[27]

While Duncan busied himself with land acquisitions, he also sold off assets, such as a Homochitto River tract and 18,000 feet comprising two commercial lots in the city of Natchez.[28] In the spring of 1837, he also sold over 2,500 acres of land obtained in the Choctaw and Chickasaw land cessions, spread over seven counties in central and eastern Mississippi, to one of the wealthiest individuals in Natchez, Francis Surget, for almost $30,000 in cash.[29] Perhaps the land did not live up to its potential for planting; more likely, it was investment property that Duncan acquired cheaply and sold for a profit. By 1837 the depression had hit Mississippi, and Duncan might have needed a substantial and quick infusion of cash, especially given the liquid nature of his financial portfolio. As a prime example of his liquidity, in 1835 he sold his Saragossa plantation, located five miles outside of Natchez, for $24,000 in cash. The next day he turned around and paid over $100,000 in cash to purchase another plantation.[30]

With plenty of banknotes in his possession, Duncan mastered the economy of flush times, continuing to reinforce his economic power as he concentrated more on his position as planter and slaveowner. His landholdings spread from the old Natchez District of Wilkinson and Adams Counties up into the rich and fertile soil of the isolated Mississippi Delta. Such expansive holdings of prime land made him one of the largest planters in the region.

For Duncan, flush times grew sweeter as he diversified his planting operations, venturing deep into the sugar country of Louisiana. Within the first week of 1835, he purchased four tracts of adjoining land along Bayou Teche, which wound through the parish of St. Mary in southern Louisiana not far from the Gulf of Mexico. Over 123 miles long, the bayou flowed along an alluvial ridge, forming a natural levee. Its historically deep waters and slight current made the adjoining lands especially valuable, as it rarely overflowed and steamboats could navigate it.[31] Duncan's plantation lay within the rolling prairies of the Attakapas region and the sea marsh of coastal Louisiana. It consisted of three tracts on the east side of Bayou Teche and one on the west, totaling 2,760 arpents.

These rich agricultural parcels cost Duncan $120,000, which he paid in cash to his friend and former factor, Washington Jackson of Philadelphia, who had owned the plantation since the 1820s. In addition to the land and buildings, Duncan acquired the plantation's 137 slaves, as well as numerous horses, mules, work oxen, tools, cattle, hogs, and sheep.[32] This was the first of Duncan's many acquisitions in St. Mary Parish, where he eventually established the Camperdown and Oxford sugar plantations.[33]

The diversification of Duncan's operations into sugar production marked a distinct departure from his earlier enterprises. Like cotton, sugar cultivation demanded intensive labor; unlike cotton, sugar required more skill, more capital, and greater labor outlay due to the agricultural implements and cane-processing equipment, as well as the elaborate drainage systems that crisscrossed the plantations.[34]

Duncan was not completely unaware of what was required to cultivate sugar. Early in his planting career, he weathered the effects of a severe drought in which his cane was "literally dying" and was "the worst on the coast," forcing him to replant it three times. Duncan was also exposed to the vagaries of sugar planting through Thomas Butler, who purchased a sugar plantation in 1827 on Bayou Grand Caillou in Terrebonne Parish. Butler later purchased several other sugar plantations, which included joint ownership (with Richard Ellis) of one on Bayou Lafourche in Lafourche Parish.[35]

Duncan's venture into sugar country was a logical next step in building his plantation base. With this diversification, the magnitude of his operations increased significantly, illuminating the sharp contrast between his philosophy and his practice about the growth of slavery. Despite his concerns about increased numbers of slaves and absentee slaveowning, he ignored his own fears, becoming one of the largest absentee planters and slaveowners in the Mississippi Delta and Louisiana's sugar country. Always the opportunist and realist, he adapted his actions to fit his ambitions. Simply put, the money to be made by enslaving agricultural laborers was too great for him to pass up.

Duncan not only availed himself of the financial opportunities that flush times offered, but he also took advantage of the economy's downward spiral during the panic and depression years of the late 1830s. Between 1830 and 1840, he purchased 14,294 acres of land, 10 lots, and 366 slaves in Mississippi and Louisiana, for which he paid $156,109. Conversely, he sold 10,412 acres and 303 slaves, for which he received $74,060 in cash and $636,500 in promissory notes.[36] Combining Duncan's acquisitions during the 1830s with those from the 1820s, the scale of his assets becomes even more dramatic. In two decades, he amassed over 18,600 acres of land and 440 slaves, for which he paid almost $300,000.[37] In short, the explosive economy of the 1830s allowed Duncan dramatically to expand his operations. In the process, he moved into the highest stratum within the most elite echelon of the southern slaveholding aristocracy.

In addition to his land acquisitions and sales, Duncan extended a mixture of personal cash loans, credit, and endorsements to business associates or members of his social, familial, and economic networks. Personal loans and endorsements formed a constant stream of capital activity. Between 1830 and 1840, he involved himself with ten loans totaling more than $200,000, which were secured with nearly 3,000 acres, 6 city lots, and 205 slaves.[38] He made many of his loans to those who previously borrowed from him. Such was the case in 1830, when Duncan loaned Robert McCullough and Benjamin Harmann $8,000 at 8 percent interest. Under similar terms two years earlier, Duncan had loaned McCullough $4,500. McCullough also entered a co-partnership with Duncan in 1832 and became further indebted to him as the partnership evolved.[39]

Duncan also made generous loans and gave endorsements to relatives and close friends, such as William C. Conner, who borrowed $5,500 from Duncan interest-free in addition to securing his endorsement on a separate $13,000 loan.[40] Between 1830 and 1840, only two of Duncan's loans carried interest, both fixed at 8 percent. Although interest-free loans did not economically benefit Duncan, he might have considered them good business, given the fact that he was involved in other financial relationships (like joint land ownership) with the beneficiaries of his loans. The benefits of extending interest-free notes also paid off in a nonmonetary way, netting Duncan power within the white networks and within the dynamics of white reciprocity and noblesse oblige. On a more personal level, Duncan also gave interest-free loans to several individuals.[41] These personal loans that Duncan extended or endorsed reflect both the cash he had on hand and the credit available to him. Furthermore, he was willing to risk his own resources by lending his endorsement to others' notes. This practice was not only part of an economic relationship in which he was a creditor, but was also an important facet of his social relationships.

By the end of the 1830s, cotton, sugar, and slaves were a major part of the economic foundation of Duncan's wealth. Unlike many of the South's largest planters, however, Duncan did not confine his economic resources solely to slave-driven agricultural profits. His other financial pursuits and investments—in steamboats, the lumber industry, and railroads—were equally important to his monetary success. Expanding the financial interest in shipping he had developed in the 1820s, in 1838 Duncan helped launch the Natchez Steam Packet Company. The company's ownership reflected the overlapping networks that comprised Duncan's world. He was joined in this venture by brothers-in-law, financial confidantes, and political rivals and allies James Wilkins and Adam Bingaman; nephew-in-law and banking partner William Minor; and business associates Alvarez Fisk, Levin Marshall, and John Routh. The company ordered an ocean-going vessel from a Brooklyn shipyard. Bearing the name *Natchez*, the ship sailed in 1839 to the Liverpool cotton markets, carrying 41,500 bales of cotton. Direct shipment of cotton overseas eliminated, in part, the use of outsiders, keeping the wealth of Natchez elites safely within their circle.[42]

Duncan also invested in Andrew Brown's sawmill and lumber operation, which was located at Natchez-under-the-Hill. After running into financial trouble in the late 1820s and in danger of bankruptcy, Brown secured an emergency loan from his friend Duncan, who became Brown's silent but equal partner in the early 1830s. Brown increased the mill's capacity, and by 1835 it manufactured 2 million feet of lumber per year, most of which was produced by slave labor. Duncan reaped the benefits of Brown's lumber enterprise not only through the company's profits, but also through another of his entrepreneurial ventures—railroads.[43]

With the financial boom leading to the development of interior towns and new markets, rail transportation became increasingly important to Mississippi's expanding economy. In 1837, the Mississippi Rail Road Company, also referred to as the Natchez Rail Road Company, began construction of a line between Natchez and Jackson. In the conductor's seat of Natchez Rail sat Stephen Duncan, who was a principal in the venture. In a move that would reap significant profits for himself, Duncan used Brown's company to supply the lumber for the railroad's cypress crossties as well as planking for bridges and buildings. In its first year of construction, the Mississippi Rail Road Company's bill from Brown and Company totaled a modest $9,000. One year later, the railroad generated a $46,000 bill for 1.3 million feet of lumber. Eventually, however, Duncan and his fellow investors abandoned the railroad due to the economic depression of the later 1830s. Further exacerbating the railroad's financial plight was the fact that its route ran through the lesser-developed piney woods region rather than the more prosperous cotton planting areas. Duncan's desire to locate a railroad through the more sparsely populated and economically fragile piney woods turned out to be a mistake; indeed, the jettisoned project was an odd gamble for him to undertake. Yet in spite of the railroad's collapse, he profited from the deal. As Brown's partner, he made tens of thousands of dollars building it.[44]

Duncan's ability to recover from financial miscalculations helped him ride out the boom and bust times of the 1830s. His success, however, was not all due to his shrewd business acumen, but also to his exploitation of black slaves and poor white yeomen, as well as his often Machiavellian manipulation of the white elite networks in which he was central.

6

❖

PUBLIC DUTIES AND PRIVATE WORLDS

The Roles and Dynamics of the Duncan Family

On December 12, 1837, Stephen Duncan and several of his associates, friends, and relatives spent the day in downtown Natchez conducting their daily business. William Johnson, a free black barber and small farmer, noted their presence in the city that morning. Later that evening, he commented in his diary that Duncan and his companions "are the most wealthy and inteligent part of this community."[1] Johnson's opinion of Duncan was shared by many other Natchezians. By 1837, Duncan's economic position within Natchez had crystallized and, in turn, had enhanced his status as a community leader and benefactor. Yet his position within the smaller, intimate circle of family was not always so absolute. Events beyond his control, outside influences, and subtle shifts of power took place within the Duncan family as certain members took on more visible roles. These varied developments signaled that Duncan's power was not unqualified; he, too, was vulnerable. Behind Auburn's imposing columns and seemingly impenetrable brick walls, he and his family created their conjoint public and private worlds.

From the first, Duncan was involved in the Natchez community. His active involvement in the Natchez Dancing Assemblies, for example, provided fertile ground for social contacts. In the early 1820s, he helped to spearhead the construction of Trinity Episcopal Church in Natchez. The massive, columned Greek revival structure was born out of a conversation during a party at Auburn in the fall of 1821. One year later, Duncan's instrumental role on the building committee served as an impetus to complete the construction of the church. Duncan's finely tuned business acumen led him to serve as treasurer of

Trinity Episcopal until 1826, and church leaders elected him as a member of the vestry, a position he declined.[2]

Trinity Episcopal Church not only served the Duncans' spiritual needs, but it also helped to realize certain social and cultural expectations that could be fulfilled through membership in religious institutions and organizations. The ecclesiastical world of Trinity Episcopal provided a forum for Duncan's secular social and economic networks, particularly since nearly all the members of the antebellum vestry also belonged to his economic and social circles.[3]

Duncan's role in the community also encompassed involvement in the state's institutions of higher learning. Oakland College, privately established by Presbyterians in 1830 and located north of Natchez in Claiborne County, focused its curriculum on classical education of a high caliber in hopes of preventing Mississippi residents from attending northern schools. Shortly after its inception, Duncan lobbied the U.S. government to give Oakland public land. In a letter to Senator Josiah Johnston of Louisiana, he argued that "the grant of a few thousand acres of the Public domain would ensure its permanent success."[4] Over time, Oakland became a public presence and became marred by political controversy, as some Mississippians charged that its faculty members held antislavery beliefs.

In addition to Oakland, Duncan became heavily involved with Jefferson College, a public institution located just outside of Natchez in the town of Washington. The Mississippi territorial legislature established Jefferson in 1802, but it did not enroll students until the 1810s. By 1820, Jefferson's campus consisted of a three-story brick structure that contained classrooms, dorms, and a 1,500-volume library. Its curriculum centered around classical education, particularly science and math. Duncan became connected to the college through Benjamin L. C. Wailes and Wailes's father, Levin, both of whom sat on the school's board of trustees. Having secured a visible role in the Natchez community by the end of the 1820s, Duncan seemed to be a perfect candidate for the board. On December 11, 1830, the Jefferson trustees elected Duncan to the board—a position he happily accepted.[5] However, for all Duncan's work on behalf of Jefferson College, as well as neighboring Oakland College, he still chose to educate his sons at northern institutions like Yale.

Even as Duncan refined his public role, he engaged in cultivating his newly acquired lands, which left less time for his activities in the community. By 1833 he felt so overwhelmed that he resigned his position at Jefferson College. "Other duties so fully occupy my time & attention," he explained to the elder

Wailes, "that I have found it impractible heretofore, to devote the proper attention . . . as a member of the Board of Trustees." He felt that "it is due to the institution, as well as to my self, that my place should be better filled." Reaffirming Duncan's value as a member of the community and his potential contribution to the college, the board promptly rejected his resignation.[6] A few days later, the trustees offered him a compromise whereby he could "render important services to the institution without giving . . . personal attendance at the meeting of the Board." In this way, Jefferson College could continue to benefit from his "extensive acquaintance" with financial matters. Not wanting to offend his colleagues, Duncan did not "press the acceptance" of his resignation.[7] Reluctantly, but efficiently and effectively, he carried out his duties as board member, particularly those associated with financial matters and the hiring of new faculty. In spite of the compromise limiting his involvement on the board, he continued to lobby for his resignation throughout the 1830s, finally meeting with success in January 1840.[8]

Duncan's involvement in public and community affairs went beyond the local level. In the early 1830s, one of his most visible roles was that of delegate to the state constitutional convention, where he, along with John Quitman and Spence M. Grayson, represented Adams County.[9] In September 1832, Duncan became annoyed with the politics that unfolded in the state capitol. The winds of Jacksonian democracy, which swept across the nation, affected Mississippi as well, challenging his belief—typical of that of elites—in an organic hierarchy and a social order based on class, race, and gender. Disgruntled, he wrote Levin Wailes, "I regret to say we are making slow progress in the business of the convention." Referring to the proposed measures for democratization, he continued, "But this is not the worst—for the little we are doing—is anything but wise or discreet." As he continued, "Our convention is composed of the most complete radicals you ever saw." Duncan scoffed at the popular election of judges and other public officials. Questioning such "democratization," he asked Wailes, "What would you think of electing the circuit judges from the *people*—without regard to their *profession* or *occupation?*" He concluded, "This is an absurdity." Finally, he pledged to Wailes, "You may, know—, rest assured, we will give you a constitution much more than the one we are considering & much more *democratic* than any other in the U.S. Not *republican*—but down right & absolute *democracy.*"[10] After this experience as a delegate, Duncan limited his future political activities to lobbying on the local level for the national Whig cause.

Duncan fashioned his private world as precisely as he did his public one. He was adept at negotiating the intersections between them, as can be seen in his appeal to his brother-in-law James Wilkins not to run for Congress in the early 1830s because of Wilkins's alcoholism.[11] As family patriarch, Duncan exercised considerable influence over his immediate and extended family members, but events beyond his control sometimes challenged his authority. Further undermining Duncan's authority was the emergence of individuals who assumed more visible roles within the family.

External forces also altered his friendships. Feeling the loss of other companions, he wrote to one of his closest confidantes, John Ker, "There are few, very few, whom I can call friends . . . and now more than ever do I feel the necessity of clinging more closely to those who are left." Ten days later, worried about Ker's health, he expressed to his friend the hope that "we may both be spared many years. I really feel as tho you were about my *last* friend, and certainly I claim none, whose loss I would more bitterly lament." Both men would come to rely upon their relationship over the years, particularly when profound events touched their lives.[12]

Duncan's deep trust in the haven of friendship was equaled and surpassed by his belief in the sanctity of the family. By the mid-1830s, Stephen and Catharine's family had grown to four children: Charlotte, Henry, Maria, and Samuel. In 1836, they became parents for the last time with the birth of their son Stephen Jr. In spite of the significance Duncan placed on family loyalty, the near abandonment of his children from his first marriage illustrates the limits and complexities of that loyalty. Though he was close on some level to both John and Sarah Jane, ultimately an emotional distance remained, which was only exacerbated by a geographical one.[13]

Though these issues were present, Duncan went about constructing his life in Mississippi. Stephen and Catharine and their children anchored their lives at Auburn, which soon became known as one of the finest plantation homes in the region. Duncan would often direct his New York factors to purchase the best china, furniture, wines, and liquors for use at the homestead. "I wish you would send me 10 gallons of the oldest & best *cogniac* Brandy that can be procured— without regard to price," he ordered on one occasion. Another time he demanded that he be sent the "very best Hillsak Champagne for after all, I believe it is the purest & soundest wine. I want the *very best*—without regard to cost."[14] Though Duncan spared no expense when it came to Auburn, he later moralized against the dangers of extravagance.[15] Nonetheless, it was not unusual for

him to desire the best regardless of cost, or to purchase material goods that symbolized the family's social position and power.

Though the Duncans made their southern homestead one of grandeur, they
spent considerable time away from it; every summer, they sojourned in the
North. Beginning in late May or June, the Duncans traveled to Philadelphia and
spent a month with Sarah Blaine and Emily and Matilda Duncan. From there,
the family journeyed to Saratoga Springs, where they stayed for the rest of the
summer and early fall, returning to Natchez in late October or November. Occasionally, their routine would be punctuated by travels with extended family
to Europe or within New England.[16] They also frequently visited New York
City en route to Saratoga Springs. The Duncans' connections within New York
and the surrounding region eventually prompted him to purchase a nine-room,
three-story townhouse at 12 Washington Square.[17]

Many of Duncan's Natchez associates also had ties to the North and spent
their summers there, escaping the heat and sickness of Mississippi summers. So
dramatic was the departure that it prompted Duncan to observe in early June
1831 that "our city & neighd is nearly depopulated all or nearly all—the '*success*' of the community has gone, or about to go North for the season." Such a
pattern of travel might have also been a relief to Duncan, who could be assured
that little in the way of financial or even political transactions would occur in
his absence.[18]

In addition to extremely strong familial ties to the North, Duncan maintained vital financial connections to the region. Among other ties, Charles and
Henry Leverich, his cotton factors, whom he engaged in the mid-1830s, based
themselves in New York. Duncan's extended network of family, friends, business partners, and acquaintances in the North fed his enormous desire to live
there. While he was a fervent believer in the vitality of political and economic
nationalism, he preferred the northern cultural landscape. He thought it to be
a "morally superior" region compared to the South and a far better locale in
which to raise children.[19]

In light of Duncan's dual residency in the North and the South, to what extent did he identify with either region? His roots and many of his economic and
social ties were solidly northern, yet he reaped the ever-growing rewards of the
southern slave system, in addition to cultivating close bonds with many white
Mississippians. His identity cannot be reduced to northern businessman or
southern planter and slaveowner. For Duncan, these two identities merged into
a complex hybrid that resulted in his being neither strictly northern nor south-

ern. Keenly aware of the nation's growing political sectionalism and intensified regional identities, Duncan was in the 1830s still able to straddle the line between what were becoming two distinct arenas. The familial roots and economic connections that he maintained in both the North and the South, coupled with his nationalistic politics, allowed him to connect his identity to both regions in very specific ways and to see himself, at least publicly, as belonging to neither. The ideas and implications of sectionalism and regional and national identity in antebellum America are even now more contested, complex, and blurred than historians, the historical actors themselves, and contemporary discourses have presented them to be. The life of Stephen Duncan, as well as many of the elite enslavers with whom he associated, proves this to be the case.

Duncan's connection with the North grew even stronger in 1833, when daughter Sarah Jane, at the age of nineteen, married into a well-established Pennsylvania family, the Irvines. Since the early nineteenth century, the Duncan and Irvine families had been friendly and related through marriage. Sarah Jane thus deepened the historical relationship between the two families by exchanging vows with William A. Irvine, a young physician, farmer, and entrepreneur on October 14. Just days before Sarah Jane's wedding, Duncan sent her a letter wishing her "all the happiness this world can give." Yet he harbored some skepticism about Irvine's business acumen, which prompted him to send Sarah Jane money as well as good wishes. "Your husband may not be engaged in any profitable pursuit, for several years," he warned, reminding her that she and Irvine would need to watch their expenditures. Protecting his daughter by making her self-sufficient, and perhaps at the same time protecting Irvine from potential financial embarrassment, Duncan urged Sarah Jane to use the money so that "[you] might not have to call on your husband immediately after your union." This gesture may have been a way for Duncan symbolically to maintain a connection with his daughter as she became Mrs. Irvine. It may have also been a final attempt to maintain some level of control over her through her monetary dependency upon him. To this end, Duncan proposed purchasing the Mississippi land that Sarah Jane had inherited from her grandfather Ellis, as well as her deceased brother's portion to which she was entitled. In his mind, this made perfect sense since she and Irvine did not want to live in the South and it would provide them with cash. As he explained to Sarah Jane, this was his way of maintaining "interest in your welfare." Perhaps even more to the point, it enabled him to acquire a prime land tract.[20]

For Sarah Jane, the days leading up to and after her wedding were not focused on financial matters; rather, they centered on her own desires and hopes. Almost lamenting what the future might hold, she penned on a scrap of paper her innermost feelings:

> Think not the Husband gained, that all is done.
> The prise of happiness must still be won,
> But oft too many find it to their cost,
> The Lover, in Husband may be lost.[21]

After their marriage, the Irvines moved into a house they purchased next door to Sarah Jane's grandmother, Sarah Blaine, and her aunts Emily and Matilda. With this arrangement, Sarah Jane did not have to move away from her family. A few years later, however, the Irvines moved to Warren County in western Pennsylvania, to a vicinity that later became known as Irvine. Perched on the banks of the Allegheny River was Brokenstraw, the home that William Irvine's father had built at the turn of the century. Initially, Sarah Jane, William, and their first child, Margaret Ellis (born on May 12, 1835) spent their summers at Brokenstraw. Shortly before the birth of the second child, Callender, on February 22, 1838, the Irvines moved there permanently.[22]

Though Sarah Jane was familiar with Brokenstraw and its environs, she often experienced isolation and loneliness. Integral to these feelings was the fact that she could no longer see her aunt and grandmother on a daily basis. Her father and stepmother's yearly visit to Philadelphia also passed her by. She desperately wished for a railroad to come near Irvine so that she could see family members more easily. If a railroad would pass near Brokenstraw, she believed, her grandmother would be more inclined to visit, which might act as a drawing card for her father to come as well.[23] To bridge the distance between herself and her family, she thought that she might "very pleasantly pass a winter South—a part of the time at Auburn & some time with Aunt Butler, who is anxious for me to visit her." During this visit she hoped to connect with her past, as she would "endeavor to visit all of my Mothers relations."[24]

Sarah Jane's homesickness for her family was somewhat relieved through daily and weekly letters to and from the Philadelphia homestead. Casting about for some type of small comfort, she requested that a portrait of her grandmother be sent to Irvine. "Oh dear Grandmother, so far away from you, you know not how delighted I am to have that picture," she confided, continuing, "When I think of it—it seems *almost* as if a friend had arrived to cheer me & I can look up at you when alone & *try* to fancy you are with me."[25]

Contributing to Sarah Jane's loneliness was the frequent absence of her husband, who often traveled on business. In December 1838, she fell into a state of despair over the possibility of Irvine's absence during the holidays and her own distance from her beloved relatives. In a letter to her grandmother, she revealed that she would "be *very much* disappointed if he is not home on Christmas—It will be quite enough to feel that I am for the first time so far from *you* all."[26] Typical of many nineteenth-century women, Sarah Jane built her world around her family. Without them, she felt the existence of a profound void, a heavy emptiness that seemed to haunt her.

Though thoughts of family aggravated Sarah Jane's emotional state, they also served as a way to soothe her distress. She found some comfort in focusing on her home and her children, which helped her to feel more optimistic. "I have the prospect of getting a motherly woman to take charge of things & of *me* too when I am sick—& of the dear children," she wrote to Matilda Duncan. Wanting to maintain the outward symbols of their social class, as well as to have help and companionship when she was ill, she hired Comfort Budge at $1.25 per week. At Brokenstraw, Budge joined three Dutch girls who worked in the kitchen and did the wash. Perhaps taking a cue from her father that higher pay garnered a better class of employee and more efficient work performance, Sarah Jane paid her servants the highest wages in the area. "We must endeavor to keep our girls *wages* as secret as possible in this Country—as they are very high for this part of the world," she explained to her aunt, continuing, "We would very cheerfully give much higher wages than be dependent on the people of county or neighborhood who have so poor a character."[27]

In spite of her staff, children, and husband, Sarah Jane continued to yearn for a person to keep her company and assuage her loneliness and anxiety. Writing to her beloved aunt Emily, she remarked that she hoped for a woman who had "knowledge of country life, & country work, a respectable woman that I could *make* a *companion of & could sit at the table with* us & yet who would be willing to put her hand to many things."[28] Though clearly this mythical servant would be white and of a lower class, she would nevertheless be a friend, and perhaps even a quasi-equal—even as Sarah Jane retained ultimate authority over her.

In her desire for the ideal domestic servant and companion, Sarah Jane revealed how radically life at Brokenstraw differed from life at Auburn. In all of her many writings, she never once commented on her father's world or compared his black slaves to her white servants who could "sit at the table" with her.

To her, as well as the rest of the Duncan family, Stephen Duncan's hundreds of slaves remained invisible. Even Sarah Jane's devout Christian ideals failed to inspire her to question the morality of slavery. Indeed, they may have provided the rationale for enslavement, in that it was God's will.

Religion played an extremely important part in Sarah Jane's life—more than any other member of the Duncan family—and doubtless served as the impetus behind her many acts of charity to individuals in need.[29] At times, however, her religious devotion reached a near-obsessive level. She placed great faith in an omnipotent God, which provided an outlook that she considered calming; however, this conviction also can be seen as a negative force in her life, as she believed that she had little will of her own. Her fatalistic outlook might have helped to foster the devastating depression from which she suffered. The Duncan family dynamic—based on fear of disappointment, exaggerated expectations, and stifling overprotection—further contributed to the fragile nature of her conflicted emotional state.[30]

While marriage somewhat emancipated Sarah Jane from familial pressures, she now had to deal with being subordinated to her husband. After several years of marriage and the responsibility of motherhood, she again found herself caught in the familiar family dynamic of trying to please by meeting others' standards. Regardless of what she wanted, the needs of others came first—particularly those who had power in the family, such as her father and her aunt Emily. Her loyalty and devotion to them prompted her to forego her own wishes; yet she could not escape the awful bind that came when her own desires conflicted with her family obligations.

This played out on all levels, from the most trivial incident to the gravest of issues. For instance, shortly after Christmas 1838, Sarah Jane found herself sheepishly apologizing to Emily for what her aunt judged to be an inattentive and carelessly written letter to her grandmother Blaine. Sarah replied, "I know that I *ought not* to write carelessly to anyone & above all to one for whom I feel the respect & gratitude I owe to dear Grandmother." In an attempt to offer her aunt an explanation, she noted, "I had an ugly headache that increased as I wrote so that I felt hardly able either to pen or compose a letter." On a more serious occasion, when she fell critically ill and Emily was en route to tend to her, Sarah Jane wrote, "I only hope you will not be disappointed in our dear children—You must dear Aunt remember what an inefficient & miserable mother they have had this winter."[31] This type of interaction only served to demean Sarah Jane's already low self-esteem, while placing Emily in a superior position within the family hierarchy. Out of this dynamic, historical patterns of familial power were enhanced; yet the stage was set for new ones to emerge.

By the fall of 1838, Sarah Jane had sunk into physical and mental illness. Nonetheless, her husband, children, and other family members—as well as her deep religious beliefs—helped to buoy her spirits, as did the fact that she was expecting another child in spring. Sarah Jane could not count, however, on any emotional support from her father. Feeling overwhelmed by the demands of his plantation and other financial activities, Stephen Duncan chillingly withdrew into his own world. "Tell Sarah she must expect no letters from me until the idle season returns," he wrote in a shocking letter to William Irvine, explaining that "this is just the onset of my busy season; and I have recently been left [executor] to a very large Estate—which will add considerably to my labors."[32]

While Duncan surely loved and felt concern for his daughter, his actions demonstrated his obvious limitations as a father. He abandoned her when she was physically suffering and emotionally vulnerable. Why he had Irvine break this crushing news to Sarah Jane rather than telling her himself is not known. Perhaps it was symbolic of handing over the reins to William Irvine, letting Sarah Jane's husband have control over her—the ultimate transfer of ownership and property—and simultaneously wrenching Sarah Jane out of her dependency upon her father. Alternatively, Duncan, who was keenly aware of his daughter's depression, might have wanted Irvine to cushion the blow of what must have felt to Sarah Jane like abandonment. Regardless of the reason, his news only added to his daughter's already distressed state.

As winter abated, Sarah Jane continued to decline physically, and she plunged into an even deeper depression. She desperately sent to Emily for help. Reflecting upon her situation to her grandmother, she wrote, "I am cheerful more so than you might expect considering how much I am unwell & how *natural* depression is to a woman in my situation." With a fatalistic approach to her upcoming delivery, she noted, "I endeavor to look forward to either life or death as our Heavenly Father may choose." Yet even in her failing condition, Sarah Jane still felt compelled to apologize for calling Emily away; she thanked her grandmother "for this sacrifice of *your comfort* in parting with her."[33] The dysfunctional nature of the Duncan family and the Duncan-Blaine household, in which Sarah Jane grew up, fostered her adult belief that she remained a burden even in extremity. This kind of perspective and family interaction helped to keep her locked in her excessive overdependency on them as well as in her own despair.

On May 19, 1839, shortly after calling Emily to her side, Sarah Jane gave birth to Sarah Duncan Irvine. Several weeks after Sarah's birth, William Irvine gathered his composure long enough to confide in his father the recent news regarding his wife. "Sarah is now lying by me in a very critical Condition. Her relapse has been a severe one indeed. She is today nearly exhausted, lethargic and her mind wandering. Without some immediate change her recovery is impossible. No one can be better prepared for the change than herself," he wrote, admitting, "My grief at the prospect of losing her is selfish indeed." The next day he penned a postscript to the letter, informing his father that "my dear Sarah lies now nearly insensible, her end cannot be far off. I have no expectation of her surviving." He bleakly stated, "It is a heavy blow to me, breaking up the plans of a life." Later that day, with her husband and Emily at her side, Sarah Jane Irvine died. In an attempt to comfort his grieving son, Callender Irvine offered, "None could have been better prepared for another world than Sarah; She was in every sense . . . a religious and most valuable woman."[34]

For Stephen Duncan, the last days in June 1839 brought back memories of the autumn ten years earlier when his son John had died in his arms. But whereas his presence during John's illness and death eased his pain, that was not the case with Sarah Jane. Scrambling to get to Brokenstraw, and without the knowledge that his daughter had passed away a few days earlier, he wrote his sister Emily that it would take him six days to travel from Philadelphia to western Pennsylvania. Fearing he would be too late, he sadly wrote, "I could be of no service to my poor Sarah for by that time she will have obtained relief or her suffering will be over. I wish that I could be with you . . . to see her suffer this—could only increase my anguish."[35] Once again, Duncan was reminded that his carefully constructed world was vulnerable to forces beyond his control.

One week after Sarah Jane's death and two days prior to what would have been her twenty-fifth birthday, Duncan arrived at Brokenstraw, where he tried to soothe William Irvine's intense grief. Several weeks later, he suggested that Sarah Jane's death was all part of God's plan, which she had fully prepared for during her last months on earth. "There is something . . . in the reflection that she was prepared—ever prepared—for the world of spirits," her father concluded, adding "that she will know no pain—no sorrow & no suffering hereafter." In hopes of providing additional comfort, Duncan assured Irvine that he would not abandon him or the Irvine children, stating, "Believe me—I shall ever feel a deep interest in you & in your dear children. They shall be to me—

as my own dear Sarah was."[36] Over the years, Duncan kept a close connection with Irvine.

Almost immediately after Sarah Jane's death, discussion began about what would become of the children. The general feeling was that they needed a mother, and family members discounted the possibility that they would remain with their father. The first person to indicate a desire to take on the maternal role was William Irvine's aunt, Mary B. Lewis. Within one week of the funeral, she informed Irvine, "I have promised . . . my God that I will be to *Sara's* children a faithful Mother to the fullest extent of my power."[37] While Irvine was trying to decide whether or not he would take care of his children, Emily Duncan reminded him that "your dear children occupy my waking and dreaming thoughts, & I hope to hear through you frequently of their welfare." A few weeks later, with the issue still unresolved, Emily not only began to press Irvine into letting her take the children, but also gave unsolicited counsel on matters relating to them. Aware of her own behavior, she told Irvine, "I think my dear Nephew I see you smile, & hear you say, 'Aunt Emily is so fond of *advising.'*" She continued, "But this is not in the way of *advise*, I only suggest this, & you can think of it, besides, all this is said in Expectation of your sending the children, when you may decide on keeping them."[38]

Emily was not the only one who wanted to care for the Irvine children. Mary B. Leiper, William Irvine's cousin, who grew up with Sarah Jane in Philadelphia and was extremely close to her, offered to take the infant Sarah. Growing impatient with Irvine's indecisiveness on the matter, Leiper bluntly stated, "I wish you would make up your mind to let me have the baby to take care of," adding, "I will endeavour in all respects to act the part of a Mother towards her & it will make me more ambitious than ever to imitate her dear Mother."[39]

Stephen Duncan remained silent on the issue for several weeks. Feeling powerless over Sarah Jane's illness and death, he left Philadelphia for Saratoga Springs, carrying with him his feelings of profound loss and perhaps even guilt. "My poor brother," observed Emily, "left yesterday morning for Saratoga, with a heart too sad to enjoy any thing." Several weeks later, Duncan experienced further sadness as he empathized with his friend John Ker, whose young son James had recently died.[40] Meanwhile, when he reflected upon Sarah Jane's death, he focused on her qualities and character, as opposed to the battle of familial opinions over who should receive the Irvine children. He also addressed Irvine's suggestion to keep one child with him at Brokenstraw and send the others to Emily in Philadelphia.

Wary of this idea, Duncan thought that all the children should be with his sister. "I am sure it will gratify my sister to have them," he wrote, adding, "I think it would be wrong to separate them, and I am sure dear little Margarets of an age—when she will require now the advantage of moral counsel & Example, from one who would be to her [a] mother." Acknowledging the difficulty that Irvine would have in giving up his children, Duncan told him that "[your] feelings must be your advice for the present."[41] With that said, he removed himself from the debate and, uncharacteristically, did not attempt to influence the situation. Instead, he let his sister take control of the matter.

Ultimately, Irvine was unwilling to let the children go and had them remain with him at Brokenstraw. Deeply affected by her mother's death, Margaret confided in Emily, "I do not forget my dear Mother, & I think of her . . . & when I look at my black frock, I think it is to remember my Mother. I were twice to see her grave since you went." Ann Lewis, Irvine's cousin, informed Emily that Margaret "talks very often of her dear Mother . . . she not only has a perfect recollection of having had a Mother, but seems fully to comprehend and appreciate the tie between them & I frequently overhear her, asking little Cal if he knows where his dear Mother is; he shakes his little head and in a mournful tone answers, 'all gone.'"[42]

Despite Margaret's comprehension of her mother's death, she never mentioned where and with whom she preferred to have lived. Meanwhile, Emily Duncan, obsessed over this issue, continued to press for the children. She explained to Irvine that they so occupied her thoughts that "at times I feel too Anxious for my own comfort." A few days later, she increased the pressure, pleading with Irvine to let her have them. "Let me assure you of my *readiness & willingness*, to take charge of dear Sarahs children, & of my desire to bring them up in near as possible in the manner I think she would have done," she wrote during the last days of August.[43]

Emily's reasons for wanting the children were complex. Taking care of them not only fed her maternal desires, but also provided a way to grieve over Sarah Jane. "It appears to me I shall mourn her loss less when I have them with me," she explained to William Irvine. Her desire might have also been expressive of her power within the family. Though Emily occupied the position below her brother in the Duncan family hierarchy, being a second mother to the Irvine children, Stephen Duncan's grandchildren, would protect her place. Furthermore, she would see to it that the Irvine children would be brought up with the proper training of their class, ensuring that they would not reflect poorly on the family. Almost immediately after this last bid by Emily, Irvine relented. He let her have the baby and Margaret, while he kept Cal.[44]

Immediately after Irvine's decision, Emily, in a very odd exchange, informed him that he needed to pay for the children's subsistence, noting that "you may be sure we have no wish to *make* money, but as they will be an added expense to my good Mother, I know, you would not consent to their being here without paying for their board." She expected him to pay at least ten dollars a week for their care.[45] The fact that she felt she had to raise this subject brings into question the amount of respect she had for Irvine, suggesting her doubts about his capacity to reach this conclusion on his own. For the Duncans, family consisted of a tightly drawn circle; Irvine, without his late wife, was perhaps no longer considered a full member.

Irvine's sadness over the absence of his children became even greater when Cal went to live with Emily on an intermittent basis. Stephen Duncan tried to calm his son-in-law's grief by explaining to him that Margaret needed the attention of a woman who possessed moral qualities. If Margaret would have remained at Brokenstraw, she "would not have had [this] while with you unless you could calculate on having some of the females of your fathers family . . . in your home." For Irvine this was little comfort, and he emphasized to his children that they "can never know [Sarah's] tender love, or profit by her bright example."[46]

Over the next few years, the dynamics of the Duncan family would play out in a similar fashion. Emily took the lead, placing herself in full charge of the Irvine children. Even when Cal was not living with her, she still felt the need to instruct Irvine on every aspect of raising his son. Her controlling behavior was suffused with class overtones. In one instance, upon learning that Brokenstraw was not being kept neat and in order, she launched into an attack upon the white housekeeping staff, which ended with the conclusion that the situation "only proves that *all* domestics require an eye to watch them." Her elitism can be most clearly seen when she was in the process of hiring a governess for the Irvine children at the Blaine-Duncan household. She believed that by "having a governess [the children] will be kept from intercourse with our domestics, which I always disliked."[47]

In addition, Emily was highly critical of others, particularly Irvine, and did not hesitate to tell him—or the Irvine children—of their failings. On one occasion she admonished Margaret for talking about her sixth birthday. "Aunt Emily says I *think* & *talk* too much about it, but I cannot help it," Margaret sadly wrote her father. She added that she and Cal wanted to be with him very much, clearly indicating their displeasure and unhappiness at being stuck with their great-aunt.[48] Emily's heavy-handedness created familial tension while allowing her to feel morally superior to others in her family. Her feelings of superiority and her desire for dominance surged forth in the summer of 1842, when Irvine took Cal to Saratoga. In a tirade typical of those she directed at Irvine, she informed him, "Were I to express half the mortification I feel at your taking Cal to Saratoga you would be surprised; but I *must* say, you have treated me most *unkindly* in Exposing him among strangers." She added haughtily, "I do not deny your *right* to take your son *where* & *when* you please, but I do think I ought to have been apprised."[49]

Like her brother Stephen, Emily believed that the actions of others reflected back not only on herself, but also on the whole Duncan family. The fact that both Emily and Stephen were driven by a narcissistic attitude points to how deeply etched it was in the Duncan family. The ways in which the Duncan family interacted with one another mirrored the ways in which they functioned in society. Was the Duncan family a quasireplica of the stratified slave society they had helped build?

Sarah Jane Duncan Irvine, for example, found her family oppressive; she was enslaved by their expectations. This played a role in her severe depression, which, one could argue, contributed in a major way to her death. William Irvine's place within the family was equally fraught, especially after the death of his wife. His status as widower and father of Sarah Jane's children complicated his relationships with the Duncans, particularly Emily and the family patriarch. Stephen Duncan's relationship with Irvine was the most intertwined, compared to his dealings with his other sons-in-law. Emotionally, the two men shared a common bond through Sarah Jane and her children. Indeed, if it were not for the children, they might well have drifted apart after Sarah Jane's death. Whether it was how Irvine raised his children or how he handled his finances, he followed his own course in spite of Duncan's many criticisms of his actions. A deep level of conflict existed between the two men in regard to money, all the more so because their long economic relationship was marked by unequal positions. Consequently, Irvine usually found himself in the position of an errant child whom Duncan felt compelled to correct.

Over the years, Irvine occasionally served as a quasi-agent for Duncan in Pennsylvania, handling a variety of business transactions that included payment of road taxes and bills for lumber processing, the collection of interest on

personal loans, the hiring of carpenters for the Blaine-Duncan house in Philadelphia, and the disbursement of cash to Emily Duncan.[50]

Irvine's account book reveals the extent of the economic and familial inter-
dependency that existed between him and his father-in-law, and it raises some
interesting questions. Why did Irvine take care of some financial obligations
and not others? Was geographical proximity the only criteria? If so, why did
he handle certain economic matters for the Philadelphia household, since Emily
supposedly controlled her own finances? Just as Duncan adapted his own personal financial operations to the changing economy and environment, perhaps
Irvine and other Duncan family members did so as well. Yet the financial crash
and subsequent depression of the early 1840s placed a severe strain on the familial and economic relationship between Irvine and Stephen Duncan. For better or for worse, the main tie that bound them together throughout the 1840s
and 1850s was Irvine's perpetual indebtedness to his father-in-law.

Irvine owned and managed a number of ventures, including a farm, a tavern, a general store, a gristmill, a blacksmith shop, and five sawmills, some of
which were located at or near Brokenstraw. To complement these ventures, he
invested heavily in the railroad industry. Additionally, he invested tremendous
amounts of money in banking, particularly in southern financial institutions,
such as his father-in-law's Agricultural Bank and the Bank of Louisville, which
dealt him a severe blow in the panic of 1837.[51] Unlike his father-in-law, Irvine
did not remain immune to the financial crash, and Duncan risked his own reputation to pull the severely overextended Irvine out of several financial jams
during the depression. Irvine also borrowed heavily from his mother-in-law,
Sarah Duncan Blaine.

With the weight of the financial crash upon him, the recent death of his wife,
and a failed political bid for Congress in 1840, Irvine found himself deeply in
debt and emotionally tapped.[52] In a complex series of events that took place
over the course of the next decade, Irvine enlisted the help of his father-in-law
to assist him with his financial straits. Never before had the interconnection of
familial and economic bonds been so clear, so blurred, or so maddening.

In order to get out of debt, Irvine planned to enter the cloth manufacturing
business, hoping he could capture Duncan's business as well as that of other
planters within the Natchez network. In the mid-1840s, he constructed an eight-
loom factory that soon produced good quality linsey cloth (used for slave clothing) as well as some flannels. He also built a machine shop and foundry, where
he manufactured patented items for others. Unlike his father-in-law's success-

ful ventures, Irvine's diverse entrepreneurial base produced limited profits, as
his income barely surpassed his expenses. As each month passed, and as his operations expanded, his debt grew deeper. He soon found himself paying bills
by issuing notes, as well as borrowing more money from Duncan.[53]

In spite of Irvine's worsening financial condition, Duncan remained interested in his son-in-law's textile operations. He requested samples and a price for
five thousand yards of material. Though he purchased Irvine's linsey and jeans
cloth and was pleased with its quality, he warned his son-in-law that he could
obtain it elsewhere for a cheaper price. "I am satisfied I can do better at the factory in this city & quite as well in Kentucky," Duncan stressed. "I make this
proposal to further your plans—for I believe I can be supplied from a Factory
in this neighd. on better terms." Still hoping to help his son-in-law, Duncan purchased Irvine cloth for his plantations and sparked sales of it to some of his fellow nabobs.[54]

Though his textile business increased, Irvine's bills mounted and he sank
deeper and deeper into debt. He suggested that his father-in-law's cloth purchases be applied to the interest on his loans, but Duncan refused the proposal,
claiming that "it would not suit my [finances] to blend the purchase of my supplies with the payment of the interest that will be due by you in March & June
[of 1847]." Three years later, Irvine's debt had become so burdensome that he
appealed to Duncan to purchase his Erie property so that he could gain much-
needed cash. Once again, Duncan, appalled at the way in which Irvine handled
his finances, flatly rejected the plan: "I will not become the purchaser of your
Erie property, *at any* price." Instead, Duncan suggested that Irvine mortgage
unencumbered property to him, and he would transfer to Irvine Louisville
Bank stock worth $36,000 so that Irvine could pay off his debts.[55]

A few years later, however, Irvine had to borrow another $25,000 from his
father-in-law. His failure to be punctual with payments made Duncan bristle,
but the loans continued. Upon the next infusion of cash, Duncan warned Irvine
not to be "tempted by the frivolity thus afforded you, to waste *one cent* . . . in
new improvements in additions to your property, *of any kind* or *description*." As
his anger grew over his son-in-law's poor financial decisions, Duncan exclaimed, "If I thought that *one dollar* more, would be thus expended, or appro-
priated, I would see your whole estate sacrificed for a song—before I would
commit to your relief." He concluded with a judgment that cut like a razor:
"You have a species of monomania which has so mastered your judgment that
you are wholly blinded to your true interests. I consider your rage for im-

provement nothing short of mental derangement. But this is a subject I do not wish to discuss."[56]

In spite of Duncan's warnings, Irvine continued to enhance his property and pursue get-rich-quick schemes. The final blow came in 1854, when he purchased stock in a speculative Virginia gold-mining company. Clear out of money, he bought the worthless stock with notes. When the notes came due, he had no money and little stock to pay them off. The creditors circled like vultures. In order to settle all of his debts, Irvine's estate was seized and sold for $266,630 to his biggest creditor—none other than his father-in-law. Wanting to extricate himself from Irvine's financial problems, Duncan favored a quick liquidation of the property; but Irvine proposed an alternative arrangement in order to keep the property. Surprisingly, Duncan accepted it.[57]

Meanwhile, creditors hounded Irvine and soon brought suit against Duncan as well. By 1860, Duncan very much regretted that he made the deal with his son-in-law. He could not understand why Irvine would not sell off the property, as they had agreed. Duncan confided in his sister Emily, "I wish I had been 10,000 miles from Louisville [where they made the bargain], when I encountered him there in 1855. I now begin to think his *pride* alone stands in the way of a desire to sell. He hates to be thought a poor man. But he will never be anything else, than a poor man." Six months later, in June 1860, Duncan again wrote Emily about Irvine's refusal to sell. With the recent discovery of oil near Irvine's property, Duncan thought the land would fetch a high price. "If I could only see him *commence* sales, I would have hope of living to see this whole affair—which has proved so vexatious and annoying to me—brought to a final issue," he wrote. By September, he desperately sought a sale of the potentially oil-laden land, but it never came to pass.[58]

The following year, in an attempt to save something for his grandchildren, Duncan conveyed the property directly to them. With the Irvine saga nearly over, he reflected, "I will then be freed from, one source of . . . trouble. This is not the course I intended—or would desire to persue; for I feel well assured they will never induce their father to sell so long as he desires to hold on."[59] Duncan's conveyance of the property to his grandchildren eliminated Irvine's debt and the advance on their inheritance.[60]

William Irvine resisted selling the family's property, thus maintaining the memory of Sarah Jane and preserving the Duncan familial bonds. In the end, he followed his own dream. By doing so, he often paid a high personal price by not having the full respect of his father-in-law whom he tried so hard to emulate. Meanwhile, Stephen Duncan's support of Irvine over the years illustrates his own type of commitment to family. He tolerated Irvine's poor financial decisions because family bonds transcended other relationships.[61] Perhaps he propped up his son-in-law for so long because he felt that the future of his grandchildren was at stake. In order to protect their legacy, he had to adapt his business practices as well as risk his reputation. And only within the context of the immediate, familial network would Duncan allow this to happen.

7

+>-<-

SURVIVAL OF THE FITTEST

Preservation of Wealth and Family

In the late 1830s, as Stephen Duncan grieved over the death of his daughter, loss of a very different nature swept across the nation. The panic of 1837, which hit Mississippi the hardest of all the states, wreaked havoc on the antebellum economy and caused widespread financial ruin. Setting the disaster in motion was the Specie Circular Act of 1836, advocated by Andrew Jackson, which mandated only gold and silver as acceptable specie for public lands. In the vanguard of the fight against the act was Senator Robert J. Walker of Mississippi, an ardent Jacksonian (and a cousin of Duncan's), who chaired the Senate Committee on Public Lands. In spite of vigorous protest, the act went into effect, creating a run on gold and silver supplies at so-called "pet banks."

Senator Henry Clay's Deposit Act of 1836 was even more disastrous for Mississippi. Under the terms of this act, the Federal government distributed surplus revenues from the sale of public lands to the states. Mississippi, which led the nation in such revenue ($6 million alone in 1835 and 1836), received $510,000, far less than what was anticipated. In combination, these two acts put the squeeze on Mississippi's financial institutions. Banks issued less paper money, and gold and silver remained in short supply. Moreover, as a result of the Specie Circular Act, pet banks began to call in loans in order to meet their obligations as well as to meet the demands of government drafts, which they were required to honor. The latter was exceedingly difficult to do and was exacerbated by the fact that little money was received from the Deposit Act.[1]

Further contributing to the economic crisis were plummeting cotton prices, domestic crop shortages, and the suspension of specie payments by New York banks. The rise in British interest rates and the curtailment of specie flowing to the United States also caused American interest rates to rise. Although Mississippi's crop was never more abundant, cotton prices held more or less steady during the early years of the depression and the bottom fell out of the market by the middle of 1839. Prices plunged sharply with the crop year commencing on September 1, 1839, and they remained low through the mid-1840s. In New York, where Duncan sold nearly all of his crop, the price of cotton lost between five and nine cents per pound for most of the 1840s. This situation was exacerbated by the overproduction of British textiles, which decreased the demand for the American staple.[2]

As the financial crash landed Mississippi in a deep economic crisis, Duncan confronted its reality. Perhaps the front-page article about Mississippi in the October 2, 1839, edition of the *Philadelphia Gazette and Commercial Intelligencer* prompted his pessimistic mood that day. As the article stated, "It was confirmed without a doubt, that in this section of the State the crop would be less than that of last year . . . in the counties of Jefferson, Claiborne, Hinds, Madison, and Yazoo . . . there will not be over half a crop—half as much as was fairly expected three weeks ago." The article also noted that "the destruction is *very* great in all the uplands," as a result of a severe drought that choked Mississippi at the time.[3]

The economic implications of the loss of the cotton crop were disastrous, particularly when figured into the already negative financial picture. "I see no prospect of relief," Duncan wrote to Charles Leverich later that day, adding that "the only source of relief is the sale of Am. [American] securities in London." Challenging Leverich's economic optimism, Duncan continued, "You seem to think, the present state of things can't last long. *I* think they will last until the Banks back ⅘ of those who are in trade,—& then break themselves." He remained pessimistic, believing that the bad economy and any remedy for it would be a "complete 'Kilkenny Cat' business." Two days later, Duncan again challenged Leverich's confidence by noting, "I think if you[r] New York Banks are as strong as you think then they show a different face to the Philadelphia Bks."[4]

The nationwide financial failure had the potential to affect Duncan on multiple levels—as a planter, a slaveowner, and a banker, and also as an owner-investor in railroad, shipping, and manufacturing businesses. Of his many roles, that of banker ensured that he would confront the crisis on a daily basis. Even before the panic fully hit, he tried to use his influence to ward off disaster.

With Duncan and William J. Minor at the helm, the Agricultural Bank, along with the rest of the banks in the country, suspended specie payments in May 1837. The following year, Duncan rejoiced that the Sub-Treasury Bill, which proposed to pull public funds from state and private banks and place them in Federal depositories, failed to pass. Had it done so, he predicted, "We would have had a year or more of intense suffering from pecuniary embarrassments." Yet the bill's demise did not alter his fundamental outlook. As he concluded, "I hope I may prove a false Prophet, but I must confess—I have gloomy forebodings."[5]

Contributing to Duncan's agitation over the economy was Henry Clay's suggestion to identify publicly those who—like Duncan—received bank discounts. Feeling a potential loss of control as well as pecuniary benefits, Duncan noted in a letter to his friend Clay that neither he nor his associates "have any desire to see our names figure on the list of discountees." He believed that Clay's plan would "inflict a severer blow on commercial confidence and credit than the far famed 'specie Circular' or the 'removal of Deposits.'" He went on to reason that "it would ruin thousands, when it would benefit hundreds. It would check enterprise—break up speculation—and paralize mercantile energy. Thousands are served daily by small discounts, who would be deprived of them altogether; if the amounts previously discounted for them, by other Banks were made public."[6]

As the Mississippi economy continued its downward spiral in 1839, Duncan managed affairs as best he could. In July of that year, the Agricultural Bank did not offer dividends. In a letter to William Irvine, Duncan noted that it would be "doubtful, whether she will make one in Jany." Yet he told Irvine (who owned stock in the bank), "If I could with any conscience spare $1000—it would afford me great pleasure, to accomodate you & take an order for your divid[end] when declared."[7] Hundreds of miles from Mississippi, Emily Duncan also felt the effects of the financial panic. Concerned over the state of banking affairs, she wrote Irvine that the failure of the Schuylkill Bank in Pennsylvania had caused "much conversation," declaring, "I begin to think the Banking System is pretty corrupt." In another exchange with Irvine, she asked, "What is to become of our banking institutions? there is Much commotion here." Anxious about the stability of the banking system, she added that her "brother is authorised to sell our Agricultural Stock as soon as he can, at par value, if we get less interest, it may be more secure in land or houses."[8]

Though the Agricultural Bank failed to pay dividends and the future of banking looked precarious, Duncan believed his bank to be sound. In contrast, Daniel W. Coxe, a prominent Philadelphia businessman, charged that Duncan misrepresented the solvency of the Agricultural Bank. In a sharp response, Duncan vigorously defended his institution:

> I also regret, that you should suffer by misplaced confidence in my representa-
> tion. I only represented the truth, in plain language. The Agl. Bk. was all I rep-
> resented her to be, at the time—and is yet, the soundest & best Bank in this
> state—and far more sound than *many* of the Philad. Banks, and *fully* as sound,
> as the *best* of them. But you might well hold me responsible for event that are to
> transpire . . . as to attribute any pertaining your present loss & embarrassment
> to my representations. All I have said to you of the Agl. Bk. was that she was by
> far the soundest & best in the state. I say the same now.[9]

A year and a half later, in spite of the depression, the depreciation of cotton, and the continued suspension of Agricultural Bank dividends, he still thought that the bank was on firm ground.[10]

Despite Duncan's claims, he sold his stock in the Agricultural Bank sometime during 1839.[11] Perhaps he took the cautious course of action and sold his stock despite his beliefs; perhaps, having inside information, he knew what lay ahead for his institution and got out in time while letting others later sink. In spite of his liquidation of his stock and eventual resignation of his position at the Agricultural Bank, Duncan continued to advise his nephew-in-law, William J. Minor, about the bank's business, particularly with regard to reducing the bank's debt to the Federal government. In a confidential letter to Minor written in December 1839, he intimated that he had held private meetings to discuss the bank's finances. He proposed that Minor pay $200,000 of the debt by March 1, 1840, which would solve the whole debt fiasco. He predicted that "the Judgement against the Bank & her Bondsmen—you will hear no more on the subject." He assured Minor, "Of this, I feel as confident, as I do that your Bank is solvent." In the same letter, Duncan advised Minor on how to carry out the debt reduction, offering what amounted to a primer on the subject.[12]

Wondering whether "it may seem strange that I not [a] stockholder should be anxious about the Bank," he offered the following justification: "I am anxious for the reputation of the Bank—& I would dislike to hear it said that she lost 33 percent on cotton taken in payt. of debts—when no other Bank in the state lost a cent." This statement serves as yet another illustration of Duncan's obsession with control, the maintenance of power, and his ever-present concern with reputation. Probably correctly, he believed that negative reports about the bank would reflect back upon him.[13]

The economic troubles of the late 1830s lay beyond the scope of Duncan's influence; he could not solve them by convincing the legislature to extend the bank's charter or to create a new bank, as he had done in the past. Nevertheless, the Agricultural Bank weathered the economic storm. And the disposal of Duncan's Agricultural Bank stock, combined with the final cessation of the Bank of the State of Mississippi's corporate powers at midnight on December 31, 1843, signaled the end to a crucial chapter in Duncan's life. Banking had helped propel him to the pinnacle of economic power in Mississippi; two decades later, the effects of its disarray prompted him to end his banking career forever.

The financial crash and the resulting depression hit Mississippians hard. Even the inner circle of the Natchez elite were not spared. A classic example is that of Frederick Stanton, who was financially destroyed. By 1842, the successful Natchez commission merchant had judgments against him and his partners that totaled more than $700,000. William J. Minor also found himself overextended; he was forced to borrow large amounts of money in the form of personal loans from Duncan.[14]

Duncan himself was not immune to economic blows. On a searing summer day, he wrote William Irvine that "the great depreciation of the price of cotton in Europe has deprived me of the power of drawing, & will, I fear, oblige me to pay bills already drawn." Wrongly thinking that he would not have enough money, he anticipated a situation that would "greatly embarrass me."[15]

Further compounding Duncan's economic difficulties was the general state of affairs in Natchez. A few weeks after Duncan wrote Irvine of his troubles, a fire destroyed a valuable commercial section of the city. As the ashes cooled, a burning problem of another nature began to smoulder—yellow fever. In September 1839, the disease claimed twelve lives in little over a week.[16] And the season of disasters was not over. A spring tornado ripped a two-mile-wide path through Natchez, destroying a good part of the river landing and a portion of the city atop the bluff. The twister killed over three hundred people, many of whom drowned in the waters of the Mississippi, and caused over $5 million in damage. The day after this catastrophe, William Johnson, a free black barber in Natchez, declared in his diary, "Oh what times, no One Ever seen such times."[17] Shocked by the news of the storm, Emily Duncan asserted that "Natches appears to be a doomed place." Perplexed and annoyed that she had not heard any news from family or friends about the recent events, she commented, "Every one is so engaged in aiding the sufferers as to forget how anxious their friends must be." After several days, she finally received word that no relatives or close friends had suffered any personal harm.[18]

Though none of Stephen Duncan's property was damaged in these natural events, he felt the stress of the multiple disasters, suffering a bout of vertigo. A few weeks later, he found out that he had lost much of the cotton on his river plantations. In order to make up for this loss, he sold a tract of land in Pennsylvania known as Port Royal, for which he received $12,500 in cash. Emily Duncan regretted the transaction: "I am sorry that it is sold for I think he [Stephen] ought to live there & leave a country subject to such Tornados, Fever, Fires, & a country so evidently under the frown of God."[19]

Duncan weathered these setbacks, despite his protestations to the contrary. In a feisty exchange with Daniel Coxe over which of the privileged two suffered more from the depression, he expostulated, "I might as well complain, because my fortune is reduced nearly one half, by the general depreciation of every thing." Less than two months later, in another letter to Coxe, Duncan ruminated upon the general situation. "I regret—truly regret—that the state of things here,—is not only bad—but growing worse daily," he wrote, adding, "I have no hope left. I look upon the prospect as most gloomy and I can indulge no hope of immediate relief." Relinquishing all expectations for a quick recovery, he exclaimed, "We are under the govt. of knaves and blackguards—who seem resolved to crush every thing."[20]

One year later, rumors began to spread in Philadelphia that the invincible Duncan had gone under. Emily Duncan appeared to doubt such claims, observing that "Brother does not appear worried at the reports in circulation here about his failure." Duncan wrote to his sister several weeks later and squelched any such news. "I had a letter from Brother last week," Emily wrote William Irvine, "he puts our minds at rest about his failure, & is at a loss to conjecture how the report originated."[21]

During the depression years, public perceptions of Stephen Duncan's economic health thus varied. And even in his own mind, Duncan was not always clearheaded. In his lamentation to Coxe, he believed that he was entitled to complain because his fortune had dwindled.[22] Though land values plummeted by at least half, Duncan, unlike many others, owned his land outright and did not lose it. His ability to pay cash for his land and slaves enabled him, and others who did the same, to survive the panic and depression.

As Duncan navigated the dangerous waters of national economic insolvency, he continued to chart the economic course he had mapped out twenty years earlier. He engaged in timely acquisitions, as well as the vigorous sale of land at a profit, and he extended cash loans that were secured by property. During the two years immediately following the crash, he made several opportune transactions, some of which were sparked by the financial misfortune of others. In March 1837, for example, he acquired 1,700 acres in Washington County and 124 slaves from Elijah Atchison when Atchison apparently defaulted on notes granted earlier by Duncan. The following month, Francis Surget paid Duncan $29,879 in cash—an astounding amount, given the economic climate—for 2,576 acres of land in seven central and eastern Mississippi counties.[23] All totaled, between 1835 and 1839, Duncan acquired 5,700 acres of prime land in Washington County, one Natchez city lot, and 134 slaves. Meanwhile, he received $34,879 in cash for property sales between January 1839 and December 1840.[24]

Even more striking proof of Duncan's solvency are the loans he granted during this period. Utilizing his deep pool of liquid cash, he granted nearly $69,000 worth of loans between 1837 and 1839, which were secured by one city lot, 1,392 acres of land, and 51 slaves. As others scrambled for money in the wake of the panic, Duncan lent his endorsement to $60,000 worth of notes secured by very little—four lots and two slaves. Of his five recorded loans and endorsements in Adams County, none carried interest, and none of the recipients were part of his inner circle except for his uncle, Henry Postlethwaite. This lending behavior was a departure from Duncan's previous practice; those who received earlier interest-free loans from him were usually relatives or part of his inner circle. One explanation for this shift may be that in the context of panic, Duncan did not want to charge interest. If the borrower defaulted, Duncan would come out on top anyway by receiving the land and slave property used to secure the loan. His deal with William Hall was one such example of this. If Hall, whose delta property bordered Duncan's, defaulted on his $44,000 note to Duncan, Duncan would gain these valuable parcels near his own holdings.[25]

Duncan's loans and endorsements illustrate the importance of his liquidity, particularly during a time when cash was difficult to obtain. With such resources, he created new opportunities to build his asset base by investing more money in land and slaves. However, as Richard Kilbourne Jr. notes, "Wealthy planters had good cause to seek stable income streams beyond their own plantations and thus to diversify the risks inherent in growing cotton or other staples." Stephen Duncan followed such a plan. He did not plow all of his resources back into land and slaves, like some of the planter elite did; rather, he diversified into stocks, bonds, securities, and other investments. Having a varied portfolio that was not solely based on monoagriculture and massive slave labor allowed him to master the economy of the financial crash.[26]

Throughout the slow economic recovery of the 1840s, Duncan managed his resources in the same manner that he had for the previous two decades—selling and buying when prudent. The 1840s proved to be an opportune time to make extensive acquisitions, especially since Duncan had cash and others desperately needed it. He also sold almost 4,000 unproductive acres in Louisiana and Mississippi, along with 145 slaves, for a total of $80,000.[27] Of the eleven land transactions involved in the sell-off, Duncan based only three on promissory notes, revealing his ability to garner mostly cash sales in the midst of an economic crisis.

Another example of Duncan's ability to take advantage of a depressed market can be seen in his deft handling of a property acquisition and sale in Tensas Parish, Louisiana, located along the Mississippi River approximately thirty miles north of Natchez. At the beginning of the depression, William Smith of Tensas Parish purchased 1,280 acres and twenty-nine slaves, on which Duncan and his business associate, Ayres P. Merrill, held the mortgage. In April 1844, for unspecified reasons, Duncan released Smith from his mortgage. Smith died within the year, and the court in Tensas auctioned off his property at a probate sale in February 1845. Duncan then bought the plantation for $20,000 in cash. Within three months, he sold the land, slaves, and cotton gin, as well as the horses, stock, and farming implements, to Ann E. Flowers for $45,100, to be paid in seven promissory notes. Given the fact that cash was scarce and the economic recovery tentative, Duncan offered Flowers the option to pay off the notes in cash or in cotton. Flowers chose the cash option, from which Duncan profited more, but he still would have made a significant profit from the cotton. By 1850, however, Flowers had defaulted on all the notes that were due. In turn, Duncan cancelled the notes and took the title to the property.[28]

Duncan also purchased land from, as well as for, acquaintances who could not afford it. One such instance arose when a neighbor of Duncan's relative, A. D. Postlethwaite, lost his land in a lawsuit and the court directed the sheriff to sell it at public auction. On the day of the sale, Duncan successfully outbid everyone for the parcel. Less than a year later, he sold it to the neighbor's relative, Phoebe Beaumont, for $3,140, payable in three promissory notes.[29]

Duncan's indentures with Beaumont and Flowers constituted some of his first transactions with women acting on their own behalf. Even though Flowers was married, she bought the property in her name (as was legally allowed under the Louisiana Civil Code). It is not clear if Beaumont was also married, but if she was, the Mississippi Married Women's Property Act of 1839 granted her the right to own property free of her husband's control and protected it from her husband's creditors. In a time of economic depression, the law might have forced husbands to look to their wives' new legal status as a protection against creditors, which perhaps explains Duncan's transactions with women.[30]

The transactions with Beaumont and Flowers were unusual for Duncan, since the women were not part of his economic or social networks and had no previous connection to him. He extended personal loans to other strangers as well. All totaled, during the bad economy of the 1840s Duncan loaned over $27,000, which was secured with 5,386 acres of land, 222 slaves, two Natchez city lots, a textile mill, and the merchandise of a saddlery store. He also likely extended loans that were not recorded through legal channels.[31]

Few of the loans Duncan made in the 1840s carried interest. He might have thought that grantees had a better chance of paying off the loan without interest during financially strapped times; therefore, interest-free loans outweighed the benefits of a steady stream of income. As much as he had an eagle eye for a deal and swooped down from his watchful perch to pluck a good prize, he remained conscious of the economic difficulties of the time and made adjustments in some cases. In 1843, for example, he returned $20,000 worth of notes executed before the panic of 1837 to his former partner, Andrew Brown Jr. Duncan also refused loans if a potential debtor failed to exhibit financial stability, as can be seen in the case of John C. Jenkins. In 1849, Jenkins owed Duncan $5,000, but he needed more cash. He approached Duncan about this, offering to secure the loan with his land and slaves. Duncan replied, "Why your security is not good. Your cotton lands sell for a song and an *Epidemic disease, may, in a month, sweep off all your negroes.*" Jenkins concluded that Duncan was a sharp man of business—"I now see he was right," he later wrote—and dropped the matter.[32]

In light of his varied economic approaches and ventures, Duncan helps to illuminate the grander entrepreneurial scope that existed among the slaveholding elite. Perhaps those who diversified their economic activities handled the crush of the depression better than those who did not. For Duncan, the meticulous and measured construction of his asset base during the previous thirty years enabled him not only to survive the difficult decade, but also to increase his holdings.

During the 1840s, Duncan continued to amass property at a phenomenal rate. Between 1840 and 1850, he acquired 11,572 acres in Louisiana and Mississippi, three City of Natchez lots, a textile mill, and 275 slaves. Although some of these acquisitions were the result of borrowers who defaulted on their notes, most of them were outright purchases, for a total cost of $182,500. Of this amount, Duncan paid $76,003 in cash, with the remaining $106,500 to be paid in notes. Clearly, the hard economic environment did not deter him from acquiring more property. Yet his ability to do so may have been somewhat curtailed. For the first time ever, he failed to purchase certain properties outright and incurred over $106,000 worth of notes.[33] His property transactions may have been limited because of the economy; it might have been more advantageous for him to enter into debt than to spend his cash. Duncan's grantors also benefited, since the interest-bearing notes—backed by Duncan's sound credit—produced a guaranteed cash flow.

Duncan acquired some prime parcels of land—such as the Robertson, Osgood, and Wells textile mill in Natchez—when borrowers defaulted on their notes to him; in this way, he also acquired many slaves.[34] In one instance, Frederick Stanton, a member of the Natchez elite, declared bankruptcy on November 8, 1842. Stanton's personal residence, situated on forty-four acres a mile and a half outside of Natchez, and his business properties, which included warehouses and cotton sheds on the corner of Pearl and Franklin streets in downtown Natchez, were sold at public auction for next to nothing. Duncan walked away from the auction with Stanton's residence and commercial buildings for a mere "$10 cash in hand" for each property. Three years later, he turned his ten-dollar investment into $18,000 when he sold the downtown warehouses and cotton sheds back to Stanton and his partner, Henry Buckner.[35]

For Duncan, these acquisitions were fortuitous; for his debtors, they signaled the disintegration of a last hope to gain or regain an economic footing. Perhaps more than any of Duncan's borrowers, Zenas Preston and Robert McCullough felt the sting of their indebtedness. The ten-year saga of copartnerships, land sales, and loan agreements that Duncan engineered in the early 1830s between himself, Preston, and McCullough came to an end in the early

1840s. No longer able to pay on the $216,000 worth of promissory notes he owed Duncan, McCullough conveyed to Duncan all of the property in his possession. On April 22, 1841, Duncan received McCullough's land and all but nineteen of his slaves. In return, Duncan released McCullough from his remaining notes and, on his behalf, paid off a $5,600 debt to the Agricultural Bank, a $5,300 debt to the Lake Washington and Deer Creek Railroad Bank, and a $574 balance on a plantation account. Duncan also transferred, "without recourse," five notes totaling $70,000 that had been executed by his relative, Dr. Samuel Gustine. If McCullough had been able to pay off the promissory notes to Duncan, he would have been able to capture prime delta land and slaves with a small amount of cash up front. However, the depression and the slump in cotton prices hit him hard; what was once an opportunity now turned sour. Though he was left with the five mortgage notes on Gustine's plantation, those notes may have been worthless in light of the prevailing economic conditions. In a similar but less involved agreement, Zenas Preston also lost land for failing to pay Duncan's promissory notes. In this case, Duncan simply returned the notes to Preston; in exchange, he gained sixty-seven slaves and over one thousand acres of prime land adjacent to his property in Issaquena County.[36]

As Duncan acquired these massive amounts of property, he began to transfer some of his assets to his children upon their twenty-first birthdays. Beginning in 1844, he allowed his son Henry to take partial control of his own finances. A few years later, "for and in consideration of our natural love and affection we have and bear for and unto our beloved son," Catharine and Stephen Duncan gave him Ellislie plantation. They also gave Henry 113 slaves from Ellislie, as well as Harry, who was enslaved at Auburn. Like his father, Henry would build upon these lands over the years. By 1850, he owned eighty acres in Adams County and 2,680 acres in Issaquena County, as well as 207 slaves.[37]

Duncan's transfer of wealth to his children allowed land and slaves to stay within the family while reducing his own responsibilities. It also allowed his sons and sons-in-law to assume positions of power within the inner circle of the Natchez network by catapulting them to the status of elite planter without draining economic resources from the family through additional acquisitions. This new phase in Duncan's financial activities enabled the perpetuation of his family's wealth while creating a domain over which he remained sovereign.

The 1830s and 1840s were anything but a financial failure for Stephen Duncan. Instead, these years were a critical building period, during which his assets grew exponentially. In 1840, Duncan owned 18,600 acres of land and 440 slaves in Louisiana and Mississippi. Within ten years, he had increased his land more than 5 percent (to 19,629 acres) and had more than doubled his number of slaves (to 895). His land, livestock, and implements, excluding his slaves, was valued at a total of nearly $335,000 at the end of the 1840s.[38]

In Mississippi, Duncan's Issaquena plantations held the greatest cash value. The rich delta soils of Carlisle, Duncannon, Holly Ridge, Oakley, and Reserve plantations plus all the farm implements, machinery, and livestock on them were worth over $100,000. Further to the south, Duncan's Adams County plantations carried a $57,000 value. Even though his holdings in Louisiana were smaller, his land, equipment, and livestock were worth more in that state. His main sugar plantation in St. Mary Parish was valued at $122,000—almost as much as all of his plantations in Mississippi combined.[39]

Nor was this all. Factoring in the property Duncan gave to his son Henry, the family's land amounted to over 22,000 acres, as well as livestock and equipment, worth nearly $400,000 by 1850. This figure does not include landholdings in the North, personal property, stocks, securities, and other ventures, or unsold cotton, sugar, and other staples.[40] Nor does it include one of the Duncans' most significant assets—the value of their human property. By the end of the 1840s, over one thousand slaves labored in the fields of Carlisle, Oakley, Holly Ridge, Duncannon, Reserve, L'Argent, Camperdown, Oxford, and other Duncan-owned plantations.[41]

Ultimately, Duncan emerged from the 1840s not only with an extremely sound asset base, but also with a reputation among whites as one of the most exceptional planters in the region. In fact, his reputation as an astute entrepreneur with an extraordinary ability to handle financial matters was so well-known that he was considered within upper-level Whig political circles for the position of Secretary of the Treasury if the Whigs triumphed in the 1852 presidential election (which they did not).[42] The fluidity of Duncan's regional identity also contributed to his potential political viability, as his advocates believed him able to tap into both northern and southern bases of support.

As much as the 1840s demonstrated Duncan's fiscal acumen, the decade also represented a time during which his familiar networks began to shift slightly and to reflect a variety of tensions. Such changes and strains appeared most dramatically when familial and economic networks criss-crossed and sometimes collided. One notable example of this can be seen in the connection between the Duncan and Leverich families. Natives of Newtown, Long Island, brothers Henry and Charles Leverich launched their mercantile careers during the early 1820s when they joined the financial house of Peter Remsen and Company in New York City. There they were mentored by George Rapalje, a merchant-shipper also associated with Remsen. Rapalje served as one of the first points of connection between the Duncan and the Leverich families. He was the itinerant, alcoholic husband of Jane Ellis, the aunt of Duncan's first wife.[43]

In light of Stephen Duncan's familial relationship with Jane Rapalje, it is probable that he might have had indirect knowledge of the Leverich brothers. This is even more plausible considering the fact that Charles and Henry's older brothers, James and Edward, had a mercantile business in New Orleans. James and Edward's clientele consisted of leading Natchez planters, such as John Routh and the Metcalfe family. Given the intimacy of the Natchez network, Duncan surely would have been aware of James and Edward Leverich, as well as the nascent merchant trade of the younger Leveriches in New York. Gradually, Charles and Henry built a southern trade; by the end of the 1830s, Duncan—and other members of the Natchez elite—numbered among their clients. They became the consummate brokers, cotton and sugar factors, plantation suppliers, and coastal shippers for Duncan and his cohorts.[44]

Because of their Natchez trade, Charles and Henry visited the city on an annual basis, which gave them ample opportunity to meet Stephen Duncan's nieces, Matilda and Margaret Gustine, who lived there. A courtship between the Gustine sisters and the Leverich brothers began during the 1830s; by the end of the decade, the two couples had married. Matilda's and Margaret's marriages firmly rooted this branch of the Duncan family into an elite northern social and economic circle that was also intimately connected to the South. The marriages between Stephen Duncan's nieces and the Leverich brothers cemented the pre-existing relationship between Duncan and the Leveriches. Whether the Gustine-Leverich courtships and marriages were encouraged by Duncan or not, the marriages reinforced critical economic ties with familial bonds. The importance of this new connection between the Leveriches and the Duncans cannot be underestimated. As Emily Duncan exclaimed in response to news of the impending marriage between Matilda and Charles, "We are to be doubly connected with this family now."[45]

On the most obvious level, Emily's remarks referred to the fact that with Matilda's marriage, both Gustine sisters would now be part of the Leverich family, thus forming the double connection. Given Emily's astute awareness of social and economic position, however, she also might have intended to imply that the Duncans were to be connected to the Leveriches through both an economic and a familial relationship. No longer were Stephen, Charles, and Henry just business associates and friends; they were now also extended family, where loyalty and service held significantly greater meaning and value.

Duncan entrusted the Leverich brothers and their firm with nearly all of his varied financial arrangements, including cotton and sugar factoring and transportation of cotton directly to foreign markets. The brothers also provided extra, though common, services, such as offering investment opportunities and financial advice, ordering plantation supplies, and advancing cash, as well as procuring fine wines and household furnishings, securing hotel rooms, or looking after relatives and friends who were passing through Manhattan.

Along with other members of the Natchez elite, including the Surget, Mercer, and Marshall families, the Duncans vacationed at the Leverich family homesteads on Long Island or at Newport, where much financial wheeling and dealing took place. These sojourns provided Duncan with priceless entrees to northern financial and social circles. Yet the relationship cut both ways. While the Leveriches supplied Duncan with valuable acquaintances, Duncan furnished the Leveriches with access to a vast pool of potential clients from the social and economic dynasties of Natchez. Ultimately, they enabled one another to build their respective bases of wealth and power.[46]

The Duncans' excitement over the September wedding of Matilda and Charles coexisted uneasily with their sadness about Sarah Jane Duncan's death, which had occurred earlier that summer. The financial crash added to the tension in both the Duncan and Leverich families. Charles Leverich's sanguine attitude toward the economy was not shared by his brother Henry, who contemplated leaving the business in the fall of 1839. "Mr. Leverich has almost decided to give up business in N. York, & retire to the Newtown Farm," Emily Duncan confided to William Irvine, noting, "perhaps I ought not to mention this, but with you it is safe." The thought of moving to the family's homestead on Long Island disheartened Margaret Gustine Leverich. "Sister G. does not appear to like the place," Emily remarked, "but Margaret as a good wife, will go very cheerfully."[47] Much to Margaret's relief, Henry remained in business in New York.

In spite of these familial strains, Stephen Duncan's family network continued to expand through the marriages of his children. In the winter or spring of 1849, Maria married John Julius Pringle of Charleston, South Carolina. The Pringles were related to many of the leading slaveowners in the low country region, and the family ranked among the state's wealthiest. And Charlotte married the affluent Samuel Davis of Natchez, which further ensconced the Duncan and Davis families within the Natchez inner circle by combining their social power.[48]

Over the course of the 1840s, Duncan's social, economic, and familial networks fluctuated, expanding with marriages or contracting as some members crashed upon hard times. For Duncan, the decade signified only forward movement. He took risks to help those who had fallen behind, but he also profited from others' misfortune. He felt no ethical concern over his behavior, seeing it as perfectly natural and, perhaps, "survival of the fittest"—certainly a worldview typical of elites. Like a chameleon, Duncan adapted himself to the new economic environment and emerged an even wealthier man from the financial ruin that surrounded him. He was one of the largest planters, slaveowners, and entrepreneurs in Mississippi. By 1850, his quasi-empire was well positioned to become even larger.

8

✦➤◄✦

AN EMPIRE REALIZED

The Concentration of Wealth and the Negotiation of Shifting Networks

In the winter of 1853, the prominent Natchez geologist and agriculturalist Benjamin L. C. Wailes reflected that Stephen Duncan was "perhaps at this time the wealthiest cotton planter in this state," adding, "Dr. D. is one of the most systematic observing and calculating planters. . . . He promises me from the stores of his experience as much information as he can on the subject of agriculture."[1] As much as Duncan was a systematic and calculating planter, he was also a meticulous businessman and an astute entrepreneur who successfully merged the seemingly incompatible worlds of slave agriculture and high finance into a profitable capitalistic venture.

In spite of Duncan's diverse economic ventures, slavery remained a pillar of his economic enterprises. Without the labor of thousands whom he and other members of his family enslaved, the enormous amounts of cash derived from plantation agriculture would not have been available to prime other projects. Conversely, Duncan's business activities helped to foster his plantation economy. No single engine powered Duncan's economic machine; rather, all of his ventures worked in a dynamic fashion to contribute to the operation of his empire.

Though recognizing slavery's limits and arguing periodically for its dissolution, Duncan continued to expand his labor force throughout the 1850s. In doing so, he relied upon familiar economic strategies; he also called upon his political, social, and familial networks, which changed form to some extent during the 1850s. A significant key to Duncan's economic success lay in his ability to use these networks to his advantage, but this ability depended on balancing resources and connections in both the North and the South. In the end, Duncan once again translated hardships into success, expanding his holdings while also streamlining his operations in some areas to concentrate his wealth and power as the nation became more deeply sectionalized over the question of slavery and all it encompassed.

Duncan's networks within the South began to erode first. The familial and economic connections that had propelled him to the higher echelons of society in the 1820s had developed when Natchez was a nascent frontier community. Founders like Duncan were accorded the status of "pioneer." Subsequent generations of white newcomers looked upon him and his fellow pioneers as role models. Yet by the late 1840s and 1850s, the social and economic networks of Natchez began to shift. Some of the men whom Duncan relied upon most were suddenly absent.

The first hint of the changes that were to come was the death of Duncan's brother-in-law, business associate, and longtime friend, Thomas Butler, on August 7, 1847. En route from New Orleans to New York aboard the steamboat *Old Hickory*, Butler became severely ill and died of apoplexy at the age of sixty-two. News of his death traveled slowly. Some three weeks later, while in Saratoga Springs, Duncan stumbled upon his friend's death notice in a Philadelphia newspaper. In great shock, he immediately wrote Butler's son, Pierce: "I have just recd. the melancholy intelligence, of the death, of my most highly esteemed friend—your Father." Of all Duncan's friendships, his relationship with Butler spanned the greatest number of years. "I am sure that no one can more sincerely sympathize with his bereaved wife & children—in this severe dispensation, than I," Duncan claimed. "I was attached to him by the strongest friendship, from my early youth."[2] Less than six months later, Duncan's sister, Matilda, also died. Then his mother, Sarah Duncan Blaine, entered a period of declining health. In September 1848, during Duncan's annual visit to Philadelphia, she took a turn for the worse when she fell down the stairs and struck her head. In light of all these events, Duncan contemplated leaving the South altogether and taking his family, including his mother, to live in New York.[3]

Weighing his options, Duncan returned to Natchez in late October 1848. Hoping that life would be more stable, he instead faced more uncertainty as a particularly virulent strain of yellow fever snaked its way through the city. Even as the epidemic relinquished its grip, high waters along the Mississippi River in December threatened his crops. Duncan feared that the "destruction of property will be incalculable" if a flood ravaged the region. He concluded that he was "doomed to have a short crop year," grousing that "with Flood—Frost—Cholera & Grass—our prospect is indeed gloomy." Additionally, a severe cholera epidemic swept through his plantations shortly after Christmas. "The cholera is committing frightful ravages on the plantations in the Reach," he relayed to Charles Leverich, adding that there were no "symptoms of abatement." By May 1849, cholera had killed 130 slaves on Duncan's plantations. As the slaves died in their quarters, the crops died by the acres in the fields. Duncan's attention seems to have been more focused on the latter: the destruction of his crops occupied much more space in his letters than the slaves' suffering. Commenting on the devastation of both crops and slaves, John C. Jenkins, a nearby neighbor of Duncan's, remarked, "The loss (about $100,000) is a bagatelle to the Doctor, as he has large sugar Estates in Louisiana and in this country . . . large cotton places."[4]

With the cholera epidemic still raging during the summer of 1849, acute grief once again gripped the Duncan households in Natchez and Philadelphia. On August 16, the family matriarch, Sarah Duncan Blaine, died. Shortly thereafter, Emily closed the fashionable Walnut Street home, which had served as a haven for the Duncan family for decades, and moved to New York to be with her sister, Mary Ann Gustine, and the Leveriches.[5] With her mother's death, Emily Duncan no longer had to compete for the role of family matriarch; she was now fully in charge. The family circle had certainly been refigured.

The personal losses that Stephen Duncan experienced during the late 1840s continued to dog him into the 1850s. In late spring of 1850, his twelve-year-old grandson, Callender Irvine, died while examining a loaded gun that accidentally discharged, killing him instantly. Jolted into deep despair, William Irvine scribbled a quick note to his cousin Galbraith in nearby Warren: "Please Telegraph to No. 190 2nd Avenue New York to Miss Emily Duncan that Callender accidentally shot himself dead a few minutes since. What my anguish is no one can conceive but those who know his noble nature." Irvine's grief was so insurmountable that he could only bear to record the year of his son's death in the family Bible. His relatives were stunned by the news. "I was so shocked to hear of the calamity which has befallen you that I scarcely know how to write to you," wrote cousin C. I. Lewis. Another cousin, Mary Leiper, offered Irvine some consolation: "With what joy he [Callender] must have been greeted by our Sainted Sarah." But little is known of Emily and Stephen Duncan's reactions to Callender's death. The tragedy was so difficult for Irvine that he might have destroyed their expressions of condolence. Irvine struggled intensely to make sense of his son's death and eventually sought solace in spiritualism, reading deeply on the subject and attending seances.[6]

Losses of longtime friends and business associates compounded Duncan's familial ones. In early January 1850, he received the devastating news that his devoted friend and associate in Natchez, John Ker, had succumbed to heart failure. Duncan and Ker had been "united in the bonds of closest and dearest friendship," as Duncan once put it, helping one another weather life's gravest storms.[7] Duncan's wider circle of economic and social partners also narrowed: William St. John Elliott died in the mid-1850s; Adam Bingaman fell into troubled times, spent much of his resources, and eventually moved to New Orleans; Levin Marshall, who named his son "Duncan" in honor of Stephen, spent more time at his Pelham Bay, New York, residence; and relative, friend, and economic associate William Newton Mercer divided his time between Natchez and New Orleans.

In spite of these changes, the network of Natchez elites remained vital. For example, Duncan (as well as Marshall and Mercer) continued to serve as an economic resource for others; during the late 1850s Duncan was one of the few local creditors. Throughout the decade, he loaned significant amounts of money to friends and associates. Between 1850 and 1860, he recorded nearly $100,000 in loans at the Adams County Chancery Clerk's Office. Some of these loans went to individuals outside his inner circle and even outside his larger economic network. He often provided modest loans to small Natchez businesses, such as clothiers and tailor and saddlery shops. His relatives, however, borrowed the largest sums of cash. Duncan loaned Alex and Mary Postlethwaite nearly $40,000, interest free, over the decade and helped to sustain their dry-goods store.[8]

In addition to the loans Duncan recorded through official channels, he provided countless private grants. Between July 1861 and June 1862, he floated nearly $77,000 in private loans. These personal arrangements carried interest rates between 4.15 and 7.2 percent and produced almost $3,000 in annual income.[9] Such revenues were not significant compared to his plantations or other investments; nevertheless, they comprised an integral part of Duncan's larger enterprise—they helped him maintain power within the white community.

As Duncan extended his frequency of private and public loans, he also extended his management of family finances. Throughout the antebellum period, he oversaw, in a general fashion, the finances of his extended family. Despite this, his sister Emily fiercely guarded her economic independence and continued to retain control over some monies, building an impressive portfolio based on stocks, bonds, and securities, as well as private loans to individuals. Throughout the 1850s, Emily continued to maintain her financial autonomy, even as her brother increasingly attempted to involve himself in her affairs. Stephen was doubtless increasingly worried by the political circumstances that engulfed the nation; he might also have feared that his own days were coming to an end. In any event, he desired to see Emily more financially secure and perhaps believed that, as a woman, she was incapable of handling her own affairs. "When I am gone, if no one else can be found here, to invest for you," he explained to his sister, "you will have to be content with 6 percent Int[erest]."[10]

Yet despite this brotherly advice, tensions between Stephen and Emily mounted. Sparked by the political turmoil of potential secession, Duncan became obsessed with finances. It was all too clear that his most valuable source of income—slave agriculture—hung in the balance. He realized that planters needed to adapt, and to do so quickly, in order to fend off the economic damage that would come from secession or war.

In December 1860, with secession looming, Duncan attempted to convince his sister to follow his lead. As he wrote, "It is but too true—*lamentably true*— that there is an impending crisis, & *near at hand too*—which will reduce us all— both rich & poor—& those who make up their minds to this result, sooner & will prove to be the wisest." He then made his emotionally charged appeal: "You and sister have occupied much of my thoughts, & I believe, as the result of such meditation & reflection—it would be wisest & safer move, to try & guard against the evils. . . . I am sure, you & sister will cheerfully submit to a reduced income provided it is sufficient to render you *independent*. But you ought both to concur, *now*—the system of *retrenchment*."[11] Under his plan, he would take over much of his sisters' finances, including bills receivable. In return, he would give Emily a note for $20,000 at 7 percent interest, which would give her an extra $1,400 of yearly income. He also would give a note to Mary Ann for $27,500, which would yield $1,925 in interest per year.

From Duncan's point of view, this plan protected his sisters financially, but gave him the use of their income and kept the money within the family. He sought to assuage any fears that Emily might have had by stating point-blank, "I can Make nothing By it." He gave Emily some time to consider the arrangement, but he wanted her answer by March 1861, since he predicted Mississippi might then secede.[12]

Emily interpreted Stephen's plan as a crass attempt to make money rather than to protect her or Mary Ann. Implicit in her response was the feeling that she was being controlled and manipulated. Resolving to fight to maintain her independence, Emily challenged her brother. She questioned not only his authority, but also his character, which was a definite blow to Duncan. He defended himself by calling upon the most intimate of bonds. "I am sure—very sure," he pleaded, "neither you nor sister Gustine—could for one moment entertain a thought, a suspicion,—that I *could* or *would* desire to *speculate* on you—the *only relics of a sainted mother.*"[13]

In spite of tensions over this matter, the siblings remained close confidantes, particularly as war approached and Emily assumed the role as family matriarch. Upon the death of Sarah Blaine, there was no question as to who would take her place. The ease with which Emily assumed her mother's position was due, in part, to the fact that she had always played a significantly more active role within the family than her sister Matilda. And Mary Ann Duncan Gustine had always been less central to the family network, perhaps because of her marriage and her ties to her husband's family, which continued to bind her even after she was widowed. In contrast, Emily's unmarried and childless state gave her more power within the family, since she was totally independent.

Though Stephen Duncan's wife, Catharine, was never considered the family matriarch, she was still the mistress of Auburn, which carried considerable weight at least in Natchez. By the mid-1850s, only Stephen, Catharine, and Stephen Jr. lived at Auburn, while eleven black house servants labored to make their existence a comfortable one. The Duncans made extensive additions to the Natchez homestead in this period, enlarging the house to accommodate guests—including their children and grandchildren—for extended visits. In a letter to her sister-in-law, Mary Ann Gustine, Catharine noted that the additions "are big great improvements to both . . . *appearance* and *convenience.*"[14] For many of Duncan's contemporaries, life at Auburn set the standard to emulate.

Behind Auburn's imposing facade, however, difficulties existed. Catharine Duncan exercised power as a slaveowner and as the direct master over eleven house slaves; she also enjoyed significant status in the Natchez community as a Bingaman and as Stephen Duncan's wife. Yet she still experienced severe limits to her power as a result of both her sex and internal family dynamics. Auburn's location on the outskirts of Natchez carried with it a sense of isolation, which could become overwhelming for her, as it did in the winter of 1857. Though the weather that season was generally good, the roads in Natchez were nothing but a "sea of mud and water and deep holes." Deploring their condition, Catharine wrote Mary Ann that she was doomed to "stay at home as the roads are *impassable* for *Carriages*." Unable to leave the house for weeks at a time, she noted that the previous day had been "the first time in *two months* that I [and daughter Maria] have been in the *Carriage*," and then only "at the *risk* of our lives." Whether Catharine's days of being housebound were by choice or by the direction of her husband, she felt trapped. She deplored her situation, particularly since Stephen traveled into town every day.[15]

The winter of 1857 was indicative of Catharine's daily existence. As a result, she craved visits, particularly by her children and their families, who came regularly to Auburn. Perhaps because of her neediness, her son Stephen, the youngest child, felt pressure to remain at home; he never married and lived at Auburn as an adult. When the elder Stephen gave his namesake the Carlisle plantation in 1857, Catharine was relieved that their son would remain in Natchez. "Do not think by this that Stephen will *leave us. No indeed!!*" she wrote her sister-in-law. "This is *his home* and he will only go up there now and then to see about his business." Reflecting upon Stephen Jr.'s recent twenty-first birthday, she remarked, "Oh Me! how . . . children seem to grow up," adding, "I *hate* to think Stephen is of age—often wish he was '*a boy again.*'"[16] This was perhaps as much a parent's lament over her children growing up as a statement about Catharine's own loneliness and sense of purpose.

The reasons behind Stephen Jr.'s decision never to marry and to remain at home can be explained by a number of possibilities, from sexuality to dysfunctional family dynamics. Whether his parents ever pressured him to marry is unknown; but in light of the elder Duncan's intense focus upon maintaining the family's elite status, Stephen Jr.'s marriage into a prominent family would surely have been desirable. The younger Duncan might have refused a match based solely on social and economic power, since marriage for his generation was based more on intimacy and desire than parental direction.[17]

If Stephen Jr.'s bachelor status was by choice, his aversion to marriage might have been influenced by his parents' relationship. As he wrote in 1859, "Marriage is a mirage which is only lovely at a distance." He also noted his views on women: "Men are the play things of women—& *women* of the Devil."[18] Stephen Jr.'s views on marriage might have also been influenced by his mother, who believed that marriage was not always a good choice and that it could be oppressive. Commenting on her sister-in-law's paid white housemaid who was contemplating the bonds of matrimony, Catharine remarked, "I hope that she has not been such a *goose* as to do so *foolish* a thing." She believed that the prospective bride was far better off remaining single. Certainly Catharine's opinion was influenced to some extent by the fact that a marriage might cause Mary Ann Gustine to lose a laborer. Whether or not it was a reflection of her views about marriage more generally, it doubtless reflected her own sense of white women's lack of power in the South's patriarchal society. She was keenly aware of gender dynamics and openly worried when female relatives gave birth to girls. Confiding in her sister-in-law, she astutely observed, "I know how much *Fathers* prize *boys* and how it has almost become a matter of *regret* to them (judging by my *sons in law*) when a little *girl* is announced." Nonetheless, she added, "But for myself—I *love* little girls."[19]

By virtue of her marriage, class, and race, Catharine possessed a certain amount of power, and her position as a white slaveowner gave her instant authority over blacks. Yet between the gender hierarchy of the nineteenth-century South and the marital dynamics of the Duncan family, she was clearly a subordinate. Even her mastery over those directly under her, the house slaves, may not have been complete. In a letter to Mary Ann Gustine, she griped that her own servants "seemed all the time *complaining*."[20] In this instance, the source of Catharine's vexation might have been a verbal altercation with the house slaves, which they followed by acts of resistance.

As a white woman, Catharine was perceived within the planter culture as inferior to her husband and the other patriarchs among whom she lived, but superior to those whom she enslaved. Caught amid this tangled mixture of power, quasi-power, and powerlessness, she never assumed the role of Duncan family matriarch. She did not even appear to play a significant role within the Duncan family. Perhaps even more telling is the fact that her closest confidante among the Duncan clan was Mary Ann Gustine, whose own sphere of influence within the family was severely limited. Perhaps their close relationship was a conscious alliance between two women who had diminished private family roles, yet who exerted great class and racial authority publicly. For Catharine Duncan, as well as for other plantation mistresses, the politics of identity and power were very much intertwined with the politics of family.

For Stephen Duncan, the needs of family were enmeshed with those of finances and politics—connections that presented fewer internal contradictions. During the 1850s, Duncan shifted away from his earlier strategy of aggressive acquisition, focusing instead on fewer new acquisitions, steady growth of his existing assets, and the transfer of those assets to his children. His more limited interest in land acquisition had disparate causes. He turned seventy in 1857, and he remained extremely concerned about the future of slave labor and the deepening sectional crisis. He also wanted to consolidate his legacy to his children. In order to do so, he concentrated his wealth.

During the 1850s, Duncan expanded his acreage on the Camperdown and Oxford plantations in St. Mary Parish, adding over 550 acres to his sugar empire.[21] In December 1858, he purchased a lot in Natchez, known as The Bluffs, from Hester Cummings, a free black woman. Cummings resided in Natchez and was a good friend of free black barber and businessman William Johnson. She bought the freedom of her sister and niece, and she owned several slaves. In July 1858, she bought a parcel of land for $700. Five months later, she sold the same parcel to Duncan, along with ten slaves, for $3,000. Duncan probably knew Cummings through Johnson, who held money for her, loaned her small sums, and made tax payments on her behalf. Five years later, Duncan gave the land to Nanette, also a free black woman, for the sum of one dollar. The relationship between Duncan and Nanette is not clear, but a woman of the same name was listed among the ten slaves Cummings originally sold Duncan. How Nanette gained her freedom remains unknown; Duncan might have manumitted her, or she might have purchased her freedom outright. In any event, the fact that he sold her the land for only a dollar suggests that he felt some extensive obligation to her.[22]

Unlike the Cummings transaction, Duncan's other acquisitions during the decade directly benefited his children. In March 1850, on his sixty-third birthday, he purchased a 1,203-acre sugar plantation and 78 slaves from the estate of Thomas Butler for $80,000. He paid $26,000 in cash; the remaining balance was to be paid in two notes over two years at 8 percent interest. He soon gifted a portion of the property to his daughter, Maria Duncan Pringle. The following November, he and Catharine deeded Maria the entire plantation, plus an additional twenty-seven slaves. The following year his son Henry and his daughter-in-law Mary decided to leave the South and move permanently to New York City. In the wake of their departure, Duncan bought Henry's forty-acre plantation, Stump Lawn, as well as two slaves, Wilson and John, for $19,000, to be paid in three promissory notes.[23] In spite of the more limited growth of Duncan's assets during the 1850s, his acquisitions were still significant: he purchased 1,758 acres of land and over 100 slaves for a total of nearly $124,000, most of which he paid for in cash.[24]

For Duncan, these purchases were less important than his improvements to what he already held. Perhaps the political climate of the late antebellum period tempered his economic actions. Keenly aware of national debates over slavery, he might have been preparing for what he predicted throughout the 1850s—the inevitable end of slavery. With tens of thousands of acres under cultivation by a slave force numbering in the thousands, he began to sell off less productive land, primarily in Adams County, and to sell or usually give land to his children. As a result, his own holdings became concentrated in the Mississippi Delta county of Issaquena and St. Mary Parish in coastal Louisiana. Due to the varied locales of his plantations, it was impossible for Duncan himself to keep as close an eye on them as he would have wished, and some were clearly in a neglected state. While visiting Holly Ridge in the delta during the winter of 1848, Duncan noted, "I expect to be here another week & I ought to remain a month for things here require looking after." Ten years later, he echoed the same sentiments, writing, "I . . . never saw it [Holly Ridge], in so backward a state."[25] Others noticed the condition of Duncan's land as well. Wanting to get rid of his less productive and older property in Adams County, Duncan offered Benjamin L.C. Wailes his Homochitto plantation for $10,000. Wailes mulled over the offer, visited the plantation, and jotted down his impression: "[I] got a horse and rode with the overseer over the plantation, which I find in a most worn and ruinous condition, and all the land worth anything, protected by a long and precarious levee. All the buildings in a very decayed and ruinous condition." He concluded simply, "Place not worth having."[26]

Over the course of the 1850s, Duncan unloaded some 2,600 acres in Adams County, including the plantations of Walnut Grove, Ellislie, and Sunnyside, as well as Homochitto. Sunnyside, a forty-acre plantation and residence next to Auburn, he sold to his son-in-law, Samuel M. Davis, for $17,000. Duncan also divested himself of almost 1,500 acres in Wilkinson County and over 2,000 acres in Tensas Parish. While concentrating his plantation base, Duncan continued to transfer wealth to his children. Just prior to presenting Maria with the former Butler plantation in Pointe Coupee Parish, he gave his daughter Charlotte the Holly Ridge plantation and 105 slaves. During the late 1850s, he handed over L'Argent, the Tensas Parish cotton plantation, to Samuel, along with 173 slaves; he also gave Carlisle plantation and 149 slaves in Issaquena County to Stephen Jr.[27]

In spite of these transfers, Duncan still wielded tremendous influence over the operations of his former property. For instance, he routinely traveled to Holly Ridge to keep a close eye on Charlotte's husband, Samuel Davis, who ran the plantation. By giving his children property, both land and human, Duncan created a period of apprenticeship during which he could watch over the heirs to his empire. Catharine Duncan once remarked that her husband "makes it a *rule* when his sons are *21* to give them their *property* so that *he* can see how they will *manage* it and he can *advise* them." By 1856, the elder Duncan had given each of his five children an average of $212,500 in land and slaves, for a total of $1,062,500 in property and assets.[28]

At this time, Duncan also entered into a partnership with the manager of his Oxford and Camperdown plantations. Since the 1840s, Andrew McWilliams had managed Duncan's sugar operations. He also supervised the neighboring sugar estate of Mary Porter, widow of Alexander Porter and an intimate of the Leverich family. McWilliams maintained frequent contact with Charles Leverich, informing Leverich in April 1859 that "I have bought one half interest in both places with the Dr." For $430,000 to be paid over the course of eleven years, McWilliams purchased interest in 5,230 arpents (4,393 acres) in St. Mary Parish, 1,019 acres in neighboring St. Martin Parish, and 326 slaves. Under Duncan's direction, he would continue to manage the plantations and crop shipments. For his services, he would be paid $3,500 per year, which would be charged to the expense account of the partnership—a distinctly different arrangement than the one Duncan had made with Robert McCollough and Zenas Preston in the early 1830s. Duncan controlled all crop sales and divided the proceeds equally between himself and McWilliams.[29]

Though the arrangement was supposedly an equal partnership, Duncan maintained more control and had more power than McWilliams. In the fall of 1859, the two men disagreed over what to do about planting seed for the following crop year. Duncan adamantly opposed McWilliams's desire to plant seed during a dry spell. Conversely, McWilliams believed that "if I had waited for rain—we would been without any seed for next year." Further exacerbating the situation, much of the current crop froze to the ground in a severe cold snap, which was preceded the night before by a hurricane. Duncan disagreed with McWilliams's desire to cultivate what remained after the storm and freeze, believing that his partner was "in too great a hurry to roll with a short crop." As the situation unfolded, the crop indeed turned short, which caused McWilliams great anxiety, particularly since Duncan had "warned" him not to plant the seed cane when he did. Worried that the short crop would anger Duncan and cause him economic troubles, McWilliams pressured Leverich to "exert" himself and "make it bring a good price" to make up for the loss.[30]

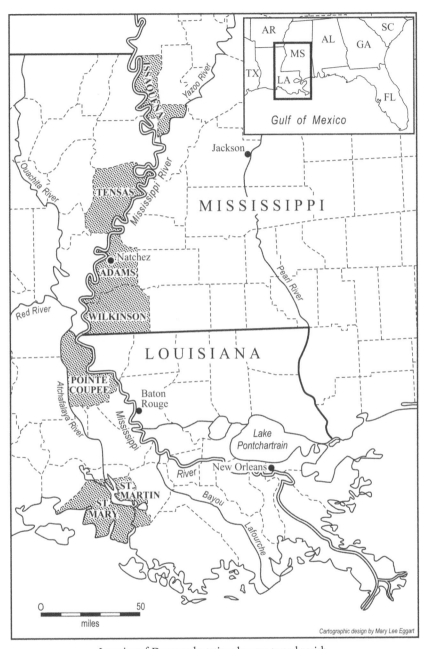

Location of Duncan plantations by county and parish

McWilliams was intimidated at times by Duncan, who leaned hard on him for perceived mistakes. Magnifying this dynamic even more was the fact that, unlike his ultra-wealthy partner, McWilliams could not afford hard times. In light of the short crop, McWilliams informed Charles Leverich, "the Dr says he will be short of funds this year" and wondered in confidence, "and if he is what do you suppose will become of poor me[?]"[31] Despite some successes, within two years McWilliams had sold two-thirds of his share in the partnership back to Duncan.[32]

The McWilliams case demonstrates that when Duncan tried to transfer some property outside of his familial circle in ways that allowed him to maintain control, these arrangements did not work. The transfer of property to his heirs, in contrast, allowed him to maintain absolute authority. Meanwhile, he divested himself of less profitable assets. Over the course of the decade he sold nearly 17,000 acres, 11 lots, and 685 slaves, netting himself $114,701 in cash.[33] Simultaneously, the number of improved acres on Duncan's plantations steadily increased. In 1850, slightly over 3,000 acres in Issaquena County lay ready to be cultivated on the plantations Duncan owned. Ten years later, the amount of ready-to-use, productive acres had risen by 67 percent, and the number of unimproved acres had dropped from 4,650 to 2,610.[34]

On the eve of the Civil War, Duncan still owned almost 13,000 acres of land in Mississippi and Louisiana, which were valued at over $1.3 million. Additionally, he owned $55,000 in equipment and $44,650 in livestock. Even without counting slaves and personal property, the total cash value of his own plantations was $1,434,650 by 1860—an increase of 328.3 percent over the previous decade. In addition, Duncan gave his children nearly a million dollars worth of property during the 1850s. These plantations, combined with Duncan's own holdings, totaled almost 25,000 acres. The value of the family's assets grew exponentially over the course of the 1850s. At the beginning of the decade, Duncan family holdings in land, equipment, and livestock totaled $431,158; this increased to a phenomenal $2,346,790 within ten years.[35]

The Duncans' slave force increased dramatically as well in the 1850s. According to a combination of Federal census and family records, in 1860 the Duncans enslaved 2,241 women, men, and children. This included the 1,400 slaves Duncan owned, plus the 841 slaves he transferred to his children, making them among the largest slaveowners in the entire South.[36]

On the eve of the Civil War, Stephen Duncan's empire had reached its zenith. His cautious decision making, conservative approach to credit and cash, and adaptability to the ever-changing economic environment allowed him to build in one generation what took others far longer to achieve. Vital familial, social, and economic connections helped propel him to such high realms. Yet Duncan's status as one of the wealthiest planters and capitalists in the region was not entirely due to fortuitous alliances with family members or other elites; nor was it entirely founded on the fruits of his own labors. Most of his empire was built row by row on the backs of the thousands of women, men, and children whom Duncan enslaved. The ultimate key to Duncan's power and wealth resided less in his web of white associations, and more within the black slave quarters of the Mississippi Delta and the sugarhouses of gulf coastal Louisiana.

9

⇥⊷⊰⇤

UNDERGROUND NETWORKS

Slave Communities and Slavery on the Duncan Plantations

I n the late spring of 1849, Stephen Duncan anxiously informed Charles P.
Leverich that cholera "of unusually virulent character" had broken out in
the Mississippi Delta. In an attempt to protect his massive slave force from
the deadly effects of what had become a nationwide epidemic, Duncan traveled
to his delta plantations to provide homeopathic treatment. Though he claimed
that his medical solutions had met with "great comparative success," cholera's
ravages could not be prevented. This was particularly true for the more than
one hundred enslaved men, women, and children on Carlisle plantation, where
most victims died within six to twelve hours of its onset.[1]

Although many of Carlisle's slaves warded off the disease, its effects continued to resonate within the slave community. Women of childbearing years
found it difficult to carry pregnancies to term, and the average number of years
between recorded births within Carlisle's slave families was significantly higher
than that for slave families in other locales throughout the South.[2] While disease played a part in this reality, other facets of enslavement contributed to it as
well. Factors such as the environment, the labor regimen, disease, slave sales,
transfers, and deaths caused instability within the Duncan slave communities.
Nevertheless, slave women and men sought to counterbalance this instability
with efforts at community building. Through a dynamic kin system comprised
of extended families and living arrangements, the Duncan slaves built underground networks and communities that they could rely upon for comfort,
strength, and daily survival.

Duncan enslaved the smallest number of people at Auburn, where between eleven and nineteen women, children, and men labored as his family's personal and household slaves. Other Duncan plantations had extremely large slave forces. The Camperdown sugar plantation in Louisiana consistently remained one of Duncan's largest operations. In 1850, he enslaved 169 people in the cane fields; ten years later, that number had increased 21.3 percent, to 205 slaves. Duncan's plantations in the Mississippi Delta also had significant numbers of slaves, ranging from 88 to 174 slaves in 1860.[3]

Of the plantations Duncan transferred to his children, the largest was the sugar and cotton plantation in Pointe Coupee Parish that he gave to his daughter Maria and her husband, John Julius Pringle, in 1850. By 1860, the Pringles were the second largest slaveowners in the parish. Like all the Duncan plantations, the labor regimen in Pointe Coupee was intense, resulting in high output: in 1860, 318 slaves produced 653 hogsheads of sugar, 60,000 gallons of molasses, and over 900 bales of cotton.[4]

The slaves on the Duncan family's other plantations produced as much as their counterparts in Pointe Coupee. And the labor regimen was just as unrelentless on the five delta plantations still owned and operated by the elder Stephen Duncan. They yielded over 3,600 bales of cotton, while Camperdown and Oxford produced 820 hogsheads of sugar, 1,645 gallons of molasses, and 15,000 bushels of corn. On the eve of the Civil War, production on the Duncan family plantations reached its apex: 1,473 hogsheads of sugar, 61,645 gallons of molasses, 7,209 bales of cotton, and 60,000 bushels of corn, for a conservative cash value of $438,000.[5]

The enormous proportions of Stephen Duncan's land- and slaveholdings shaped his management style and his relationship with his slaves. Duncan remained a hands-off, absentee planter focused primarily on the business rather than the human dimensions of his empire. However, during the cholera crisis, as at other times when he felt that his plantations would benefit from his direct management, Duncan undertook the arduous journey from his comfortable Natchez mansion to the isolated world of the delta. Given the geographical reach of his far-flung holdings, it was impossible for him to manage certain plantations personally, and it is doubtful that he had many one-on-one relationships with his slaves except those at Auburn or in the immediate vicinity of Adams County. Within Duncan's world, paternalism was simply not relevant. This was as much a function of the size and diverse nature of his holdings as it was of his worldview.

The scholarly debate over the nature of the master-slave relationship has taken many forms over the years. The inner dynamics of a relationship in which one human being is owned by another can never be known on its deepest level, but historians are afforded glimpses into this world. Large, sweeping models can be useful in providing ways in which to think about master-slave relations, but, in the end, they cannot take into account the extensive variables, particularly human variables, that comprised and shaped such a system.

In the past thirty years, one of the most enduring interpretations of slavery has been that of paternalism, put forth by Eugene Genovese. Though Genovese's model has fostered much scholarly debate and challenge, much of the core argument remains, even among revisionists. As he contends, "Paternalism's insistence upon mutual obligations—duties, responsibilities, and ultimately even rights—implicitly recognized the slaves' humanity."[6] Such mutual obligations formed part of the basis of the master-slave relationship. An examination of slavery under Stephen Duncan challenges this framework, however. Duncan did not practice paternalism to any significant degree, nor did he ever indicate that he "implicitly recognized the slaves' humanity." In his world, slaves were simply cogs in a larger (and largely) capitalistic machine. It is difficult to imagine that slaves in such a regime—or any other regime, for that matter—would feel any obligations to or identify with their enslavers.

Over the decades, Duncan, a prolific letter writer, scarcely mentioned his slaves or discussed slavery in any detail. The absence of over two thousand individuals is haunting, and it speaks loudly of Duncan's views: slaves were barely human and hardly worth the ink on paper. Occasionally, however, Duncan did exhibit some acknowledgment of his slaves' humanity—usually in conjunction with major loss of life due to disease or an epidemic. Perhaps this was rooted in the fact that Duncan was a physician, and the lives of his slaves were among his greatest economic assets.

Nonetheless, it is striking that Duncan, the consummate businessman who discussed his financial affairs in painstaking detail, was so silent about one of his largest asset bases, which was worth, by exceedingly conservative estimates, at least a million dollars. Unlike some planters, Duncan did not wrestle with the gripping moral and racial questions of bondage. In all his writings, he never questioned the ethics of owning another human being. Perhaps his silence on this issue was a form of denial; alternately, it might have reflected sheer indifference to his massive labor force. His worldview was grounded in economics, and slaves were simply economic units.

The Duncan slaves' lives were thus regulated by the needs of the Duncan economic empire. When not laboring in the stifling cane fields off the Louisiana gulf coast or in the cotton fields of the eerily withdrawn world of the Mississippi Delta, the Duncan slaves found some refuge in their families and households, which formed the backbone of their slave communities. Yet those communities could be ripped apart at any given moment by a Duncan directive of sale or transfer, disease, or simply the awareness that by sunset of any given day, a family, household, love relationship, or friendship could be destroyed.

Though relational and familial bonds were fragile, slave women and men strengthened them as much they could within the context of slavery. The households in which they lived, either voluntarily or involuntarily, formed a significant facet of their lives. Of the 336 slave households recorded on Auburn, Camperdown, Carlisle, Duncannon, Ellislie, Homochitto, L'Argent, Oakley, Middlesex, Oxford, and Reserve plantations between 1851 and 1862, a majority contained children, and the slave force was almost evenly divided between men and women. Well over half were adults—sixteen years and older—and most were between twenty and fifty years old.[7] Slightly more than half of the households with children were headed by a male and female adult (referred to as a "two-parent household"), and 29 percent were headed by two parents plus at least one other related or unrelated adult (referred to as a "two-parent extended household"). The most common type of all households on the Duncan plantations, either with children or without, was that of two parents with children, which comprised 35 percent of all slave households. The next most common form of household (19.9 percent) was that of two parents and their children plus at least one other related or unrelated adult. A childless couple, either married or unmarried, was the third most common form of living arrangement (14.9 percent), while the least common form of living arrangement was that of a group of single, childless females residing together (0.3 percent). Interwoven among these less common household formations were groups of females and males with children and single males and females with or without children.[8]

Though the most common type of slave household seemingly replicated nuclear familial structures, the evidence from the Duncan plantations suggests that living arrangements were more complex and wedded to a larger network than households consisting simply of a mother, father, and children. According to Duncan's records, 37.9 percent of all slaves lived in two-parent households. But, interestingly, nearly a third lived in two-parent extended family household structures, even though this configuration comprised only 19.9 percent of the households on the Duncan plantations. Most slaves thus grouped themselves or were grouped in extended, non-nuclear family living arrangements. Even more significant is the fact that 62.1 percent of all Duncan slaves lived in arrangements other than that of the traditional two-parent paradigm, which remains at the center of scholarly debates over slave family and household structure. This suggests that slave families and households increasingly experienced disruption, instability, and reorganization, which forced them into more extended living arrangements. In spite of this pattern, some individual plantations reflected more nuclear familial models. For example, 68 percent of Middlesex slaves lived in households that consisted of two parents and children. Likewise, almost 57 percent of L'Argent slaves lived in a nuclear two-parent household.[9]

Regardless of their living arrangements, Duncan slave communities possessed vibrant kin networks of support. Though the deeper meanings of such networks remained hidden from whites, their existence was of paramount importance to blacks. The slave communities on the five delta plantations of Oakley, Duncannon, Carlisle, Reserve, and Homochitto illustrate the dynamic nature of slave households and extended kin networks. Between 1851 and 1862, these slave communities changed shape: old members disappeared, new ones were gained, families and households broke apart and reconstituted themselves. In spite of this, a majority of the households and families present in 1851 could be found on the same plantations eleven years later, during wartime, when external factors might have disrupted slave family life even more than usual. On Duncannon, 55.3 percent of the slave families recorded in 1851 were still present in the same form in 1862. Likewise, 77.3 percent of families on Reserve in 1851 were still there eleven years later. This points to seemingly stable communities.[10]

The addition of new households over the years often resulted from members breaking off from their original family units to form new families and living groups. Carlisle illustrates this well: between 1851 and 1862, twenty-five new households were formed, 36 percent of which were composed of members who had lived on the plantation for at least five years. In many cases, the new households consisted of children who had left their parents and formed their own family units.[11]

Between 1851 and 1862, the number of two-parent extended family households increased, while the number of two-parent nuclear households with children declined. At Oakley, for example, more nuclear family structures decreased by 28.6 percent, while extended family structures increased by 150 percent. These changes affected the overall proportion of two-parent and two-parent extended family households in relation to all the households on Oakley. In 1851, two-parent extended families comprised 12.6 percent of household types; by 1862, however, they had dramatically increased to nearly one-third of all households.[12]

Mirroring this shift in household type were the number of slaves who lived in these households. Between 1851 and 1862, the number of Oakley slaves in two-parent families plunged 65 percent, while the number of slaves in two-parent extended households jumped 173.9 percent. Clearly, Oakley slaves increasingly grouped themselves—or were grouped—into more extended family units. This suggests rising levels of instability within slave communities, due either to the planned forces of white mastery or the unplanned forces of nature.[13]

The situation at Oakley was mirrored on other plantations as well. On Duncannon, the total number of two-parent extended families increased 166.7 percent between 1851 and 1862, while strictly two-parent households with children decreased 26.7 percent. These shifts were not exclusive to families with children: the number of childless male-female headed households on Duncannon increased over 1,000 percent. The importance of these changes should not be underestimated.[14] The evolution of household patterns suggests that slavery on the Duncan plantations shattered, to varying degrees, family and household structures. This sparks further questions about the day-to-day realities of enslavement and its emotional and physical effects on slave family life. Out of a sense of individual and collective survival and resistance, slaves formed families and living groups that were not entirely shaped by the prevailing nuclear paradigm. Instead, the immediate support system for individuals, as well as for larger networks within the slave community, may have been much broader and more unstable than previous historical inquiry has suggested.

While the two-parent family was central to the Duncan slaves, other types of family groupings were just as strong, reflecting the diversity of slave family life and living arrangements. Though two-parent and two-parent extended families comprised 55 percent of Duncan's slave households, nearly 62 percent of those households were made up of non-nuclear two-parent families, with extended families being especially numerous.[15] Most slaves lived within some sort of family structure—biological or not—in which members cared for other members, and very few slaves lived alone.

The evidence from the Duncan plantations challenges the portrait of slave families posited by many scholars, who argue that the dominant form of living arrangements among slaves was the two-parent nuclear household with children and that slave families experienced stability. As Herbert Gutman contends in his landmark study, *The Black Family in Slavery and Freedom,* such households were characterized by long-term marriages among slave couples (as well as dominance of the two-parent familial arrangement), thus indicating that slave families and communities were extremely stable. Subsequent scholarship has largely supported Gutman's argument, refining his conclusions rather than offering outright challenges to them. Yet large questions still loom in regard to the structure of slave families and communities, particularly in the Deep South.[16] In her examination of slave life in Loudoun County, Virginia, Brenda Stevenson challenges the prevailing view, concluding that "most slave children in Virginia did not grow up in two-parent homes" and that "Virginia slave families . . . essentially were not nuclear and did not derive from long-term marriages. The most discernible ideal for their principal kinship organization was a malleable extended family."[17]

As Stevenson argues, the structure of slave communities was not everywhere a predominantly two-parent, nuclear one. Indeed, many of the slave family structures on the Duncan plantations were very similar to Stevenson's slave families in Virginia. Given the difference in time and location between eighteenth- and nineteenth-century Loudoun County and the Mississippi Delta, however, perhaps a more useful comparison can be drawn with Ann Patton Malone's study of slave families in Louisiana in the nineteenth century. There, according to Malone, the two-parent nuclear household and family structure prevailed. Nearly three-quarters of all slaves in Louisiana lived in simple families, consisting of two-parent households, childless couples, and single people with children. The remaining slaves lived in multiple, extended, and non-nuclear households or as solitaires.[18] Overall, and particularly within certain categories, dramatic differences existed between the slave communities on the Duncan plantations and those studied by Malone. Whereas Malone states that 73 percent of Louisiana slaves lived in simple families, barely 50 percent of Duncan slaves lived in this type of household. A mere 1.3 percent of Duncan slaves lived as solitaires, compared to 18.3 percent in Louisiana. Perhaps most interesting, Malone notes that 7.5 percent of Louisiana slaves lived in extended and multiple family households. In sharp contrast, 36.2 percent of Duncan slave adults with children (including the children themselves) dwelt in households of extended or multiple families.[19]

Whether connected through blood or not, or whether children were present or not, slaves on the Duncan plantations lived together in families and households. Few slaves chose to (or had to) live by themselves—only 17 of the 1,328 slaves sampled lived alone. Extant records do not reveal whether these arrangements were the slaves' choice, that of plantation management, or an amalgam of both. Nor do the records reveal whether the extended families or group households were reconfigurations of previous slave communities that had been ripped apart by sale, death, transfer, new purchases, or escapes. Nonetheless, this was the context in which the Duncan slaves lived. Their networks and communities provided some type of structure upon which they could count, in some form or fashion, to help them survive the devastating realities of enslavement.

Within such networks, Duncan's slaves formed relationships, perhaps married, built new families, and demonstrated the ability to endure their bondage.[20] The case of one family on Duncannon plantation offers an example of slave family patterns. In 1851, Andrew, Lewis, and Frank—who ranged in age from fifteen to thirty-three—lived with their parents, Ralph and Frances. Sophy also resided with them, but she was not a sibling. By 1862, Lewis and Sophy had entered into marriage or a committed relationship, moved out of Ralph and Frances's house, and become the parents of Richard, age seven, and Sam, age two. Given Lewis's and Sophy's young ages in the 1862 records, they might have simply decided to remain with Ralph and Frances until they had their own children.[21]

The scope of the extended kin network and two-parent extended household is also seen in the families who labored in the cotton fields of Reserve. By 1851, slaves Essex and Elsy had six children between twelve and one: Ishmael, Gilbert, Charles, Hannibal, Pleasant, and Dennis. They also took in Jim Taylor, who was fifteen. By the end of the decade, Jim, now in his mid-twenties, resided in the household of Washington and Phillis and their five children.[22] Jim Taylor's shift in residence illustrates that slaves who were single or without their biological parents would still generally belong to an extended family.

One of the better examples illustrating the dynamic nature of kinship networks can be found within the slave community of Carlisle plantation. In 1851, Charles and Ellen were either married or living together and had a one-year-old child, Moses. The birth of their second living (or recorded) child, Charles Jr., occurred in 1852 and was followed by the birth of Lorenzo. Shortly afterwards, Charles and Ellen's relationship ended either voluntarily or involuntarily; by 1856, Ellen lived alone with her three sons. Sometime within the next five years, they began to live with William, the son of Nat and Little Harriet. Meanwhile, Ellen's previous partner, Charles, had formed a new family with a single mother, Minerva, and her daughter, Kiah. By 1861, Charles and Minerva had become the parents of two daughters, Cely Ann and Elizabeth.[23]

The shifting nature of the Carlisle slave community is also illuminated by another pair of households. In 1851, Zack and Sally headed a household that included their son, Simon; a thirty-three-year-old man, Bob; and an eight-year-old boy, Jacob. The familial relationship of Bob and Jacob to each other and to Zack and Sally is unclear. Anthony and Betsey and their two children, Jim Henry and Daniel, formed another household. By 1856, the unions of both Zack and Sally and Anthony and Betsey had dissolved. Zack and Betsey had formed a household, along with Betsey's two sons and a son of their own, Martin, born in September 1856. Simon, Zack's son from his previous relationship with Sally, was not listed as living with Zack and Betsey in 1856, but he had joined their household by 1861. Meanwhile, Bob and Jacob disappeared from the slave lists, and Anthony had formed a new family with Amanda. By 1861, Anthony and Amanda had four children: Paulena, Mary Magdalen, Emerson, and Rubin.[24]

To what degree do the examples of Zack, Sally, Betsey, Anthony, and Amanda demonstrate that slaves made their own decisions to end relationships or marriages? Herbert Gutman addresses this question, using the Carlisle slave community to illustrate slaves' autonomy and ability to make choices. He argues that since there were few marital breakups between 1851 and 1861 on the Carlisle plantation, it was evident that "Carlisle plantation managers did not force slave couples to remain together as husband and wife. Because their earlier marriages had produced children, it cannot be argued that these couples had been separated forcibly for failing to increase Stephen Duncan's assets. Duncan's plantation managers probably permitted the slaves to marry and separate at will."[25]

From Duncan's perspective, it would be to his advantage for slave women to reproduce. A meticulous and detailed planner, Duncan might have forced certain relationships to break up and some to be kept together, although no evidence exists to demonstrate whether this actually happened. Nevertheless, it suggests an explanation for the disappearance from the records of some Carlisle slave families. Though a majority of the 1851 families were present a decade later, a significant proportion cannot be found in surviving slave lists. On Carlisle, 25 percent of slave households completely vanished, thus challenging some of Gutman's assertions about the stability of the Carlisle community. According to Samuel B. Smith, a former Mississippi resident who testified before the American Freedmen's Inquiry Commission in 1863, "Dr Duncan . . . was very careful in keeping up the [slave] family intercourse."[26] It is unclear whether this was accomplished by various means of white control or by allowing slave families to form and reform on their own. What is clear is that according to Smith's testimony, Duncan was mindful, if not desirous, of slave reproduction. For Duncan, as well as other enslavers, economic production and biological reproduction went hand in hand. And for masters like Duncan, whose slaves were nothing more than assets in human form, reproduction of capital was essential to maintaining individual power and enforcing the larger frameworks of the system. In spite of Duncan's concern with slave reproduction, however, a significant percentage of slave households on Carlisle, as well as other plantations, simply disappeared from the records over time. The loss of 25 percent of a given community surely would have created a profound disruption of slave life on Carlisle, affecting the stability of the slave communities as a whole as well as their individual families.

Another way of exploring the extent of power relations, white social control, and black autonomy on antebellum plantations is through slave naming patterns. Slave parents on Carlisle, Camperdown, Oakley, Reserve, Ellislie, Duncannon, Middlesex, Homochitto, Oxford, and L'Argent practiced naming patterns that clearly demonstrate the importance of family and kinship networks as well as the roles of religion and even African culture in their lives during the mid-nineteenth century.[27] As previous studies have shown, slave naming practices serve as windows into one of the most intimate facets of slave life.[28]

The Duncan slaves' naming practices suggest that they displayed a consciousness of issues of identity and drew particularly upon familial and historical memories. Of 223 slave families sampled, nearly a quarter (23.7 percent) named at least one of their children after their father, mother, grandparent, or other family member. Compared to other studies of slave naming paradigms in the slave South, however, Duncan slaves named their children after relatives less frequently. One explanation for this may be due to the inability to trace family names on the Duncan plantations over a long timespan.[29]

Like Abram and Betsy of Homochitto, who named their son Little Abram, over 23 percent of the parents on Homochitto named at least one of their children after their father. Though this naming pattern wove its way through the slave communities on other Duncan plantations, it was most prevalent on Homochitto. Slightly over 14 percent of parents on all Duncan plantations named at least one of their children after a father. Compared to families on other plantations across the South, a far lower percentage of Duncan slave families named their children in this manner.[30]

Although historian Herbert Gutman believed that it was extremely rare for girls to be named after their mothers, subsequent studies have found that many infant girls carried the historical memory of their mothers, grandmothers, or other female relatives. On the Duncan plantations, 5.5 percent of slave parents named daughters after the mothers. Yet slaves also named their female children after grandmothers, aunts, and sisters. On Ellislie, Lidda named her daughter after herself; Billy and Nancy named their third surviving daughter Nancy. In another family, Easter named her only surviving child, Little Lucy, after an older woman by that name—probably Easter's mother, aunt, or sister, who lived in the household. If, as Gutman concluded, there once was an African or slave taboo against naming a child after the mother, by the middle of the nineteenth century this cultural taboo had diminished among the Duncan slaves, as well as among slaves across the South.[31]

In addition to naming a child after themselves, parents also honored other relatives, living or dead, by giving their children the names of grandparents, siblings, uncles, and aunts. Overall, almost one-quarter of all slave families named a child after some family member; on certain plantations, the percentage was even higher. Forty percent of slave parents on Ellislie and Homochitto named at least one child after some family member, while over 25 percent of the slave families on Carlisle practiced this naming pattern.[32] This suggests that slave families on the Duncan plantations maintained some measure of cultural autonomy for themselves in regard to naming their children. Many chose to keep alive familial memories, indicating cross-generational connections as well as the importance of familial networks both large and small.

Duncan slaves also named their children after biblical figures. Names like Isaac, Ishmael, Moses, Israel, Rachel, Ezekiel, Luke, Matthew, Sarah, and Mary Magdalen dotted the slave registers. The symbolic naming of a child Moses or Israel might have been intended to evoke images of those who were eventually freed from oppression by the will of God, sending a subtle signal to the Duncans, other slaveowners, and the white community that their mastery was not complete. Within the Duncan slave community, 15.7 percent of all slave families named at least one child after a biblical figure. On some plantations, this pattern was more popular than on others. One-third of Ellislie families gave at least one child a biblical name; on Camperdown, in contrast, barely 4 percent of slave families did so.[33]

An equally important naming practice was that of giving a child a name that reflected consciousness of African roots, and perhaps a familial memory as well. This is particularly significant given that such names were less frequent in late antebellum slave communities than in the colonial era or even the early nineteenth century. In all Duncan slave communities, with the exception of Ellislie, 8.5 percent of parents gave at least one child an African name.[34] On Oxford, almost one quarter of slave parents named their children in such a manner. In the quarters, fields, woods, and bayous of the Duncan plantations, parents called out to children named Quash, Sabina, Kiah, Kiziah, Maika, and Phebe. These names held deep meanings within the context of enslavement, meanings perhaps impossible for modern scholars to understand.[35] This naming pattern supports Drew Faust's findings about James Henry Hammond's Silver Bluff plantation in South Carolina, where the "active sense of familial and cultural heritage was . . . evident in the perpetuation of African names in the Bluff community." Interestingly, the Duncan slave communities engaged in this naming practice to a much greater extent than slaves on the Ball plantations in South Carolina.[36] Such naming practices might have sent a message to whites that the slave system could not totally obliterate cultural identities, even in the mid-nineteenth century.

These naming patterns suggest that Stephen Duncan, his overseers and managers, and other Duncan family members had little influence on the slave naming process. Further supporting this argument is the fact that few children on the Duncan plantations were named after historical or classical figures, which generally reflected a master's involvement in the naming process. Some children on the Duncan plantations did indeed carry the names of Caesar, Cornelius, Delpha, Clay, Jefferson, and Washington. But only 6.7 percent of slave parents named their children after such figures.[37]

Interestingly, parents did not choose the names of Duncan family members for their children more frequently than other English names. Of 223 families, 24.7 percent had at least one child who shared a name with a Duncan family member. However, 88.8 percent of slave parents gave their children English names other than the ones associated with Duncan family members, which included such common slave names as Samuel, Henry, and Maria.[38] In some instances, perhaps some slaves consciously chose not to name their children after their enslavers. But given the Duncan family's overall absence from their plantations, slaves might not have even known the names of their masters, excepting Duncan himself or some of his sons.

Though we can never know for sure, it is a reasonable assumption that the Duncan slaves named their own children, imbuing this practice with its own private meanings. Given Duncan's management style and the fact that he lived hundreds of miles away from many of his plantations, naming slaves might not have been a priority for him. For many Duncan slaves, in contrast, names frequently demonstrated a consciousness of African cultural ties or familial bonds that affirmed connections to the larger slave network. Some slaves appear to have practiced naming patterns that steered completely clear of replicating that of the whites who owned them. This autonomy was reinforced by the fact that most of the Duncan slaves in the isolated worlds of the Mississippi Delta or the Louisiana Gulf Coast did not have regular contact with great numbers of whites. Even though Stephen Duncan and his sons visited their plantations several times a year, the Duncans basically remained absentee masters. In these areas of black majority strongholds, the slaves comprised anywhere from 70 to 92 percent of the parish or county population.[39] As a result, they were able, to some extent, to foster higher levels of cultural autonomy, transcending their mere chattel status.

Slave naming practices and family relationships within extended kin networks suggest some level of internal stability, familial memory, and independent slave culture on the Duncan plantations. However, factors such as long intervals between the births of surviving slave children, the late ages at which most slave mothers gave birth, and the low number of surviving infants per family suggest instability as well. This instability was triggered by external forces, such as disease, overall health, environment, punishment, social control, and an oppressive work regime.

Across the antebellum South, the average age at which slave mothers gave birth for the first time was 20.6 years. This varied not only from region to region, but also from plantation to plantation within the same region. The average age at which Virginia slave mothers gave birth was 19.71 years; in Orange County, North Carolina, first-time mothers were seventeen on average. Slave women in Louisiana gave birth to their first child at an average age of nineteen or twenty years old.[40] In comparison, slave women on the Duncan plantations gave birth to their first surviving child at 21.12 years.[41] On some plantations—such as Reserve, Carlisle, Homochitto, and Oxford—the average age was younger; on others—such as Ellislie, Middlesex, and L'Argent—it was even later, ranging from 22.93 years on L'Argent to 24.60 years on Ellislie. Precisely what accounted for such disparities cannot be known, but certainly differing work regimes, punishment and social control, environmental conditions, disease and sickness, malnutrition, overall community stability, and slave resistance could have influenced slave women's ability to reproduce.[42]

Another statistic representing the power of external forces that affected slave family development was the low number of live births per family. Compared to the average for the South, mothers on the Duncan plantations had fewer live births. In Virginia, the average number of live births per woman was 4.94; in Louisiana, the average was between five and seven. One study that focuses on the entire antebellum South concludes that the average number of live births per mother was 9.24 children.[43] Between 1851 and 1862, slave mothers on the Duncan plantations had an average of 3.41 live births. Women on Homochitto experienced an even lower average—2.39 live births per mother—while other plantations, like Reserve, had higher averages.[44]

The longer intervals between surviving children suggests that slave women on the Duncan plantations had a very difficult time carrying pregnancies to term. Studies thus far have shown that child spacing among slaves across the South ranged from 2.06 to almost three years. Within the Duncan slave community, child spacing averages were far greater, ranging from a low of 2.61 years on Ellislie to a high of 4.39 years on Homochitto. Some individual women had extremely long intervals between live births, such as six or seven years. Women on most plantations hovered near the three-and-a-half year interval.[45] Accounting for this pattern might have been the harshness of the work regime, which caused fertility problems and prevented slave women from carrying pregnancies to term. Miscarriages and stillbirths, as well as the deaths of infant children, might also have resulted from the dire conditions of enslavement. Moreover, some slave women might have induced abortion as a means of resistance. As Deborah White and others argue, slave women were well versed in plants that caused miscarriages, and they could thus control their fertility for a number of reasons. Finally, and even more chillingly, it is feasible that Stephen Duncan sold some infants and very young children before he ever recorded them on his slave lists.[46]

Slave women's fertility differed dramatically among Duncan plantations (even those located next to one another), as the example of Middlesex demonstrates. Between 1851 and 1862, the average slave woman on this plantation gave birth to her first surviving child at almost twenty-five years of age and averaged only 2.69 live births. Furthermore, the average space between children was nearly three-and-a half years.[47] Slave reproduction provides a window through which we can ascertain slave community stability. As in the case of Middlesex, external and internal factors challenged this stability to such an extent that community survival was threatened.

In spite of the profound instability on some Duncan plantations, slave families, households, and communities sought to counterbalance sources of disruption with efforts at community building. Again, Middlesex serves as a good example of this, particularly since the community experienced the crushing effects of ill-health, an unhealthy environment, and an oppressive labor regimen. Middlesex naming patterns reveal that families engaged in cultural resistance on some level and wielded considerable autonomy as they sought to instill cross-generational memories via family names. Over 26 percent of parents on Middlesex named at least one child after a family member, and over 13 percent of parents gave their child an African name. At the same time, Middlesex had the lowest percentage of slave children who shared a name with a member of the Duncan family. Because the Middlesex slave community possessed what would be considered both very unstable and stable characteristics, the question becomes how connected these factors were within slave communities. Stability and instability were not mutually exclusive, but worked in a dynamic fashion with one another. Did the fact that Middlesex slave mothers had difficulty carrying pregnancies to term, or the fact that disease and the sale of infants and children decimated the slave populations, foster more familial memory and make slave communities more tightly knit? In the case of the Duncan plantations, it is likely that the greater the destruction of slave communities, the greater the black effort to create stability. Of all the Duncan slave communities, Middlesex fared among the worst in terms of surviving births and child spacing, yet it represented some of the strongest characteristics of internal slave family stability and familial memory through naming practices.

Even as the Duncan slaves practiced cultural resistance, their daily life was characterized by an ultra-demanding labor regimen in the fields, combined with survival levels of an exiguous material existence. In the slave households, in which so many men, women, and children found some measure of comfort, or at least companionship, the Duncan slaves found themselves crushed into living conditions not much better than that which livestock endured. The Duncans packed their slave quarters more tightly than many southern slaveowners.

Throughout the antebellum South, most slave housing was no more than crudely built, one-room log or wood cabins with dirt floors, which usually measured twelve by twelve (at most, twelve by fifteen) feet. On exceptional plantations, slave cabins measured sixteen by eighteen feet and had elevated plank flooring and brick chimneys.[48] Generally, the cramped slave quarters contained at least two families, or five to six slaves per cabin. According to the 1860 census, housing on Stephen Duncan's Issaquena County plantations averaged 8.3 slaves per cabin. The worst conditions for his slaves were on his delta plantation overseen by Jacob Garrett, where 147 slaves jammed into 12 housing units, an average of 12.3 slaves per cabin. Stephen Duncan Jr. housed his Issaquena County slaves in a similarly cruel fashion. Slaves on Samuel Duncan's L'Argent, Henry Duncan's Ellislie, Samuel Davis's Homochitto, and J. J. Pringle's Pointe Coupee plantations found themselves living in comparatively better conditions: these plantations averaged between 3.1 and 4.8 slaves per cabin. For each cabin, the Duncans provided their slaves with the customary and minimal implements necessary to cook, clean, and wash: coffee pots, buckets, cups, plates, knives, forks, and spoons, as well as "blue gray" blankets.[49]

For the Duncan slaves, the harshness of material life encompassed not just housing, but other facets of daily life. The food and clothing allotments they received were barely average. Throughout the antebellum period, slaves, regardless of locale, received fairly similar rations, which consisted of one peck of cornmeal, between two and four pounds of meat (usually salt pork), and a quart of molasses a week. Many slaves supplemented their meager rations with vegetables that they grew, as well as fish, rabbit, and an occasional chicken that they raised or hunted.[50] Such supplementation was crucial, as it enabled slaves to survive the nutrient-deficient diets their white masters provided. Like the majority of those enslaved, the Duncan slaves' main diet consisted of pork. Because of the family's enormous slave force, it was not unusual for Stephen Duncan to order seventy or eighty barrels of pork per month. Duncan slaves also supplemented their daily rations with fish and other meat (perhaps rabbit), as evidenced by the large quantities of fishhooks and dozens of jackknives purchased for their plantations.[51]

In keeping with the concept of self-contained, self-sufficient plantations, the Duncans purchased cloth from which slaves could make a variety of items. Yet they also bought finished products, which they issued to slaves twice a year. From the Mississippi Delta to Natchez straight south to the Louisiana Gulf Coast, the annual ritual began on the first of every April: each adult male and

One of the original slave cabins (ca. 1820s) on Duncan's Saragossa plantation.
Photograph by James Butters for the Historic American Buildings Survey, 1936.
Courtesy of the Library of Congress.

boy received two fine cotton shirts and two pairs of Lowell pants, while women and girls received two fine cotton shifts, one fine cotton gown, and one Lowell petticoat. On November first, as winter approached, overseers distributed one pair of heavy jeans, one fine cotton shirt, and one jeans overcoat to all males. Female slaves received one linsey gown, one fine cotton shift, and a jeans overcoat. Shoes and boots were distributed as well. However, slaves who did not work outside or who remained near the quarters received no overcoats or spring shoes. Like the adults, slave children also had their allotments: three fine cotton slips in April and one linsey slip in November. Like most slave children across the South, they endured fieldwork and other labor barefoot. And, perhaps to fulfill the Duncan family's sense of "Christian duty," at Christmas slave men and boys received a wool hat, while women and girls were given one calico gown and two headkerchiefs. As indicated by Stephen Duncan's ledger ("Presents—6 Headkerchifs and 1 pair shoes"), he occasionally gave slaves extra clothing as gifts throughout the year; however, given the scant number of relevant ledger notations and the enormity of his slave force, such gifts were extremely rare and probably for favored slaves.[52]

The quality of clothing issued varied widely from master to master. Slaves found the typical material—particularly "osnaburg," or jean cloth—to be extremely rough. Stephen Duncan always bought the highest quality of cloth available (though it was still grossly uncomfortable for those forced to wear it) and referred to his purchases as the "very best," "all of a better quality," and "thought very superior."[53] Though he did not reveal why he bought such a high quality of clothing, he might have thought that he could extract more labor from his slaves if they had better clothing. And given Duncan's obsession with how other whites viewed him, he might also have wanted his slaves to reflect well on him.

While there is ample evidence about the material conditions of life for the Duncan slaves, there is far less testimony about another facet of daily slave existence—slave punishment and control. As we saw earlier when Thomas Butler called upon Duncan in 1823 to handle a violent altercation between an overseer and his slave, Old Gloster, Duncan did not advocate extreme forms of punishment, as he believed it fueled more slave dissent. He advised Butler to sell the troublesome slave, instead of following one of the more usual recourses: execution by hanging.[54] In general, Duncan sought overseers and managers who mirrored his philosophy of restraint. Yet he sometimes had troubles with his overseers. On a trip to his delta lands, he remarked while at Holly Ridge, "I have had a very busy time here charging & discharging Agents & overseers & reforming . . . many abuses."[55]

Over the years, Duncan maintained the same position on slave management and punishment—restraint when possible as the first course of action. This stance did not come out of a position of benevolence or consciousness of a slave's humanity, but out of the belief that less punishment reduced slave resistance and at the same time extracted more labor. But Duncan's managers did not entirely avoid the lash. Few letters from Duncan's managers or overseers have been preserved, and those that survive never speak of whipping or other forms of punishment. But other evidence, such as the direct testimony of slaves, indicates that brutal and extreme forms of punishment took place. In 1863, a Duncan slave saw Federal troops opposite Louisiana's Lake Providence and hid himself in a swamp for ten days to wait for an opportune time to abscond behind Union lines. The slave later revealed that before he could escape, he was found and "put in the stocks & severely whipped."[56] While this is only one example of an extreme form of punishment, it suggests that corporeal punishment was not unknown on the Duncan plantations. Likewise, the existence of stocks on the Louisiana plantation testifies to a permanent structure used for slave punishment.

Just as Duncan rarely mentioned methods of social control and punishment, he also did not mention slave resistance. Aside from certain specific cases and scattered brief remarks about maroon formations and work slowdowns, Duncan seldom, if ever, wrote about slaves challenging whites. Likewise, Duncan's manager and one-time partner of the Camperdown and Oxford plantations, Andrew McWilliams, hardly mentioned slaves in any context, let alone resistance, within his abundant correspondence about day-to-day plantation activities.[57]

Nonetheless, slaves plotted, absconded, activated work slowdowns, formed maroons, engaged in verbal resistance with Duncan's wife, and brandished firearms. In a rare discussion of slaves in a series of letters dated March and April 1859, McWilliams reveals an incident that suggests such activities. Both Oxford and Camperdown were located along an accessible bayou where the Duncan slaves loaded sugar and molasses directly onto the boats that would take them to market. In 1859, a sailor on one of the shipping vessels apparently purchased sugar directly from some of the Oxford slaves. In response to this incident, McWilliams noted, "The Boy had no sugar nor was he allowed to sell sugar out of the Sugar House." He concluded that the sailor "must have encouraged the Negro to take it to him," adding, "They know it was not right to buy or trade with the people."[58] Not wanting to believe that Duncan slaves engaged in such activities, Charles Leverich, who was to receive the shipment, thought that maybe McWilliams had sold the sugar to the sailors. In defense of himself, McWilliams responded to Leverich that "in regard to the Sugar & Molasses in possession of the Sailors of the Vessels—I sold none nor caused to be sold from any of the places any Sugar, Molasses . . . only what I *advised you of,*" repeating that the sailors "caused it to be stolen by *the Negroes* or pilfered it from the cargoes." One week later, McWilliams addressed the issue again with Leverich: "I am surprised to hear the Crew of Gregory has Sugar & Molasses in their possession Said to be purchased from Negroes. I do not believe a word of that—they have pilfered it from Cargo of the vessel—or had the Negroes to Steal it from the Sugar Houses."[59]

Did the Duncan slaves on Oxford actually sell sugar on the side? If so, was it an act of resistance, an avenue to make extra money, or both? Perhaps some of the Duncan slaves formed a class and status bond with the sailors, many of whom were presumably lower-class whites, and mutually planned such activities. In any event, Duncan's manager unequivocally denied that he stole from Oxford. Perhaps even more telling is the fact that he relayed this information to Charles Leverich. The fact that McWilliams chose to write Duncan's confidante about the incident when he usually said nothing about slaves may indicate that he did not want Leverich—and therefore Duncan—to think that he could not manage the slaves. By asserting that white sailors prompted the slaves to steal, McWilliams might have been trying to cover up the fact that he knew the slaves engaged in this activity.

The limited nature of this and other evidence affords only brief glimpses into slave activities and certainly not enough to gauge the scope of slave resistance on the Duncan plantations. Given Duncan's voluminous correspondence, it is striking that he remained silent on such a matter. Yet this silence does not mean a lack of resistance. Duncan might also have refused to comment on those he enslaved, as doing so would force him to face, on levels he usually failed to see, his enslavement of thousands. The perception that slavery for Duncan existed in a vacuum may only be that, a perception due to lack of evidence. If Duncan purposely was silent about his slaves, what does that mean about him as a slaveholder? Does it reflect a sheer indifference to his gigantic labor force? After all, for him, slaves were property and assets just like bank notes and bonds, ploughs and pillared porches of stately mansions—things in which no humanity could ever exist.

Duncan's silence was not necessarily shared by his slaves. In the grip of bondage and an extremely harsh labor regimen, the slaves carved out a measure of independence and culture within the landscape of the Mississippi Delta and the sugar country of Louisiana. When a slave mother called to her child who was named after her grandmother, it spoke volumes—not necessarily to whites, but to the slaves themselves. Naming practices and other activities of the underground and extended slave networks helped build a community that slaves could draw upon—on some days for bolder acts of resistance, but on most days for strength and daily survival. Privately, they embodied small moments of humanity within the horrors of enslavement.

EPILOGUE

"We Are in the Midst of Perils"

"We are in the midst of perils all our lives—& at this particular juncture, we are beset with troubles on all sides," Stephen Duncan wrote his sister, Emily, on the eve of secession in December 1860. "A *universal bankruptcy,* was [*sic*] about to take place," he proclaimed, and "nothing can avert it but the preservation of union." If the Union did not survive, he predicted, "no man in this region will escape, without a great, *very* great reduction of his fortune." With regard to his own fortune, he believed that "I can afford to lose over half & still have enough & more than enough, left for all my *wants.*"[1] Exclusive of personal property and slaves, as well as certain investments, Duncan was worth at least $2.6 million in 1860, while his family's fortune could be conservatively estimated at $3.5 million.[2] In addition, the family's slave force was conservatively worth $1.7 million. In one generation, Duncan amassed over 25,000 acres of land, out of which he carved at least fifteen plantations. In short, he created an empire, most of which was built on the backs of the 2,241 black women, men, and children enslaved on the Duncan plantations.[3]

Duncan recognized the liabilities of absentee slaveowning and planting, but the economic rewards gained from enslaving black laborers outweighed his apprehensions. Intimately connected to this were his views about the growth of slavery and his fear of a black majority's potential to revolt. Though he perpetuated the institution on a grand scale, he advocated not only tighter control over the increase and spread of slavery, but also argued privately for its gradual elimination. The Nat Turner revolt sparked Duncan's philosophy of gradual emancipation. In the aftermath of the revolt, Duncan connected his anxieties about slavery to his concerns about the southern economy, cotton overproduction, and the opening of new territory to settlement. He proposed a national solution to these issues, which included the use of tariffs and the colonization of slaves and free blacks to locations outside the United States. His proposal called for the diversification of the southern economy and the employment of slave labor in manufacturing to siphon slaves away from the fields. He believed that his plan would effectively solve the issues of cotton overproduction and the South's overreliance upon agriculture. It would also eliminate white anxieties about an ever-growing black population by implementing racial cleansing through colonization.

In light of Duncan's position on slavery, his deep connections to the North, his ability to reap tremendous benefits from the southern slave system, and his cultivation of close bonds with many white Mississippians, his identity was complex and ever-changing. He was not simply a northern businessman or a member of the southern slaveocracy. For him, these two identities operated in a dynamic fashion that merged and meshed into a complex hybrid. The familial roots and economic connections that he maintained in both the North and the South, as well as his nationalistic policies, allowed him to connect his identity to both regions in very specific ways. At least publicly, he saw himself as neither a northerner or a southerner, but simply as an American. Duncan's presence brings into focus the flexible nature of personal, regional, economic, political, and social identities during a time when sectional and cultural demarcations are assumed to have been distinctly delineated. Rarely did he join either side of the sectional debates that flared during the antebellum period. Instead, he focused on the national picture. As secession drew nearer and the impetus to claim regional loyalty became stronger, he found himself standing on the edge of a deadly crevasse. On the eve of the Union's dissolution, Duncan found himself no longer able to maintain his fluid identity. Political battles, both real and imagined, and the loss of his hegemony pushed him to take a position.

Two months after Harper's Ferry, in a politically, racially, and emotionally charged exchange with Charles P. Leverich, Duncan cast his loyalty with the South. "I—myself—have always favored a conciliatory view," he explained, but "*I can do so no longer.*" Prompting this change of heart was his belief that free-soilers wanted to dismantle slavery where it already existed. Assessing his potential for colossal financial damage and loss of social power that would come with slavery's dissolution, he funneled his anger through familiar political and racial channels. Even though he had long advocated for the restriction of slavery's growth and the gradual emancipation of slaves, he bristled at the thought that free-soilers wanted "not only to *interfere with slavery* in the States, *but to lock it up by all means*—destroy the *welfare of the whites.*" If this happened, he promised that "the *whole* South, is prepared to act, in resistance." He further proclaimed that when northerners threatened not only "our *real tangible rights* . . . but *absolutely invaded* [them]—there *will*—be—*can* be—but one sentiment." His sentiment was clear: if the North did not change course with regard to the concept of southern property rights, "I will say—*farewell, a long farewell to the North*—I will never again visit it & never again hold commercial intercourse with it."[4] Duncan failed to keep his promise. Given the breadth of his financial network as well as his familial and social circles, such a vow was an unrealistic, impulsive response to a situation that he found intolerable.

As secession drew nearer, Duncan remained loyal to the southern belief in the right to own slaves, but he still supported the Union. Just five days before South Carolina seceded, he optimistically wrote his sister Emily in Philadelphia, "I have better & brighter hopes now than I have had—that the Union *may yet* be preserved,—or than I had 10 days ago." Believing that all would "depend on the action of the Free States," he supposed that if they "manifest a desire, to do us *simple justice* & interfere no more with the rights, guaranteed to us, by the institutions—all may yet be well."[5]

Yet a week after South Carolina left the Union, Duncan shifted the responsibility for the looming civil war onto the South. In another letter to Emily, he concluded that nothing would stop disunion except a "radical change—in the tone, sentiment & feeling, of the Southern people—on the subject of slavery: and such a change, I think,—*impossible.*"[6] Was this reversal a result of his multiregional American identity? Did the secession crisis prompt him to distinguish more sharply how he defined himself? As war became a reality, Duncan shifted his position yet again. He now condemned both sections for the crisis. He firmly believed that the battle between the North and the South would determine which section "can go furthest in folly & madness," concluding that "both seem to have lost sight of their country's good." As spring turned into summer, he wrote Emily that "impartial history" would determine that "the madness of the South in originating the trouble" was equally as responsible for the war as "the selfish pride . . . of the North." By June 1861, deeply upset over the fact that the nation was falling into increasing disorder and disintegration, he proclaimed, "I look forward to the hugest & most bloody war in History," and he doubted whether the nation would ever recover. "Can any sane man believe," he asked his sister, "that the two sections *can ever again be united*"?[7]

Though Duncan felt that the North and the South shared responsibility for the conflict, his financial interests forced him to align himself with the southern cause for property rights. In spite of his financial diversity, many of his assets were tied into the southern slave system, and its demise would destroy a main pillar of his economic house. Even though he never defined himself in terms of region, the eradication of this regional facet of a national economy pushed him to do so. By June 1861, Duncan's fluid identity seems to have disappeared. He coolly distanced himself from northerners, whom he referred to in a letter to Emily as "your people, [who] seem determined to . . . subjugate [the South]."[8] For all of his defiant declarations, however, Duncan was at the nexus of the nation's divide: he was both friend and foe, depending upon one's perspective. Contradictory though it may be, Duncan's economic and political identity ultimately rooted itself in a united country and economy.

Indeed, Duncan maintained a strong loyalty to the Union and believed that its preservation should be the overarching goal. Yet this loyalty would prove to have a high cost. Because of his status as one of the nation's largest and most powerful slaveholders, he encountered difficulties maintaining his political and economic positions, particularly while living in the South—a fact that was not lost on him. By the summer of 1861, his unionism and the multiregional context in which he operated began to feel like a noose around his neck. Stephen Duncan found himself caught between warring identities: northerner and southerner, nationalist and regionalist, slaveowner and capitalist.

Increasingly, Duncan felt the strain and bind of his competing identities as his economic, political, and social networks grappled with the nation's dissent into civil war. In May 1861, he received a letter from Andrew McWilliams, his Louisiana manager and former partner, who anxiously wrote that "the war excitement runs high here [in St. Mary Parish]." In particular, hostile sentiments were focused against Duncan's friend, nephew-in-law, business associate, and cotton factor, Charles P. Leverich, who allegedly gave $8,000 for "equipment of Soldiers to come South for the purpose of subjugation [of] it back in to the '*union*.'" Because of this, opposition against Leverich and other northerners who owned property in St. Mary Parish intensified; McWilliams believed that "they would hang Mr Leverich . . . if they could get [him] here." With Duncan's connection to Leverich and his brothers well-known, and with his own holdings in St. Mary's extensive, Duncan surely wondered to what extent opposition against him existed in the parish. In spite of McWilliams's grim news, Duncan maintained his political position and supported his fellow unionists. In response to his manager, he scribbled on the back of McWilliams's letter, "Mssrs L[everich] have done just as you or I or any other good citizen would have done. They submitted [money] towards the protection of the Flag of the Union the gov't under which they lived." He noted candidly that if he had given the money, "I would be damned as a traitor."[9] And some of his peers did just that. Wade Hampton III of South Carolina, who owned plantations in the Mississippi Delta adjacent to Duncan's and who also was in debt to Duncan for $200,000, wrote his youngest sister that "Duncan should be sent away, for I regard him as a contemptible traitor."[10]

Eventually Duncan's loyalty came under scrutiny by officials from both governments. Because of his northern ties and unionism, the Confederate government thought him a traitor. Conversely, he received the scorn of Federal officials, who viewed his slaveholding and planting activities as disloyal in spite of his proclaimed support of the Union. As a result, both sides attacked the tangible manifestations of Duncan's wealth and power. In 1863, Confederate troops destroyed 2,080 bales of Duncan's cotton on Carlisle worth $279,008; they also stole eighty mules before marching down the road to Duncannon, where they stole another $8,000 worth of mules. According to a statement filed by Rear Vice-Admiral David Dixon Porter of the Union forces, the Rebels "drove Mr. Duncan from the country after burning his house [in Issaquena] and injuring his property and doing all they could to annoy him." Federal troops demonstrated equal animosity toward Duncan; they seized 123 bales of his cotton and stole $2,000 from Carlisle.[11]

Outraged over the Federal government's failure to protect them from Union troops, Stephen Duncan's daughter-in-law, Mary Duncan, wrote letters to President Lincoln, Adjutant General Lorenzo Thomas, and Secretary of War Edwin Stanton outlining the abuses on their plantations, which, according to her, had "been literally *rifled* and *stripped*." Furthermore, she argued, the protection papers given by General Ulysses Grant to the Duncan family were worthless. In a lengthy letter to Lincoln, she angrily wrote that some troops "in the name of the 'Treasury Dept' (taking books, curtains & *all* they wanted) [and] certain officers (acting under orders from *Genl. Thomas*) have forcibly seized & *impressed* our remaining negroes . . . & carried them off for service either as laborers or soldiers." In her litany of charges against the government, she asked the president "if Mr Chase [Secretary of the Treasury] can seize all cotton—Genl. Thomas seize all negroes (despite their *freedom* & our *wages*) & if *armed blacks* can roam over the property at pleasure, May I ask, My Dear Sir, in *what shape* 'protection' *is* to come?" Demanding that Lincoln give the Duncan family protection for their property as well as reimbursement for their losses—particularly the losses of slaves—she concluded that "owing to the depradations of the Union troops & the *enormous* loss in negroes—*Millions* would hardly cover our losses, consequently it is somewhat natural that [we] ask due protection for the fragment that remains of a once princely fortune."[12] Defying the typical role of an elite white woman, Mary Duncan boldly entered the political realm and presented the case for her family. Meanwhile, Stephen Duncan prepared his.

Duncan's longstanding belief in a national economy and his social and familial roots in both the North and South fostered a worldview that was national and even international in scope. He believed in the Union even though he firmly supported the argument that the North and the Federal government trampled upon the rights of southerners who wanted to maintain the right to all of their property. His Whiggish views about a national economy, paradoxically coupled with his belief in states' rights, illuminates the contradictions in his ideology— contradictions that grew even starker as war engulfed the nation. The Federal government's position on the property rights of southerners aggravated him to no end, particularly after President Lincoln issued the Emancipation Proclamation. Arguing for himself as well as his fellow planters who held similar political views, Duncan noted that Lincoln "had the right to proclaim freedom to the slaves if he deemed the exercise of the right necessary & essential to the suppression of the Rebellion." But in a last-ditch effort to save the backbone of his fortune and empire, Duncan argued to Mary Todd Lincoln, in hopes that she could influence her husband, that there was "*just ground* of *complaint* against its *indiscriminate* application to *friends* as well as *enemies*," concluding that "its *injurious* effects are felt." Even with blood flowing, Duncan still failed or refused to see the moral dimensions of slavery. Instead, he believed that he and other "friends" of the Union should be exempt from the proclamation and should be permitted to enslave their labor force with a gradual emancipation over time so as not to "reduce the value of the lands" . . . by "the extinction of our entire prosperity." Meanwhile, some of his slaves began to run away to Union lines.[13]

For Duncan and those who held similar perspectives, it was difficult to remain in the South. Yet it was also problematic for Duncan to return to the

North, as he was forced to leave the tangible assets of his power base and face some northerners who condemned him for his participation in slavery. Increasingly a man without a country, the Civil War forced him to make the choice he had spent a lifetime postponing. Reluctantly, he and Catharine left Natchez in late 1863, retreating to his Washington Square home in New York City. He left behind his southern empire to the mastery of his children. On Christmas Eve, 1864, Duncan gave up hope that there would be "a future South to return to," and he lived out the remainder of his days in New York.[14]

From afar, Duncan dispensed advice to his sons and sons-in-law about plantation and slave management, but the familiar context in which he operated had drastically changed. At the beginning of 1863, Stephen Duncan Jr.—recalcitrant and displeased with slavery's apparent demise—engaged in the process of making the transition from slave to free labor on the elder Duncan's plantations. In a letter to his father, he wrote, "I have at last paid off all the Negroes— & a more unpleasant, disgusting business I ever have attended to." As the former Duncan slaves exercised whatever power they could grasp, they began to dismantle Duncan's seemingly invincible empire. Squarely facing what was once considered inconceivable, Duncan Jr., with much disgust, informed his father that the ex-slaves "tried very hard to make their own terms—& wished to exact a great many things that I could not allow. The result was that about ½ of Oakley, Holly Ridge & Duncannon have decided to leave." As slavery began to crumble, Duncan Jr. remained defiant, barely complying with the new regulations regarding paid labor. Even more disturbing to him was that his world, built on the basis of white supremacy, seemed to be endangered. "*Schools,* are to be established for the instruction of the youthful darkies—& everything managed in such a manner that idleness will be encouraged," the younger Duncan wrote, adding that "any thing like *labor* totally destroyed." Believing that wartime Reconstruction would not work, he branded it an "insane & stupid programme" and hoped it would "fall through." And, reminiscent of his father's claims no longer to have any dealings whatsoever with the North, Duncan Jr. declared that if Reconstruction continued, "I for one shall quit the country." Eventually he did just that, spending the last decades of the nineteenth century in Biarritz, France, with visits back to the United States. Believing that the social order built on race and class had been destroyed, Duncan Jr. scoffed at the "abominable & infamous set of Regulations," which he concluded to be a plan to "ruin the planter & place the Negro upon a nearer equality with the White man."[15] The Duncans' plantation world, once tightly run, had spun out of control. "The accounts we get from Natchez are frightful," Henry Duncan relayed to his father in 1865. "The disbanding in the South, of the Negro troops will only make matters worse—what magnificent fruits, has the tree of secession produced!!"[16]

While the elder Duncan received reports from Mississippi, he (along with his daughter-in-law Mary) spent his final years trying to secure pardons— which the government eventually granted—for himself, his friends, and his family, particularly for his son Samuel, a secessionist and Rebel sympathizer.[17] He devoted most of his time to bringing order to his myriad investments, while also trying to collect on the sizeable loans, mortgages, and endorsements he had granted over the years—a difficult task because the war interrupted payment from his debtors.

As Duncan conducted his business from New York, he fell into increasingly poor health. Just a few weeks before his eightieth birthday, Stephen Duncan died on January 29, 1867. He desired that his funeral be "plain, *most plain,* without any Pall bearers—or any other parade or the invitation of any large assembly. The simpler & plainer—the better." His family took his body back to his childhood home of Pennsylvania and buried him in Philadelphia's Laurel Hill Cemetery, next to the grave of his and Catharine's infant son.[18]

Perhaps more than any other planter who has been studied thus far, Stephen Duncan fails to conform to the frameworks created by historians to explain the southern slaveholding aristocracy. He was not a one-dimensional premodern lord of the southern manor, nor was he strictly an ultramodern master of northern capitalism. He was a conservative elite who maintained his hegemony on a variety of levels and who believed in an organic, hierarchical, and wholly unequal social order that thrived in league with the free-market economy. Slavery and slaves formed as much a part of his capitalistic outlook as his other economic pursuits. Slavery and capitalism coexisted compatibly in Duncan's world. Far from a regional economy, slavery was part of capitalism and the national economy, out of which whites and free blacks, antislavery advocates and proslavery ideologues all benefited. No one was removed from slavery's specter.

Questions about the nature of the slaveholding aristocracy were assumed to have been answered long ago. However, the career of Stephen Duncan complicates those answers and sheds new light upon the multifaceted identities of slaveholding elites in the South. In turn, we can gain a fuller understanding of the lives of those at both ends of the lash, as well as of the larger system of slavery and its power dynamics.

Duncan's uniqueness lies in part in his embodiment of both North and South at a critical juncture in American history. A product of both regions, he illuminates how and when they were contradictory and when they could be made compatible. As complex as the larger world in which Duncan lived, so too was the smaller world where he constructed his power on many different levels. In spite of his authority over slaves, various white networks, and family, there were challenges, both subtle and obvious, to his mastery: challenges from those he knew intimately, those he held in bondage, and forces beyond the scope of his mastery. Nevertheless, in the end, he maintained his power. Stephen Duncan's death in 1867 meant that he did not live to see the ultimate challenge of grappling with emancipation and free labor. That fell to his family, friends, and those he once enslaved as they stood at the crossroads of antebellum and postbellum America.

→►◄←

NOTES

ABBREVIATIONS

HSP	Historical Society of Pennsylvania
LLMVC, LSU	Louisiana and Lower Mississippi Valley Collections, Louisiana State University Libraries, Louisiana State University
MDAH	Mississippi Department of Archives and History
NTC, CAH, UT	Natchez Trace Collection, Center for American History, University of Texas, Austin
NYHS	New York Historical Society, Manuscript Department

PROLOGUE

1. Stephen Duncan to Josiah S. Johnston, October 11, 1831, Josiah S. Johnston Collection, HSP.

2. These ideas and concepts, particularly that of Duncan as an "ultramodern master of northern capitalism," were first explored in Martha Jane Brazy, "The World a Slaveholder Made: Stephen Duncan and Plantation Society" (M.A. thesis, University of Wisconsin–Milwaukee, 1987), and Brazy, "An American Planter: Slavery, Entrepreneurship, and Identity in the Life of Stephen Duncan, 1787–1867" (Ph.D. diss., Duke University, 1998).

1. "TO SEEK HIS FORTUNES IN THE DISTANT SOUTH"

1. Stephen Duncan's dates may be found in Certificate of Death, Dr. Stephen Duncan, January 29, 1867, New York City Department of Records, Death Records, New York City Municipal Archives, New York. Duncan family genealogy may be found in Katherine Duncan Smith, *The Story of Thomas Duncan and His Six Sons* (New York: Tobias A. Wright, 1928), esp. 9, 41. For a detailed history of Cumberland County and Carlisle, see *History of Cumberland and Adams Counties, Pennsylvania* (Chicago: Warner, Beers, 1886). For information on the Duncan family's

involvement in Carlisle, see part 2, 27 and 200; for the history of Carlisle specifically, see part 2, 229–40.

2. Smith, *Thomas Duncan*, 44. A brief Duncan family history may be found in Nicholas Wainwright, *The Irvine Story* (Philadelphia: Pennsylvania Historical Society, 1964), 34–37. For information regarding the Postlethwaites, see *History of Cumberland and Adams Counties, Pennsylvania*, part 2, 135, 200; Morton Rothstein, "'The Remotest Corner': Natchez on the American Frontier," in *Natchez before 1830*, ed. Noel Polk (Jackson: University Press of Mississippi, 1989), 98. Fairly reliable birth dates for Duncan and Postlethwaite's children can be found in the Postlethwaite Genealogical Collection, MDAH, and are as follows: Matilda Rose, 1786; Stephen, 1787; Samuel, 1789; Mary Ann, 1792; and Emily, 1793. Much of the Postlethwaite Genealogical Collection was compiled by Mary E. Postlethwaite of Natchez, Mississippi.

3. Smith, *Thomas Duncan*, 43 (quote)–44; Wainwright, 34–35; Morton Rothstein, "The Natchez Nabobs: Kinship and Friendship in an Economic Elite," in *Essays in Honor of Arthur C. Cole*, ed. Hans L. Trefousse (New York: Burt Franklin, 1977), 108 n. 4. A detailed account of the duel can be found in a communication of Stephen Duncan Jr. to Katherine Duncan Smith, December 11, 1894, and reprinted in Smith, *Thomas Duncan*, 107. Another full account of the duel— a typescript of an extract of a letter from Carlisle dated June 22, 1793—can be found in the Postlethwaite Genealogical Collection, MDAH.

John Duncan was born on November 15, 1762, and died on June 22, 1793. These dates, as well as other birth and death dates of Carlisle's citizenry, can be found in Sarah Woods Parkinson, *Memories of Carlisle's Old Graveyard* (Carlisle: Mary Kirtley Lamberton, 1930).

4. Coincidentally, Blaine's son from his first marriage attended the fatal Duncan-Lamberton duel and served as John Duncan's second. A history of the Blaine family can be found in James Ewing Blaine, *The Blaine Family: James Blaine, Emigrant, and His Children* (Cincinnati: Ebbert and Richardson, 1920); for Colonel Ephraim Blaine, see esp. 20–42 (quote, 21). For the marriage of Duncan and Blaine, see 51–52. See also Smith, *Thomas Duncan*, 44; Postlethwaite Genealogical Collection, MDAH; Civic Club of Carlisle, *Carlisle Old and New* (Harrisburg, Pa.: J. Horace McFarland, 1907), 109–10.

5. For a history of Dickinson College, see Charles C. Sellers, *Dickinson College: A History* (Middletown, Conn.: Wesleyan University Press, 1973); for the Duncans' involvement in the college, see, 3–4, 481–84. Also see George L. Reed, ed., *Alumni Record, Dickinson College* (Carlisle: Dickinson College, 1905), 53. For a discussion of the founding of Dickinson College within the context of Carlisle social history, see Joseph B. Smith, "A Frontier Experiment with Higher Education: Dickinson College, 1783–1800" *Pennsylvania History* 16 (January 1949): 1–19. Grandfather Stephen Duncan served as a trustee of the Carlisle Grammar School from 1773 to 1788 and as a trustee of Dickinson College from 1783 to 1794. Other family members who served on Dickinson College's board of trustees were Thomas Duncan (1790–1816) and Ephraim Blaine (1792–1804).

6. Wainwright, 34–35; Blaine, 52–53, 66. Ephraim Blaine purchased from Tench Coxe two houses next to each other on Walnut Street for two thousand "Spanish Milled dollars." Agreement, Ephraim Blaine and Tench Coxe, May 4, 1780, Tench Coxe Papers, HSP.

7. Morton Rothstein touches upon Duncan's medical training in "Natchez Nabobs," 98, 108 n. 4, and "The Changing Social Networks and Investment Behavior of a Slaveholding Elite in

the Ante Bellum South: Some Natchez 'Nabobs,' 1800–1860," in *Entrepreneurs in Cultural Context*, ed. Sydney M. Greenfield et al. (Albuquerque: University of New Mexico Press, 1979), 72, 86 n. 5. No evidence has been found to indicate that Duncan received a medical degree. His name is absent from the *General Catalogue of the Medical Graduates of the University of Pennsylvania, with an Historical Sketch of the Origins, Programs, and Present State of the Medical Department,* 3rd ed. (Philadelphia: Lydia R. Bailey, 1845); and W. J. Maxwell, comp., *General Alumni Catalogue of the University of Pennsylvania* (Philadelphia: University of Pennsylvania General Alumni Society, 1917). The earliest medical schools in America were founded in Philadelphia. Ironically, Pennsylvania was one of the last states of the original thirteen colonies to craft statutes regarding medical licensing, creating a state examining board only in 1893. For a history of early medical training and licensing, see Richard H. Shryock, *Medical Licensing in America, 1650–1965* (Baltimore: Johns Hopkins University Press, 1967), 3–23, 48.

8. Additional biographical information regarding Duncan's early years can be found in *Goodspeed's Biographical and Historical Memoirs of Mississippi, Embracing an Authentic and Comprehensive Account of the Chief Events in the History of the United States, and a Record of the Lives of Many of the Most Worthy and Illustrious Families and Individuals,* 2 vols. (Chicago: Goodspeed, 1891), 1:676; Dunbar Rowland, ed., *Mississippi, Comprising Sketches of Counties, Towns, Events, Institutions, and Persons, Arranged in Cyclopedic Form,* 3 vols. (1907; reprint, Spartanburg, S.C.: The Reprint Company, 1976), 1:666.

9. Quote by his lawyer, Brief for Claimants, Executors of Stephen Duncan, Deceased, v. United States, No. 2756, Brief filed in the United States Court of Claims, December Term, 1874, MDAH. In *Natchez on the Mississippi* (New York: Bonanza Books, 1947), an undocumented book consisting of numerous folklore accounts, Harnett Kane claims that Duncan married in Carlisle at the age of eighteen, had two children, and "might have remained the rest of his life in Pennsylvania had his wife not died. Wanting to forget his sorrow in a new scene, he moved to Natchez in 1808" (p. 205). Wainwright's *The Irvine Story* also recounts this story. The Postlethwaite Genealogical Files, MDAH, notes that a daughter from the supposed first marriage died in the South from a snakebite. I have found no evidence to support a first marriage for Duncan in Pennsylvania.

10. For a highly quantitative examination of migration within America, see Peter D. McClelland and Richard J. Zeckhauser, *Demographic Dimensions of the New Republic: American Interregional Migration, Vital Statistics, and Manumissions, 1800–1860* (Cambridge: Cambridge University Press, 1982), 6–7, 50–51. Regarding migration to the Mississippi Territory within the larger story of westward migration, see Ray A. Billington, *Westward Expansion: A History of the American Frontier,* 4th ed. (New York: Macmillan, 1974), 297, 309–11; Bernard Bailyn, *Voyagers to the West: A Passage in the Peopling of America on the Eve of Revolution* (New York: Alfred A. Knopf, 1986), 475–94; Malcolm J. Rohrbough, *The Trans-Appalachian Frontier: People, Societies, and Institutions, 1775–1850* (New York: Oxford University Press, 1978), 192–205.

On the history of the region's indigenous populations, see D. Clayton James, *Antebellum Natchez* (Baton Rouge: Louisiana State University Press, 1968), 3–11; Ian W. Brown, "Natchez Indians and Remains of a Proud Past," in Polk, ed., 8–28; Richard A. Marshall, "The Prehistory of Mississippi"; Arrell M. Gibson, "The Indians of Mississippi" in *A History of Mississippi,* ed. Richard A. McLemore, 2 vols. (Jackson: University Press of Mississippi, 1973), 1:24–89.

11. See Robert V. Haynes, *The Natchez District and the American Revolution* (Jackson: Uni-

versity Press of Mississippi, 1976); James, *Antebellum Natchez*, 12–30; Byrle A. Kynerd, "British West Florida," in McLemore, ed., 1:134–57; Rothstein, "Natchez on the American Frontier," 93–94; Walter G. Howell, "The French Period, 1699–1763," in McLemore, ed., 110–33; James, 5–12.

12. Jack D. L. Holmes, "A Spanish Province, 1779–1798," in McLemore, ed., 1:158–73; Reginald Horsman, *The Frontier in the Formative Years, 1783–1815* (New York: Holt, Rinehart, and Winston, 1970), 56–58; James, 62–63; Rothstein, "Natchez on the Frontier," 94–95. A number of older studies discuss the period of territorial settlement in great detail. See J. F. H. Claiborne, *Mississippi, as a Province, Territory, and State, with Biographical Notices of Eminent Citizens* (Jackson, Miss.: Power and Barksdale, 1880); Rowland, ed., *Mississippi*.

13. Charles D. Lowery, "The Great Migration to the Mississippi Territory," *Journal of Mississippi History* 30 (August 1968): 174–79; Horsman, 56–59; William Baskerville Hamilton, "American Beginnings in the Old Southwest: The Mississippi Phase" (Ph.D. diss., Duke University, 1937); James, 160–62; John Hebron Moore, *The Emergence of the Cotton Kingdom in the Old Southwest: Mississippi, 1770–1860* (Baton Rouge: Louisiana State University Press, 1988), 118. Quote from Robert V. Haynes, "The Formation of the Territory," in McLemore, ed., 1:183.

14. Hamilton, 156; Horsman, 58; James, 31–53, 160–61; Rohrbough, 118, 194–95; Rothstein, "Natchez on the American Frontier," 95–96; Donald W. Meinig, *The Shaping of America: A Geographical Perspective on Five Hundred Years of History*, vol. 2 of *Continental America, 1800–1867* (New Haven: Yale University Press, 1993), 232. An example of economic decline in Natchez can be seen in its manufacturing values. By 1860, the total value of Natchez manufactures was less than $.25 million, whereas in Memphis, it was more than $4 million. For population figures for Mississippi in 1800, 1810, and 1820, see Moore, 118.

15. Genealogical information can be found in Wainwright, 11–18, 34; Smith, 41–46. For an exact description of Callender's land grant, see Copy of Original Patent or Grant under the hand of Montfort Browne, Esq., Lieutenant Governor, Province of West Florida, to Robert Callender, August 2, 1768, Newbold-Irvine papers, Family Correspondence, Box 1, Folder 14, and Original Copy of Grant to Robert Callender, Folder 16, HSP. The area mentioned as "great Cliffs" was later referred to as "Loftus Cliffs." For Irvine's impressions of the tract, see General William Irvine to [brother-in-law] Robert Callender Jr., January 22, 1802, Newbold-Irvine Papers, Family Correspondence, Box 1, Folder 3, HSP.

16. Haynes, "Formation of the Territory," in McLemore, ed., 1:174. Land claims granted by the British were eventually placed under Spanish rule and then ceded to the United States with Pinckney's Treaty of 1795. In spite of the treaty, some land claims and titles remained in dispute. This was particularly true of the Callender tract due to its close proximity to the thirty-first parallel, which divided the United States from Spanish territory.

17. James Dunlop to Thomas Duncan, March 17,1804, Irvine Family Papers, 1778–1843, Collection #1743 B, Folder Group 4, Section 1, HSP (quote). In *The Irvine Story*, Wainwright claims that Jesse Duncan died in Natchez in 1804. However, the son of Dr. Stephen Duncan, Stephen Duncan Jr., refuted the claim that Jesse Duncan migrated to Natchez. In an 1895 letter addressed to Kate Duncan Smith, Duncan Jr. wrote, "'I can assure you that the only members of our family and our name who came to Natchez were my father and uncles.'" Smith, *Thomas Dun-*

can, 108. Wainwright claims that Dr. Duncan settled on or near the Callender tract (p. 36), though he offers no evidence for this.

18. Rothstein, "Changing Social Networks," 72; Rothstein, "Natchez on the American Frontier," 96–100; James, passim. Regarding the Philadelphia–New Orleans trade, see C. Richard Arena, "Philadelphia–Mississippi Valley Trade and the Deposit Closure of 1802," *Pennsylvania History* 30 (January 1963): 28–45.

19. Information on Postlethwaite and Dunbar can be found in Rothstein, "Changing Social Networks," 72; Rothstein, "Natchez on the American Frontier," 96–100; and James, passim. Postlethwaite's banking career is thoroughly discussed in Robert C. Weems Jr., "The Bank of the Mississippi: A Pioneer Bank of the Old Southwest, 1809–1844" (Ph.D. diss., Columbia University, 1951).

20. Quotes from Benjamin L. C. Wailes Diary, April 23, 1859, Benjamin L. C. Wailes Diaries, Book 24, Special Collections Library, Duke University, Durham, North Carolina.

21. Pierce Butler, *The Unhurried Years: Memories of the Old Natchez Region* (Baton Rouge: Louisiana State University Press, 1948), 26; Rothstein, "Natchez on the American Frontier," 100.

22. Marriage Certificate, Stephen Duncan and Margaret Ellis, September 19, 1811, Marriage Records, Adams County Courthouse, Natchez, Mississippi. For a history of the Butler family, see Butler, 1–8, and passim (quote, 6). The note that Nancy Ellis scribbled on the wall of Laurel Hill was found during the early twentieth century when the house was undergoing repairs.

23. Butler, 1–8, and passim; Emma Louise McGin Dawes, "Judge Thomas Butler of Louisiana: A Biographical Study of an Ante-Bellum Jurist and Planter" (M.A. thesis, Louisiana State University, 1953), 31–34; Stephen Duncan to Thomas Butler, April 11, 1815, Thomas Butler and Family Papers, Box 3, Folder 17, LLMVC, LSU.

24. With regard to Margaret Ellis's dowry, see the following Rothstein articles: "Changing Social Networks," 72–73; "Natchez Nabobs," 98–99; "Natchez on the American Frontier," 100. Also see Stephen Duncan to Thomas Butler, October 14, 1814, Thomas Butler and Family Papers, Box 3, Folder 16; Stephen Duncan to Thomas Butler, April 11, 1815, Thomas Butler and Family Papers, Box 3, Folder 17, LLMVC, LSU. While in Louisiana, Butler served as a judge of the Federal District and was a representative in the U.S. Congress.

25. Thomas Butler to Ann Butler, April 30, 1814, Thomas Butler and Family Papers, Box 3, Folder 16, LLMVC, LSU (quote); Anna Eliza Farar to Benjamin Farar, January 6, 1813, Benjamin Farar Papers, Collection #65, Folder 3, Howard-Tilton Memorial Library, Tulane University, New Orleans.

26. Emily Duncan to Margaret Ellis Duncan, April 17, 1814, Ellis-Farar Family Papers, Box 1, Folder 4, LLMVC, LSU (first quote); Stephen Duncan to Thomas Butler, August 4, 1816, Box 3, Folder 18 (third quote), and May 30, 1818, Box 4, Folder 20 (second quote), Thomas Butler and Family Papers, LLMVC, LSU; Matilda Duncan to Margaret Ellis Duncan, October 25, 1814, Ellis-Farar Papers, LLMVC, LSU. Samuel P. Duncan is listed in the Dickinson College Alumni Records as having moved to Natchez after graduating. See Reed, 54. Also see Rothstein, "Natchez on the American Frontier," 101; Wainwright, 36.

27. Stephen Duncan to Thomas Butler, n.d. 1815, Thomas Butler and Family Papers, Box 3, Folder 17, LLMVC, LSU (first quote); Matilda Duncan to Margaret Ellis Duncan, October 25,

1814, Ellis-Farar Family Papers, LLMVC, LSU (second quote); Rothstein, "Natchez on the American Frontier," 101; Wainwright, 36.

28. Dawes, 70–71.

29. Stephen Duncan to Thomas Butler, August 4, 1816, Thomas Butler and Family Papers, Box 3, Folder 18, LLMVC, LSU.

30. Receipt from Abram Ellis to Stephen Duncan, January 6, 1816, Adams County Deed Records, Deed Book, Vol. H, p. 500, Office of the Chancery Clerk, Adams County Courthouse, Natchez, Mississippi. This receipt did not record the number of acres that Duncan inherited. It is unclear where Duncan's first sugar plantation was located, whether it was successful or not, and if he held on to that particular piece of property. Duncan refers to it being on "the coast" in a letter to Thomas Butler, May 30, 1818, Thomas Butler and Family Papers, Box 4, Folder 20, LLMVC, LSU. Stephen Duncan Daybook, 1816–1822, 1826, Stephen Duncan and Stephen Duncan Jr. Papers, LLMVC, LSU. The locale of Chapitoulas is unknown; Duncan referred to it only as "nearby."

31. "Arpents" was a French measure of land utilized in this area throughout the early nineteenth century. Arpents varied depending upon the locality and equaled anywhere from .84 to 1.28 acres. I have used the .84 measurement to convert arpents into acres. Thomas D. Carson to Thomas Butler, January 15, 1818, Box 4, Folder 2, and Stephen Duncan to Thomas Butler, May 30, 1818, Box 4, Folder 20 (all quotes), Thomas Butler and Family Papers, LLMVC, LSU. It was extremely atypical for slave quarters to be constructed of brick. Duncan may have been referring to the sugarhouse or dwelling house.

32. Stephen Duncan to Thomas Butler, May 30, 1818, Thomas Butler and Family Papers, Box 4, Folder 20, LLMVC, LSU.

33. Rothstein, "Changing Social Networks," 72–73 (first quote); Stephen Duncan to Thomas Butler, May 30, 1818, Thomas Butler and Family Papers, Box 4, Folder 20, LLMVC, LSU (second quote).

34. Stephen Duncan to Thomas Butler, May 30, 1818, Thomas Butler and Family Papers, Box 4, Folder 20, LLMVC, LSU; "List of Negroes Purchased by S. Duncan, Sept. 15th 1819," Stephen Duncan Daybook, 1816–1822, 1826, Stephen Duncan and Stephen Duncan Jr. Papers, LLMVC, LSU.

35. For an in-depth study of slavery and emancipation in Pennsylvania, see Gary B. Nash and Jean R. Soderlund, *Freedom by Degrees: Emancipation in Pennsylvania and Its Aftermath* (New York: Oxford University Press, 1991); for information about Cumberland County, see 4–5, 139. John Todd Howell to Colonel Ephraim Blaine, November 15, 1778, Chaloner and White Papers, Box 6, Folder 19, HSP; Receipt of Sale of Slave from Ephraim Blaine to Richard Keyes, January 10, 1781, Society Miscellaneous Collection, Box 11A, Folder 16, HSP.

36. U.S. Bureau of the Census, MS General Population Schedules, Schedule I, Adams County, Mississippi, 1820; Anna (Nancy) Butler to Margaret Ellis Duncan, February 19, 1815, Ellis-Farar Family Papers, Box 1, Folder 4, LLMVC, LSU.

37. Anna (Nancy) Butler to Margaret Ellis Duncan, February 19, 1815 (all quotes), and March 1, 1815, Ellis-Farar Family Papers, Box 1, Folder 4, LLMVC, LSU.

38. U.S. Bureau of the Census, MS General Population Schedules, Schedule I, Adams County, Mississippi, 1820. Planter status is defined as owning twenty slaves or more. For a fuller

discussion of this, see Kenneth M. Stampp, *The Peculiar Institution: Slavery in the Ante-Bellum South* (New York: Vintage Books, 1956), 30.

39. The other shareholders who had a controlling interest (twenty shares or more) were John P. Armand, William Bullitt, Samuel Davis, John Hankinson, John Minor, John B. Nevitt, and two other individuals whose names are not legible. Charter, Natchez Steam Boat Company, July 4, 1818, Natchez Trace Steamboat Collection, Box 2E536, Folder 6, NTC, CAH, UT. Other investors (like Samuel Postlethwaite), who originally owned a smaller number of shares, eventually purchased additional shares to garner a part-controlling interest. See the Natchez Steam Boat Company Stock Certificate Book, MDAH.

40. Information regarding the Natchez Steamboat Company can be found in Edith McCall, *Conquering the Rivers: Henry Miller Shreve and the Navigation of America's Inland Waterways* (Baton Rouge: Louisiana State University Press, 1984), 156–57.

41. Weems, "Bank of the Mississippi," passim; Weems, "Mississippi's First Banking System," *Journal of Mississippi History* 28 (November 1967): 386–408.

2. LAYING THE FOUNDATIONS OF MASTERY

1. Stephen Duncan to Thomas Butler, August 4, 1816, Thomas Butler and Family Papers, Box 3, Folder 18, LLMVC, LSU.

2. Ibid.

3. Marriage Certificate, Stephen Duncan and Catharine A. Bingaman, May 25, 1819, Marriage Records, Adams County Courthouse, Natchez, Mississippi; James, 137; Rothstein, "Changing Social Networks," 74, and "Natchez on the American Frontier," 101.

4. Weems, "Bank of the Mississippi," 773. Natchez prices reflect the September 1817–August 1818 crop year.

5. Ibid., 371–79.

6. Porter L. Fortune Jr., "The Formative Period," in McLemore, ed., 1:273. For a detailed account of the cotton market and the dynamics of credit and banking in Mississippi, see Weems, "Bank of the Mississippi," 145–50.

7. Weems, "Bank of the Mississippi," 145–50, 773. The date of August 31 was used to separate one cotton crop from the next crop, so the season ran from September 1 through August 31.

8. The crop of September 1824–August 1825 netted an average of twenty-one cents per pound in New Orleans and almost nineteen cents in Natchez. Stephen Duncan to Thomas Butler, July 26, 1822, Thomas Butler and Family Papers, Box 5, Folder 24, LLMVC, LSU (quote); Weems, "Bank of the Mississippi," 773.

9. The Bank of the Mississippi was chartered in 1809 during the territorial years and was rechartered in 1818 as the Bank of the State of Mississippi. See Weems, "Bank of the Mississippi," and "Mississippi's First Banking System." In both works, Weems erroneously notes that Dr. Samuel Duncan (brother of Dr. Stephen Duncan) served as the bank's president. However, in "The Makers of the Bank of the Mississippi," *Journal of Mississippi History* 15 (July 1953): 137–54, Weems correctly notes that Dr. Stephen Duncan eventually served as president. See also Larry Schweikart, *Banking in the American South from the Age of Jackson to Reconstruction* (Baton Rouge: Louisiana State University Press, 1987). Duncan family assets can be found in the U.S.

Bureau of the Census, MS General Population Schedules, Schedule I, Adams County, Mississippi, 1820; Land Deed, Henry and Elizabeth Postlethwaite to Stephen and Samuel Duncan, Adams County Deed Records, Deed Book, Vol. K, p. 68, Office of the Chancery Clerk, Adams County Courthouse, Natchez, Mississippi.

10. Stephen Duncan to Thomas Butler, July 26, 1822, Thomas Butler and Family Papers, Box 5, Folder 24, LLMVC, LSU.

11. Land Deeds, Stephen Duncan and Wife to Adam L. Bingaman, and Adam L. Bingaman and Wife to Stephen Duncan, January 21, 1821, Adams County Deed Records, Deed Books, Vol. L, p. 417, and Vol. M, p. 47, Office of the Chancery Clerk, Adams County Courthouse, Natchez, Mississippi. These transactions would be akin to the current-day practice of a seller-financed mortgage.

12. Land Deed, Joseph and Mary Texada to Stephen and Samuel Duncan, September 25, 1822, Adams County Deed Records, Deed Book, Vol. M, p. 361, and John and Anna Thompson to Stephen Duncan, May 1, 1823, Adams County Deed Records, Deed Book, Vol. N, p. 206, Office of the Chancery Clerk, Adams County Courthouse, Natchez, Mississippi.

13. The bank charged an interest rate of 6.2 percent and computed the loans utilizing a 360-day year, and deducting the interest from the principal in advance. See Weems, "Bank of the Mississippi," 289, for a discussion of this calculation.

14. For an in-depth discussion of the Bank of the State of Mississippi's lending policies, see Weems, "Bank of the Mississippi," 282–90, and "Mississippi's First Banking System," 390–91. A comprehensive discussion of interest rates throughout history can be found in Sidney Homer and Richard Sylla, *A History of Interest Rates*, 3rd ed. (New Brunswick, N.J.: Rutgers University Press, 1991). See pp. 317–26 for nineteenth-century interest rates. The open-market commercial paper interest rates during the first third of the nineteenth century ranged from 3.5 percent to 36 percent. (For the latter half of the century, call money rates ranged from 0.5 percent to 186 percent.) Homer and Sylla note that due to the lack of an organized financial market in the eighteenth and nineteenth centuries, "most borrowers depended on their personal banking connections and did not pay these high rates. The stranger who sought accommodation in the open market when neighbors were hard pressed was mercilessly made to pay for money to tide him over for a few days" (p. 317). Further exacerbating the problem of high interest rates on the open market was the fact that rates in certain locales, particularly on the frontier, were haphazard and wide-ranging. For example, during the nineteenth century in the Far West, rates ranged from 48 percent to 96 percent in some locales.

15. For an excellent overview of cotton cultivation in Mississippi, see Moore, 11–13; William K. Scarborough, "Heartland of the Cotton Kingdom," in McLemore, ed., 1:311.

16. American cotton growers responded to the speculation in Liverpool and stepped up production. Cotton prices in American markets climbed in response. In New York, prices went from twelve cents per pound to thirty, while the New Orleans market received twenty-five cents per pound. The Liverpool market increased from seven cents per pound to a high of almost seventeen cents per pound. However, when the market opened in fall of 1825, buyers were scarce and the speculation on the foreign markets did not result in a buying frenzy. James L. Watkins, *King Cotton: A Historical and Statistical Review, 1790–1908* (New York: James L. Watkins and Sons, 1908), 14–15, 29; Lewis Cecil Gray, *History of Agriculture in the Southern United States to 1860*,

2 vols. (Washington, D.C.: Carnegie Institution of Washington, 1933), 2:698. Thomas Butler to Captain Benjamin Farar, September 16, 1825, Benjamin Farar Papers, Collection #65, Folder 6, Howard-Tilton Memorial Library, Tulane University, New Orleans; Stephen Duncan to John Ker, n.d. [1824 or 1825], John Ker and Family Papers, LLMVC, LSU (quote).

17. Stephen Duncan to John Ker, n.d. [1824 or 1825], John Ker and Family Papers, LLMVC, LSU.

18. At that time, cotton prices in New Orleans were barely 11 cents, while in Natchez they were 9½ cents per pound.

19. Stephen Duncan to Josiah S. Johnston, October 19, 1827, Josiah S. Johnston Papers, HSP.

20. Ibid.

21. Ibid.; Thomas Butler to Captain Benjamin Farar, September 16, 1825, Benjamin Farar Papers, Collection #65, Folder 6, Howard-Tilton Memorial Library, Tulane University, New Orleans.

22. Samuel Postlethwaite's obituary can be found in the *Natchez Ariel*, November 7, 1825.

23. According to one historian, before Duncan became president of the bank he was "by no means the equal of Postlethwaite in general acceptability to legislators and businessmen alike." Weems, "Bank of the Mississippi," 473.

24. Ibid. Dividend payments were ten dollars in 1825, 1826, and 1828, and eighteen dollars in 1827.

25. James, 114–15; Weems, "Bank of the Mississippi," 437–74. For the growth of the Vicksburg area, see Christopher Morris, *Becoming Southern: The Evolution of a Way of Life, Warren County and Vicksburg, Mississippi, 1770–1860* (New York: Oxford University Press, 1995).

26. James, 198–201; Weems, "Bank of the Mississippi," 445–50, 490–92, 731; Schweikart, *Banking in the American South,* esp. 202–5. A fine examination of white yeomen and economics in Mississippi can be found in Charles C. Bolton, *Poor Whites of the Antebellum South: Tenants and Laborers in Central North Carolina and Northeast Mississippi* (Durham, N.C.: Duke University Press, 1994).

27. Weems, "Bank of the Mississippi," 492; James, 136–61. Both Rothstein and James employ the term "Nabob" throughout their works.

28. *Walk in the Water* appears to have been a separate and unrelated enterprise from Duncan's Natchez Steamboat Company investment. John Duncan to Sarah Jane Duncan, February 14, 1826, Newbold-Irvine Papers, Box 4, Folder 20, HSP.

29. Stephen Duncan to Thomas Butler, December 15, 1827, Box 5, Folder 27 (first and second quotes) and January 7 and 10 (third and fourth quotes), 1828, Thomas Butler and Family Papers, Box 5, Folder 28, LLMVC, LSU.

30. With regard to dividends, Thomas Butler owned a fifth of two-thirds of the boat and received a dividend of $400 in 1829. See Stephen Duncan to Thomas Butler, February 17, 1829, Thomas Butler and Family Papers, Box 5, Folder 29. For examples of Wilkins and Linton's utilization of the steamboat, see John Linton Jr. to James C. Wilkins, May 26, September 20, November 17, 19, and 29, December 17, 19, and 20, 1827, James C. Wilkins Papers, Box 2E543, Folder 7, and Box 2E544, Folders 2, 4, and 5, NTC, CAH, UT. The success of *Walk in the Water* came to a halt when it caught fire at the Natchez landing on December 8, 1835, nearly ten years after its first voyage. The loss encompassed both material goods and human life. William John-

son, a free black who lived in Natchez and a well-known barber, noted in his diary that the "Steam Boat Walk in the Water was Burned up. She took fire about 8 Oclock at night. . . . The Cotten that was Burned on the Walk Amounted to 1200 Bales. The amount of boat and Cotten was Estimated a[t] one Hundred and ten thousand Dollars—There was a runaway Boy Burned up and a pet Bear, also Harden the Bar Keeper." Diary Entry of William Johnson, December 8, 1835, in William R. Hogan and Edwin A. Davis, eds., *William Johnson's Natchez: The Antebellum Diary of a Free Negro*, 3rd. ed. (Baton Rouge: Louisiana State University Press, 1993), 82.

31. Transaction totals are derived from deeds located in Adams and Wilkinson County records, Offices of the Chancery Clerk, Natchez and Woodville, Mississippi. They should be considered a conservative estimate of the family's total holdings.

32. Information about Duncan's lease of Auburn was obtained in an interview by the author with Mary Ruth Leggett, April 17, 1986, Natchez, Mississippi. Duncan purchased the property from Daniel Vertner, who was married to Eliza Harding, the widow of Lyman Harding. Land Deed, Daniel Vertner and Wife to Stephen Duncan, December 19, 1827, Adams County Deed Records, Deed Book, Vol. Q, p. 63, Office of the Chancery Clerk, Adams County Courthouse, Natchez, Mississippi; Mary Wallace Crocker, *Historic Architecture in Mississippi* (Jackson: University and College Press of Mississippi, 1973), 19–22.

33. Crocker, 19–22; Robert J. Kapsch, "The Use of Numerical Taxonomy in the Study of Historical Buildings in the Natchez, Mississippi, Area" (Ph.D. diss., Catholic University of America, 1982), 23–26 and passim; Mills Lane, *Architecture of the Old South: Mississippi and Alabama* (New York: Beehive Press, 1989), 21–27. Weeks admired Harding for his accomplishments in his planting endeavors, particularly since Harding was also a northerner. As he wrote, "I love to think and speak of my own countrymen who will not let the saucy Virginian and supercilious Carolinian ride them down." Quoted in Crocker, 21.

34. Kapsch, 10, 17 (first quote). Kapsch focuses on Auburn as a "central piece in the puzzle of the architectural development of Natchez" as it inspired Greek (and other exotic) revival styles in the city (p. 28). Typescript of a letter from Levi Weeks to Ep Hoyt, September 27, 1812 (second quote), WPA Historical Records Survey, Adams County, Mississippi, RG 60, MDAH.

35. Stephen Duncan to Thomas Butler, February 7, August 22 (quotes), 1828, Thomas Butler and Family Papers, Box 5, Folder 28, LLMVC, LSU.

36. It is unclear to what extent, if any, Duncan invested in this factory. Stephen Duncan to Thomas Butler, August 22, 1828, Thomas Butler and Family Papers, Box 5, Folder 28, LLMVC, LSU.

37. Ibid. (first quote); Stephen Duncan to Thomas Butler, October 10, 1828, Thomas Butler and Family Papers, Box 5, Folder 28, LLMVC, LSU (second quote).

38. Stephen Duncan to Thomas Butler, August 22 (first quote) and October 10 (second quote), 1828, Thomas Butler and Family Papers, Box 5, Folder 28, LLMVC, LSU.

39. Land Deeds, William Shipp and Wife to Stephen Duncan, November 1, 1828, and Richard G. Ellis and Wife to Stephen Duncan, December 29, 1828, Deed Book, Vol. R, pp. 45 and 57, Office of the Chancery Clerk, Adams County Courthouse, Natchez, Mississippi.

40. Stephen Duncan to John Ker, December 6, 1828, John Ker and Family Papers, Box 1, Folder 1, LLMVC, LSU.

41. Indenture–Land Deed, Theodore Stark to Stephen Duncan, July 2, 1821, and April 20,

1822, Wilkinson County Deed Records, Deed Books, Vol. C, pp. 5 and 232, Office of the Chancery Clerk, Wilkinson County Courthouse, Woodville, Mississippi. Indentures in Adams County Deed Records: Archibald Lewis to Stephen Duncan, June 4, 1822, Deed Book, Vol. N, p. 393; Robert McCullough and Daniel Lippingcott and Stephen Duncan, January 1, 1828, Deed Book, Vol. Q, p. 38; William C. Conner and Wife and Stephen Duncan, December 12, 1825, Deed Book, Vol. P, p. 126; Henry C. Conner and Wife and Stephen Duncan, February 2, 1826, Deed Book, Vol. O, p. 491, Office of the Chancery Clerk, Adams County Courthouse, Natchez, Mississippi.

42. Indentures, all in Adams County Deed Records: Woodson Wren and Stephen Duncan, September 20, 1825, Deed Book, Vol. P, p. 13; John T. Scott and Stephen Duncan, May 5, 1825, Deed Book, Vol. O, p. 317; William C. Conner and Wife and Stephen Duncan, December 16, 1825, Deed Book, Vol. P, p. 126, Office of the Chancery Clerk, Adams County Courthouse, Natchez, Mississippi.

43. Articles of Agreement–Copartnership, January 1, 1816, James C. Wilkins Papers, 2E541, Folder 1, NTC, CAH, UT.

44. See Kane, 82–83; Rothstein: "Natchez Nabobs," 9; "Changing Social Networks," 71, 74; "Natchez on the Frontier," 101.

45. John Linton Jr. to James C. Wilkins, January 11, 1817, and February 1, 1827 (quote), James Campbell Wilkins Papers, Box 2E541, Folder 1, and Box 2E543, Folder 5, NTC, CAH, UT. A one- or two-cent difference could mean substantially greater returns. Using the average weight of an 1827 cotton bale (330 pounds), Duncan's 21 bales weighed 6,930 pounds. Wilkins and Linton's average per-pound price was 11.5 cents. Using this price, the Duncan cotton would equal a gross receipt of $796.95. A calculation of 13 cents per pound would yield a gross receipt of $990.90—a 13 percent higher rate of return. For an overview of cotton prices and bale weights, see Watkins, 29, 168.

46. A detailed examination of the business of antebellum cotton factors can be found in Harold D. Woodman, *King Cotton and His Retainers: Financing and Marketing the Cotton Crop of the South, 1800–1925* (Lexington: University of Kentucky Press, 1968). For commissions, see 49–59.

47. John Linton Jr. to James C. Wilkins, October 6 and November 26 (quote), 1817, James Campbell Wilkins Papers, Box 2E541, Folder 6, and Box 2E542, Folder 1, NTC, CAH, UT.

48. John Linton Jr. to James C. Wilkins, December 15, 1817, James Campbell Wilkins Papers, Box 2E542, Folder 1, NTC, CAH, UT. The next communication between Linton and Wilkins, however, reveals that Linton did purchase Duncan's cotton for thirty-one cents. See Linton to Wilkins, n.d., 1817, ibid.

49. The services cotton factors performed for their clients could be extremely varied, particularly with regard to personal transactions. For instance, Duncan, Frank Surget, and G. W. Sargent once purchased some trees, which, because of their size, they had shipped directly to Wilkins and Linton in the hope that Wilkins and Linton would ship the trees to them. Taken by surprise by the receipt of such unusual goods, a clerk in Wilkins and Linton's New Orleans office informed his superiors that "we have refused to receive [the trees] as the freight demanded is exorbitant, & we expect exceeds the value of the trees." John Linton Jr. to James C. Wilkins, August 16, 1827, and John C. Waller to Messrs. James C. Wilkins & Co., December 18, 1824, James Campbell Wilkins Papers, Box 2E544, Folder 2, and Box 2E543, Folder 1, NTC, CAH, UT.

50. Stephen Duncan to John Ker, December 10, 1828, John Ker and Family Papers, LLMVC, LSU (first quote); John Linton Jr. to James C. Wilkins, September 13, 1817, James Campbell Wilkins Papers, Box 2E541, Folder 6, NTC, CAH, UT (second quote).

51. John Linton Jr. to James C. Wilkins, August 16, 1827, James Campbell Wilkins Papers, Box 2E544, Folder 2, NTC, CAH, UT.

3. SLAVES, POLITICS, AND FAMILY

1. Quoted in Davidson Burns McKibben, "Negro Slave Insurrections in Mississippi, 1800–1835," *Journal of Negro History* 34 (January 1949): 74–76.

2. For an in-depth discussion of slave resistance during the 1820s, see Herbert Aptheker, *American Negro Slave Revolts*, 5th ed. (New York: International Publishers, 1987), 264–92 (quote, 24). Also see Gary Y. Okihiro, ed., *In Resistance: Studies in African, Caribbean, and Afro-American History* (Amherst: University of Massachusetts Press, 1986). On the existence and interpretations of the Vesey plot, see Michael Johnson, "Denmark Vesey and His Co-Conspirators," *William and Mary Quarterly*, 3rd. ser., 58, no. 4 (October 2001): 915–76; Edward Pearson et al., "Forum: The Making of a Slave Conspiracy, Part 2," *William and Mary Quarterly*, 3rd ser., 59, no. 1 (January 2002): 135–202.

3. Stephen Duncan to Thomas Butler, July 1, 1823, Thomas Butler and Family Papers, Box 5, Folder 25, LLMVC, LSU.

4. Scarborough, "Heartland of the Cotton Kingdom," in McLemore, ed., 1:329–30; Charles S. Sydnor, *Slavery in Mississippi* (New York: D. Appleton-Century, 1933), 83–85.

5. Stephen Duncan to Thomas Butler, July 1, 1823, Thomas Butler and Family Papers, Box 5, Folder 25, LLMVC, LSU. Neither Duncan nor Butler mentioned Old Gloster again, and it is unclear what happened to him.

6. Ibid.

7. They were Robert H. Buckner, Robert M. Gaines, Lyman Harding, Thomas B. Reed, and Edward Turner.

8. The junto-backed congressmen were Thomas Hinds and Christopher Rankin; the senators were Robert H. Adams, David Holmes, Thomas B. Reed, and Thomas Williams. On the Natchez junto, see Adams, 28; James, 113–14. For an extremely detailed account of Mississippi state politics, see Claiborne, chapters 27–30 and passim; Bradley Bond, *Political Culture in the Nineteenth-Century South: Mississippi, 1830–1900* (Baton Rouge: Louisiana State University Press, 1995); Christopher J. Olsen, *Political Culture and Secession in Mississippi: Masculinity, Honor, and the Antiparty Tradition, 1830–1860* (New York: Oxford University Press, 2000).

9. Duncan S. Walker was born in 1794; Robert J. Walker was born in 1801. Their mother, Lucy Duncan Walker, was Stephen Duncan's aunt on his father's side. See Smith, *Thomas Duncan*, 44. Quotes in James, 113.

10. Claiborne, 1:415; Edwin A. Miles, *Jacksonian Democracy in Mississippi* (Chapel Hill: University of North Carolina Press, 1960), 89; Stephen Duncan to Thomas Butler, February 2, n.d. (first, second, fourth, fifth quotes), and February 17, 1929 (third quote), Thomas Butler and Family Papers, Box 11, Folder 67, and Box 5, Folder 29, LLMVC, LSU.

11. See William J. Cooper Jr., *The South and the Politics of Slavery, 1828–1856* (Baton Rouge: Louisiana State University Press, 1978), 7–13, and Cooper's *Liberty and Slavery: Southern Politics to 1860* (New York: Alfred A. Knopf, 1983), 142–63; Miles, passim; Harry L. Watson, *Liberty and Power: The Politics of Jacksonian America* (New York: Noonday Press, 1990), 73–83.

12. Stephen Duncan to Josiah S. Johnston, October 19, 1827, Josiah S. Johnston Papers, HSP.

13. Stephen Duncan to Josiah S. Johnston, December 28, 1827, Josiah S. Johnston Papers, HSP.

14. Political Broadside, January 7, 1828, Benjamin L. C. Wailes Papers, MDAH. The committee consisted of Duncan, Beverly R. Grayson, Samuel Gustine, Francis Surget, Alvarez Fisk, Adam L. Bingaman, Felix Huston, and James K. Cook.

15. Ibid.

16. Ibid.

17. Stephen Duncan to Powhatan Ellis, January 23, 1828, Powhatan Ellis Papers, CAH, UT.

18. Political Broadside, January 7, 1828, Benjamin L. C. Wailes Papers, MDAH; Stephen Duncan to Josiah S. Johnston, December 28, 1827, Josiah S. Johnston Papers, HSP (first four quotes); Stephen Duncan to Powhatan Ellis, January 23, 1828, Powhatan Ellis Papers, CAH, UT (fifth quote).

19. Stephen Duncan to Josiah S. Johnston, March 28, 1828, Josiah S. Johnston Papers, HSP.

20. Stephen Duncan to Josiah S. Johnston, September 8, 1828, Josiah S. Johnston Collection, HSP.

21. Ibid.

22. John Duncan to Stephen Duncan, November 10, 1828, Thomas Butler and Family Papers, Box 5, Folder 28, LLMVC, LSU.

23. Stephen Duncan to John Ker, December 1, 1828, John Ker and Family Papers, Box 1, Folder 1, LLMVC, LSU.

24. Ibid.

25. The five Mississippi River counties were the only counties where Jackson received less than 80 percent of the vote. Cooper, *Liberty and Slavery,* 167–69, and *The South and the Politics of Slavery,* 7–13; Miles, 13–17; Watson, 93–95; Stephen Duncan to Josiah S. Johnston, September 8, 1828, Josiah S. Johnston Papers, HSP (first quote); Stephen Duncan to John Ker, December 6, 1828, John Ker and Family Papers, Box 1, Folder 1, LLMVC, LSU (second and third quotes).

26. Stephen Duncan to Josiah S. Johnston, April 10, 1829, Josiah S. Johnston Papers, HSP.

27. The six candidates were: Franklin E. Plummer, a representative since 1827 from Simpson County to the Mississippi General Assembly; David Dickson, the runner-up to General Thomas Hinds in the 1828 election; William L. Sharkey, the speaker of the Mississippi House of Representatives; Richard W. Webber, a lawyer from Franklin County; John H. Norton, a former U.S. marshal from Marion County; and Wilkins. See Miles, 29–30.

28. By 1815, Wilkins owned 277 slaves and 4,678 acres of land in Adams County. During the 1820s, he built his commission merchant business with John Linton Jr. into one of the most successful firms in Natchez. Ibid.; James, 112–16; Miles, 31 (Plummer quotes).

29. Bolton, 132.

30. Quoted in Miles, 31. Wilkins's strongest base of support was in Adams County, where Plummer received only eleven votes.

31. Stephen Duncan to James C. Wilkins, May 10, 1830, James Campbell Wilkins Papers, Box 2E547, Folder 4, NTC, CAH, UT.

32. Ibid.

33. Ibid.

34. Ibid.

35. Stephen Duncan to John Ker, December 20, 1828, John Ker and Family Papers, Box 1, Folder 1, LLMVC, LSU.

36. Stephen Duncan to Thomas Butler, November 28, 1833, Thomas Butler and Family Papers, Box 6, Folder 33, LLMVC, LSU.

37. Stephen Duncan to Thomas Butler, July 1, 1823, Thomas Butler and Family Papers, Box 5, Folder 25, LLMVC, LSU.

38. John Duncan to Sarah Jane Duncan, November 24, 1827, Newbold-Irvine Papers, Box 4, Folder 20, HSP (first quote); John Duncan to Sarah Jane Duncan, January 5, 1828, Newbold-Irvine Papers, Family Correspondence, Folder 3, HSP (second and third quotes).

39. Stephen Duncan to Thomas Butler, July 1, 1823, Box 5, Folder 25, Thomas Butler and Family Papers, LLMVC, LSU.

40. Ibid.

41. Stephen Duncan to John Ker, December 6 (first quote) and 20 (second quote), 1828, John Ker and Family Papers, Box 1, Folder 1, LLMVC, LSU.

42. John Duncan to Sarah Jane Duncan, August 18, 1829, Newbold-Irvine Papers, Box 4, Folder 20, HSP. He wrote this letter five days after his seventeenth birthday.

43. Stephen Duncan to John Ker, December 10, 1828, Box 1, Folder 1, LLMVC, LSU.

44. John Duncan to Sarah Jane Duncan, March 31 (first three quotes) and November 24 (fourth quote), 1827, Newbold-Irvine Papers, Box 4, Folder 20, HSP.

45. John Duncan to Sarah Jane Duncan, January 5, 1828, Newbold-Irvine Papers, Family Correspondence, Folder 3, HSP (quote); Report Card of Sarah Jane Duncan, 183(?), Philadelphia High School for Young Ladies, Newbold-Irvine Papers, Box 2, Folder 10, HSP.

46. John Duncan to Sarah Jane Duncan, April 6, 1829, Newbold-Irvine Papers, Box 4, Folder 20, HSP.

47. Stephen Duncan to Thomas Butler, February 17, 1829, Thomas Butler and Family Papers, Box 5, Folder 29, LLMVC, LSU (first quote); John Duncan to Sarah Jane Duncan, December 25, 1828, Newbold-Irvine Papers, Box 4, Folder 20, HSP (second quote).

48. John Duncan to Sarah Jane Duncan, February 14, 1826, Newbold-Irvine Papers, Box 4, Folder 20, HSP.

49. Stephen Duncan to John Ker, September 18, 1829, John Ker and Family Papers, Box 1, Folder 2, LLMVC, LSU.

50. Ibid.

51. Ibid.

52. Ibid.

53. Drawing and Inscription of John Duncan's Monument at Yale University, Newbold-Irvine Papers, Box 4, Folder 20, HSP; John Duncan's obituary, original newspaper clipping, no date or newspaper name, Newbold-Irvine Papers, Box 3, Folder 1, HSP (quote).

54. Stephen Duncan to John Ker, January 24 (first, second, and fifth quotes) and February 2 (third and fourth quotes), 1830, John Ker and Family Papers, Box 1, Folder 2, LLMVC, LSU.

4. "WE WILL ONE DAY HAVE OUR THROATS CUT IN THIS COUNTY"

1. Stephen Duncan to Thomas Butler, June 15 and October 4, 1831, in Thomas Butler and Family Papers, Box 6, Folder 31, LLMVC, LSU; Gray, 2:698; Watkins, 29; Weems, "Bank of the Mississippi," 773.

2. Aptheker, 293–324; Vincent Harding, *There Is a River: The Black Struggle for Freedom in America* (New York: Vintage Books, 1983), 75–100; John Duft and Peter Mitchell, eds., *The Nat Turner Rebellion: The Historical Event and the Modern Controversy* (New York: Harper and Row, 1971); Thomas R. Gray, ed., *The Confessions of Nat Turner, the Leader of the Late Insurrection in Southampton, VA* (Baltimore: Lucas and Deafer, 1831); Stephen B. Oates, *The Fires of Jubilee* (New York: Harper and Row, 1975); Henry Irving Tragle, ed., *The Southampton Slave Revolt of 1831* (Amherst: University of Massachusetts Press, 1971). For an analysis of earlier slave resistance in Virginia, see Gerald W. Mullin, *Flight and Rebellion: Slave Resistance in Eighteenth-Century Virginia* (New York: Oxford University Press, 1972). For a comparative perspective of the Turner rebellion versus other rebellions in North and South America and the Caribbean, see Eugene D. Genovese, *From Rebellion to Revolution: Afro-American Slave Revolts in the Making of the New World* (New York: Vintage Books, 1981).

3. Military aid arrived from Fort Monroe (sixty miles from Southampton County), as well as from surrounding counties in Virginia and North Carolina. See Aptheker, 300–2. Aptheker notes that prior to Turner's execution, sixteen slaves and three free blacks had been hanged as well. On the day of Turner's execution, the black community continued to see signs from God, as "the sun was hidden behind angry clouds, the thunder rolled, the lightning flashed, and the most terrific storm visited that county ever known." Quoted in Harding, 99.

4. Perhaps rivaling the white fear that the Turner rebellion elicited were the 1811 insurrections in St. Charles and St. John Parishes in Louisiana, which involved between four and five hundred slaves and is detailed in Aptheker. Numerous other studies also examine slave resistance prior to the Turner revolt. See Helen Tunnicliff Catterall, *Judicial Cases concerning American Slavery and the Negro*, 5 vols. (Washington, D.C.: Carnegie Institute of Washington, 1926–1937); Thomas J. Davis, *A Rumor of Revolt: The "Great Negro Plot" in Colonial New York* (New York: Free Press, 1985); Kirsten Fischer, *Suspect Relations: Sex, Race, and Resistance in Colonial North Carolina* (Ithaca: Cornell University Press, 2002); John Hope Franklin, *From Slavery to Freedom: A History of African Americans*, 7th ed. (New York: Alfred A. Knopf, 1994); George Washington Williams, *History of the Negro Race in America, 1619–1880* (1883; reprint, New York: Arno Press, 1968); Peter H. Wood, *The Black Majority: Negroes in Colonial South Carolina from 1670 through the Stono Rebellion* (New York: W. W. Norton, 1975). For sources on the Denmark Vesey conspiracy of 1822, see chap. 3, note 2.

5. For more on Blackhead Signpost, see Harding, 99.

6. Quoted in Sydnor, *Slavery in Mississippi*, 92; Aptheker, 311.

7. It is unclear exactly when Stephen Duncan became aware of the Turner rebellion. For his first mention of it, see Stephen Duncan to Thomas Butler, October 4, 1831, Thomas Butler and Family Papers, Box 6, Folder 31, LLMVC, LSU. In his letters at the time, Duncan never indicated whether there was any organized slave resistance on his plantations or in the surrounding area.

8. U.S. Department of State, *Fifth Census; or Enumeration of the Inhabitants of the United States, 1830* (Washington, D.C.: Duff Green, 1830); Stephen Duncan to Josiah S. Johnston, October 11, 1831, Josiah S. Johnston Papers, HSP (quotes). For slave activity in North Carolina, see Aptheker, 304–5, and passim.

9. Stephen Duncan to Josiah S. Johnston, October 11, 1831, Josiah S. Johnston Papers, HSP.

10. For a discussion of and various perspectives on slave management, see James O. Breeden, ed., *Advice among Masters: The Ideal in Slave Management in the Old South* (Westport, Conn.: Greenwood Press, 1980).

11. Stephen Duncan to Thomas Butler, September 20, 1831, Thomas Butler and Family Papers, Box 6, Folder 31, LLMVC, LSU.

12. Stephen Duncan to Thomas Butler, October 4, 1831, Thomas Butler and Family Papers, Box 6, Folder 31, LLMVC, LSU.

13. Ibid. For overseers' wages, see William K. Scarborough, *The Overseer: Plantation Management in the Old South* (Baton Rouge: Louisiana State University Press, 1966), 24–31. Scarborough notes that in Mississippi, salaries for overseers on cotton plantations ranged from $200 to $1000, with the average being $450.

14. Stephen Duncan to Thomas Butler, October 4, 1831, Thomas Butler and Family Papers, Box 6, Folder 31, LLMVC, LSU.

15. Stephen Duncan to Thomas Butler, November 16, 1833, Thomas Butler and Family Papers, Box 6, Folder 33, LLMVC, LSU.

16. Ibid.

17. Drew Gilpin Faust, *James Henry Hammond and the Old South: A Design for Mastery* (Baton Rouge: Louisiana State University Press, 1982), 99–104. Faust's study of Hammond provides an excellent microview of slave and plantation management. For other examinations of slave and plantation management on specific plantations, see Janet Sharp Hermann, *The Pursuit of a Dream* (New York: Oxford University Press, 1981), and *Joseph E. Davis, Pioneer Patriarch* (Jackson: University Press of Mississippi, 1990); Theodore Rosengarten, *Tombee: Portrait of a Cotton Planter* (New York: William Morrow, 1986). More general studies that focus on plantation and slave management through the differing perspectives of enslaver and slave are Breeden, ed., passim; Larry E. Hudson Jr., *To Have and To Hold: Slave Work and Family Life in Antebellum South Carolina* (Athens: University of Georgia Press, 1997); Norrece T. Jones Jr., *Born a Child of Freedom, Yet a Slave: Mechanisms of Control and Strategies of Resistance in Antebellum South Carolina* (Middletown, Conn.: Wesleyan University Press, 1990).

18. Stephen Duncan to Josiah S. Johnston, October 11, 1831, Josiah S. Johnston Papers, HSP.

19. Ibid. (quotes). Antimasonry started to take hold in the late 1820s, particularly in the Northeast. At its root was the popular belief in the conspiratorial nature of Masonry against Christianity, aristocracy, and liberty. Opponents of Masonry eventually founded the Anti-Masonic Party. Within the party, some members held antislavery views. See Paul Goodman, *Towards a Christian Republic: Antimasonry and the Great Transition in New England, 1826–1836* (New York: Oxford University Press, 1988); William Preston Vaughn, *The Antimasonic Party in the United States, 1826–1843* (Lexington: University of Kentucky Press, 1983).

20. For Native American Indian removal in Mississippi, see Arthur H. DeRosier Jr., *The Removal of the Choctaw Indians* (Knoxville: University of Tennessee Press, 1970); Fortune Jr. in

McLemore, ed., 1:260–66, and, in the same volume, John Edmond Gonzales, "Flush Times, Depression, War, and Compromise," 284–285; Jesse O. McKee and Jon A. Schlenker, *The Choctaws: Cultural Evolution of a Native American Tribe* (Jackson: University Press of Mississippi, 1980); Miles, 20–25, 55–56. For an excellent discussion of Native American Indian removal policies and racism, see Reginald Horsman, *Race and Manifest Destiny: The Origins of American Racial Anglo-Saxonism* (Cambridge, Mass.: Harvard University Press, 1981), 189–207.

21. Stephen Duncan to Josiah S. Johnston, February 21, 1832, Josiah S. Johnston Papers, HSP.

22. Stephen Duncan to John Ker, n.d., [either August or September 1824 or September 1825], John Ker and Family Papers, LLMVC, LSU; Stephen Duncan to Josiah S. Johnston, October 19, 1827, and February 21, 1832, Josiah S. Johnston Papers, HSP.

23. Stephen Duncan to Josiah S. Johnston, February 21, 1832, Josiah S. Johnston Papers, HSP (quotes). In the mid-1840s, Duncan invested in a Natchez textile mill that used slave labor. This enterprise eventually failed. See Moore, *Emergence of the Cotton Kingdom in the Old Southwest*, 220. With regard to employing slave labor in manufacturing, see Fred Bateman, James Foust, and Thomas Weiss, "The Participation of Planters in Manufacturing in the Antebellum South," *Agricultural History* 48 (April 1974): 277–97; John Hebron Moore, "Mississippi's Ante-Bellum Textile Industry," *Journal of Mississippi History* 16 (April 1954): 81–98, and *Emergence of the Cotton Kingdom*, 204–31; Norris W. Preyer, "The Historian, the Slave, and the Ante-Bellum Textile Industry," *Journal of Negro History* 46 (April 1961): 67–82; Robert S. Starobin, *Industrial Slavery in the Old South* (New York: Oxford University Press, 1970); Midori Takagi, *Rearing Wolves to Our Own Destruction: Slavery in Richmond, Virginia, 1782–1865* (Charlottesville: University Press of Virginia, 1999); Richard C. Wade, *Slavery in the Cities: The South, 1820–1860* (New York: Oxford University Press, 1964). For a thought-provoking discussion about the use of slaves outside of agriculture, see Thomas Hulse, "The Military Slave System and the Construction of Army Fortifications along the Antebellum Gulf Coast: Mobile Point and Pensacola, 1818–1854" (M.A. thesis, University of South Alabama, 2003).

24. Stephen Duncan to Josiah S. Johnston, February 21, 1832, Josiah S. Johnston Papers, HSP.

25. For example, New England woolens manufacturers did not believe that the tariff provided enough protection for their product. Senator Martin Van Buren of New York promptly secured further protection to woolens manufacturers. Southerners were less effective in having their concerns addressed by Congress.

26. Miles, 61.

27. Stephen Duncan to Josiah S. Johnston, February 21, 1832, Josiah S. Johnston Papers, HSP (quotes). For a general discussion of the tariff of 1828, see Watson, 88–89. A more in-depth examination of the tariff and its ramifications can be found in the classic studies of William W. Freehling, *Prelude to Civil War: The Nullification Controversy in South Carolina, 1816–1836* (New York: Harper and Row, 1966), and Charles S. Sydnor, *The Development of Southern Sectionalism, 1819–1848* (Baton Rouge: Louisiana State University Press, 1948). Also see Manisha Sinha, *The Counterrevolution of Slavery: Politics and Ideology in Antebellum South Carolina* (Chapel Hill: University of North Carolina Press, 2000).

28. For the tariff's effects in Mississippi and the state's response to it, see Miles, 59–61; Lucie Robertson Bridgeforth, "Mississippi's Response to Nullification, 1833," *Journal of Mississippi History* 45 (February 1983): 1–21 (quotes, 2, 3).

29. Stephen Duncan to Josiah S. Johnston, October 11, 1831, Josiah S. Johnston Papers, HSP.

30. For an intriguing study on community and regional identity formation, see Morris, *Becoming Southern.*

31. Most Mississippians opposed the tariff, but a minority believed that it would protect Mississippi's growing dominance in cotton production. Many within the latter camp thought that tariff protection for Louisiana sugar planters kept them from beginning cotton production, which would cut into Mississippi's market share of cotton. Other Mississippians advocated the extension of the tariff to cotton. See Miles, 59–61; Bridgeforth, 4–5.

32. For a compelling analysis of how the American government and military profited from slavery, see Hulse.

33. Stephen Duncan to Josiah S. Johnston, October 11, 1831, Josiah S. Johnston Papers, HSP.

34. Stephen Duncan to Josiah S. Johnston, February 21, 1832, Josiah S. Johnston Papers, HSP.

35. Stephen Duncan to Josiah S. Johnston, October 11, 1831, Josiah S. Johnston Papers, HSP.

36. Ibid.

37. Ibid. In spite of the similarities between Duncan's plan and Henry Clay's American System, differences existed. For example, Clay's plan called for internal improvements to be paid for through the sale of high-priced Federal lands to the states. Also, colonization was not part of the American System.

38. Ibid.

39. Ibid.

40. Stephen Duncan to William J. Minor, June 17, 1842, William J. Minor and Family Papers, LLMVC, LSU. Duncan's concerns about these issues also extended to the production of sugar. During the summer of 1842, he told Minor that with regard to the position of sugar planters, "Nothing but a high protection can save us." Stephen Duncan to William J. Minor, August 27, 1842, William J. Minor and Family Papers, LLMVC, LSU. Duncan became livid when he heard that President Tyler did not support a proposed tariff in 1842 that would protect sugar planters. As he wrote, "What a curse this man has been to this nation. He is the greatest ass—I have ever seen." According to him, Henry Clay was "the only man to get the country through the present difficulties." For detailed discussions about the tariff issue, Tyler, Clay, and the Whig position, see Stephen Duncan to William J. Minor, July 11 (above quote) and 16, August n.d. and 27, and September 17, 1842, William J. Minor and Family Papers, LLMVC, LSU.

41. On the eve of the Mississippi Colonization Society's inception, slightly over five hundred free blacks resided in the state, most of whom lived in the river counties of the old Natchez District and Natchez itself. In spite of the small black population and the frequently respected position that free blacks had within Natchez, whites from the southwestern part of the state advocated for colonization as early as 1824. Several years before the formation of the Mississippi Colonization Society, the *Woodville Republican* ran advertisements promoting settlements in Haiti. In 1826, a subscription agent for the American Colonization Society's journal began to canvass the state in search of support. In spite of some pockets of strength, the canvasser advised that the national society hold off on an all-out campaign to collect funds and formally organize a branch in Mississippi. An auxiliary society was nonetheless planned in 1828, but it became embroiled in the national politics of the presidential campaign of that year and did not materialize. For a history of the colonization movement in Mississippi, see Norwood Allen Kerr, "The Mis-

sissippi Colonization Society (1830–1860)," *Journal of Mississippi History* 43 (February 1981): 1–30; Sydnor, *Slavery in Mississippi*, 203–10.

42. Stephen Duncan to John Ker, January 24, 1830, John Ker and Family Papers, LLMVC, LSU.

43. Ibid.; Stephen Duncan to Josiah S. Johnston, April 17, 1832, Josiah S. Johnston Papers, HSP (all quotes); Kerr, 7–10; Sydnor, *Slavery in Mississippi*, 213.

44. Stephen Duncan to Josiah S. Johnston, April 17, 1832, Josiah S. Johnston Papers, HSP (all quotes); Kerr, 7–10; Sydnor, *Slavery in Mississippi*, 213.

45. Kerr, 7–11; Sydnor, *Slavery in Mississippi*, 211–16. Other state societies—such as Maryland (1831), New York, and Pennsylvania (1835)—also broke away from the national organization.

46. Kerr, 12–20; Sydnor, *Slavery in Mississippi*, 214–15.

47. Kerr, 20–22; Riley, 358–61; Sydnor, *Slavery in Mississippi*, 224–29.

48. The ruling stated that the Ross will did not violate the intent of the 1822 law, which was meant to restrict the growth of free blacks; however, since Ross had freed his slaves with the intent of colonizing them, they would not contribute to the growth in the number of free blacks and therefore were not in violation of the 1822 law. See Kerr, 21.

49. Kerr, 21–23; Riley, 358–61; Sydnor, *Slavery in Mississippi*, 227–29. A series of letters about the Ross case, as well as letters from the former Ross slaves after they arrived in Greenville, Africa, can be found in Bell I. Wiley, ed., *Slaves No More: Letters from Liberia, 1833–1869* (Lexington: University of Kentucky Press, 1980), 155–75. For insight into the protracted legal battles involving the Ross estate, see the Isaac Ross Wade Letters, MDAH.

50. Kerr, 25–30; Riley, 358–61; Sydnor, *Slavery in Mississippi*, 215–16; James, 175. Duncan was elected vice president in 1836 and appointed as life director in 1858. After his death in 1867, the American Colonization Society eulogized, "Dr. Stephen Duncan, of Mississippi, distinguished for his many excellencies of character." Eulogy in "The Fifty-First Annual Report of the American Colonization Society," found in *The Annual Reports of the American Society for Colonizing the Free People of Colour of the United States*, vol. 51 (1868; reprint, New York: Negro Universities Press, 1969), 5. See also ibid., vols. 20 and 22–51 (1818–1910; reprint, New York: Negro Universities Press, 1969).

5. POWER AND POSITION

1. The number of bales produced in Mississippi between September 1, 1832, and August 31, 1833, was 145,430. The total value of the crop was $5,196,941. Watkins, 29; Weems, "Bank of the Mississippi," 773.

2. Watkins, 29; Weems, "Bank of the Mississippi," 773; Douglass C. North, *The Economic Growth of the United States, 1790–1860* (Englewood Cliffs, N.J.: Prentice-Hall, 1962), 194–96.

3. Joseph G. Baldwin, *The Flush Times of Alabama and Mississippi: A Series of Sketches* (1853; reprint, Baton Rouge: Louisiana State University Press, 1987), 81 (second quote), 91 (first quote).

4. Quoted in Miles, 119.

5. Fortune Jr. in McLemore, ed., 1:270–72; Miles, 23–24; Weems, "Bank of the Mississippi," 489–92, 731–32.

6. Quoted in Fortune Jr. in McLemore, ed., 1:271; Schweikart, 202–5; Weems, "Bank of the Mississippi," 539.

7. Claiborne, 1:409; Fortune Jr. in McLemore, ed., 1:270–72; Miles, 23–24; Schweikart, 175; Weems, "Bank of the Mississippi," 489–92, 731–32.

8. Schweikart, 202–5; Weems, "Bank of the Mississippi," 580–90; Fortune Jr. in McLemore, ed., 1:270–72.

9. Schweikart, 202–5; Weems, "Bank of the Mississippi," 580–90, 731–32; Fortune Jr. in McLemore, ed., 1:270–72; James 198–201.

10. Minor was married to Rebecca Gustine. See Schweikart, 175, 202–5; James, 199; Rothstein, "Changing Social Networks," 77.

11. Quoted in James, 199–200.

12. Claiborne, 1:411.

13. Quoted in Miles, 71.

14. Resolution, Bank of the State of Mississippi, Stephen Duncan, President, and Gabriel Tichenor, Cashier, February 24, 1832, Gabriel Tichenor Papers, NTC, CAH, UT.

15. James, 199; Miles, 73, 119–20; Schweikart, 175–79, 202–5.

16. U.S. Department of State, *Fifth Census,* 102–3, and *Sixth Census, or Enumeration of the Inhabitants of the United States as Corrected at the Department of State, in 1840* (Washington, D.C.: Blair and Rives, 1841), 252–53.

17. Observation by Bishop Leonidas Polk, quoted in Miles, 118.

18. Malcolm J. Rohrbough, *The Land Office Business: The Settlement and Administration of American Public Lands, 1789–1837* (New York: Oxford University Press, 1968), 30, 175, 226–31; Gonzales in McLemore, ed., 1:288–89; Miles, 22.

19. Bolton, 73–83.

20. The total purchase price for the land was $2,732.57. Duncan's U.S. land patents bore the following dates: December 13 and 18, 1830; June 24, 1831; December 6, 1832; April 29, 1833; and December 4, 1834. Certificate numbers: 5721, 5723, 5772, 6445, 6646, 6447, 9336, 9337, 11412, 18851, and 19678. All in Office of the Chancery Clerk, Issaquena County Court House, Mayersville, Mississippi.

21. U.S. Bureau of the Census, Manuscript Agricultural Schedules, Schedule IV, Issaquena County, Mississippi, 1860. Totals include the value of the land, farm implements, and livestock, but not crop values or slaves.

22. The land comprised the cotton fields of Homochitto, Carlisle, Holly Ridge, Duncansby, Oakley, Reserve, Duncannon, Middlesex, and Ellislie plantations. Other land parcels were purchased, but the names of those plantations are not known. U.S. Bureau of the Census, Manuscript Agricultural Schedules, Schedule IV, Issaquena County, Mississippi, 1850 and 1860; Plantation Lists, Stephen Duncan and Stephen Duncan Jr. Papers, LLMVC, LSU; Typescripts and handwritten notes, Issaquena County History, WPA Historical Records Survey, Record Group 60, MDAH.

23. Land Deeds and Indentures, Washington County Deed Records, Deed Books: Vol. A, p. 169; Vol. B, pp. 248, 328, 379; Vol. C, p. 425; Vol. D, pp. 55, 92, 94; Vol. F, p. 343; Vol. G, p. 90. All in Office of the Chancery Clerk, Washington County Courthouse, Greenville, Mississippi.

24. Agreement, Zenas Preston and Stephen Duncan, February 1833, Washington County

Deed Records, Deed Book, Vol. B, p. 330, Office of the Chancery Clerk, Washington County Courthouse, Greenville, Mississippi.

25. Indenture, Zenas and Martha Preston and Stephen Duncan, March 3, 1835, and Stephen and Catharine Duncan and Zenas Preston, March 3, 1835, Washington County Deed Records, Deed Book, Vol. C, p. 425, and Vol. D, p. 92, Office of the Chancery Clerk, Washington County Courthouse, Greenville, Mississippi.

26. Indentures, Zenas and Martha Preston and Stephen Duncan, January 21, 1840, Washington County Deed Records, Deed Book, Vol. J, p. 38, and Vol. L, p. 327, Office of the Chancery Clerk, Washington County Courthouse, Greenville, Mississippi. In 1847, this property was given to Duncan's son Henry. See Issaquena County Deed Records, Deed Book, Vol. A, p. 255, Office of the Chancery Clerk, Issaquena County Courthouse, Mayersville, Mississippi; Indentures, Robert McCullough and Stephen Duncan, Washington County Deed Records, Deed Books: Vol. B, pp. 89, 248; Vol. D, pp. 55, 94; Vol. J, pp. 2, 4; Vol. K, p. 113, Office of the Chancery Clerk, Washington County Courthouse, Greenville, Mississippi. I wish to thank Richard H. Kilbourne Jr. for his generous help in deciphering these documents.

27. Nearly all of Duncan's land purchases outside the Mississippi Delta were in Adams County, along the Homochitto River and Second Creek. Indentures in Adams County Deed Records: Spencer and Margaret Wood and Stephen Duncan, January 19, 1830, Deed Book, Vol. R, p. 680; Benjamin F. Conner and Stephen Duncan, February 18, 1831, Deed Book, Vol. S, p. 411; William A. and Sarah Jane Irvine and Stephen Duncan, February 26, 1834, Deed Book, Vol. V, p. 417; Gustavus and Eliza Calhoun and Stephen Duncan, March 1, 1834, Deed Book, Vol. B, p. 167; Robert T. and Elizabeth Dunbar and Stephen Duncan, March 18, 1835, Deed Book, Vol. V, p. 586; James H. Cook and Stephen Duncan, March 11, 1839, Deed Book, Vol. AA, p. 574; Bill of Sale, James Gustine to Stephen Duncan, December 2, 1835, Deed Book, Vol. W, p. 462, Office of the Chancery Clerk, Adams County Courthouse, Natchez, Mississippi; Indenture, Stephen and Catharine Duncan and William Peebles, February 1, 1830, Wilkinson County Deed Records, Deed Book, Vol. F, p. 443, Wilkinson County Courthouse, Woodville, Mississippi; Indenture, Stephen and Catharine Duncan and William St. John Elliott, January 6, 1835, William St. John Elliott Papers, LLMVC, LSU.

28. Indenture, Stephen and Catharine Duncan and William Peebles, February 1, 1830, Wilkinson County Deed Records, Deed Book, Vol. F, p. 443, Office of the Chancery Clerk, Wilkinson County Courthouse, Woodville, Mississippi; Indenture, Stephen and Catharine Duncan and Lydia Dowell, April 10, 1839, Adams County Deed Records, Deed Book, Vol. BB, p. 60, Office of the Chancery Clerk, Adams County Courthouse, Natchez, Mississippi.

29. Duncan sold Surget 1,280 acres in Monroe County, 79 acres in Noxubee County, 400 acres in Oktibbeha County, 328 acres in Chickasaw County, 326 acres in Pontotoc County, 82 acres in Winston County, and 81 acres in Attala County. Land Deed, Stephen and Catharine Duncan and Francis Surget, April 3, 1837, Oktibbeha County Deed Records, Deed Book, Vol. 2, pp. 530–37, Office of the Chancery Clerk, Oktibbeha County Courthouse, Starkville, Mississippi.

30. Indenture, Stephen and Catharine Duncan and William St. John Elliott, January 6, 1835, William St. John Elliott Papers, LLMVC; Land Conveyance, Washington Jackson and Stephen Duncan, January 7, 1835, St. Mary Parish Conveyance Records, Conveyance Book, Vol. D, pp. 230–31, 262, Deed #2064, Office of the Clerk of Court, St. Mary Parish, Franklin, Louisiana.

31. Robert M. Crisler, "Bayou Teche," in Edwin A. Davis, ed., *The Rivers and Bayous of Louisiana* (Baton Rouge: Louisiana Education and Research Association, 1968), 105–12; J. Carlyle Sitterson, *Sugar Country: The Cane Sugar Industry in the South, 1753–1950* (Lexington: University of Kentucky Press, 1953), 13–16.

32. Land Conveyance, Washington Jackson and Stephen Duncan, January 7, 1835, St. Mary Parish Conveyance Records, Conveyance Book, Vol. D, pp. 230–31, 262, Deed #2064, Office of the Clerk of Court, St. Mary Parish, Franklin, Louisiana. For a description of Bayou Teche and St. Mary Parish, see Jewel Lynn de Grummond, "A Social History of St. Mary Parish from 1845–1860" (M.A. thesis, Louisiana State University, 1948), 1–3. According to de Grummond, Washington Jackson first opened up direct trade between St. Mary Parish and the North in 1825 with his brig *Attakapas*, which left laden with sugar and returned with dry goods and hardware for local merchants. Ibid., 8–10.

33. "Camperdown" came from Duncan's ancestor, Admiral Duncan, who was the "hero of Camperdown" and who "defeated the British fleet off Camperdown on the Netherlands in the time of the French Revolution." Stephen Duncan Jr. to Kate Duncan Smith, December 12, 1894 (first quote), and Lucia D. Pychowska to Kate Duncan Smith, March 3, 1895 (second quote), in Smith, *Thomas Duncan*, 107–8, 124.

34. For a good description of sugar cultivation and plantations, see Sitterson, 112–32.

35. Stephen Duncan to Thomas Butler, May 30, 1818, Thomas Butler and Family Papers, Box 4, Folder 20, LLMVC, LSU. The location of this plantation is unclear. For Butler's sugar plantations, see Dawes, 34–37.

36. These totals were taken from land deeds, conveyances, indentures, and bills of sale found in the Offices of the Chancery Clerk in Adams, Issaquena, Washington, and Wilkinson Counties, Mississippi, the Offices of the Clerk of Court in Assumption and St. Mary Parishes, Louisiana, and the William St. John Elliott Papers, LLMVC, LSU.

37. Composite totals taken from sources listed in the previous note, as well as Land Deeds, Adams County Deed Records, Deed Books: Vol. M, p. 361; Vol. N, p. 206; Vol. Q, pp. 63, 154; Vol. R, pp. 45, 57, Office of the Chancery Clerk, Adams County Courthouse, Natchez, Mississippi. The Adams County manuscript census lists Duncan as owning 378 slaves at the end of the 1830s. The census for St. Mary Parish is incomplete and does not list any slaves for Duncan, even though white members of his family are listed. U.S. Bureau of the Census, Manuscript General Population Census, Schedule I, St. Mary Parish, Louisiana, 1840.

38. Indentures, Adams County Deed Records, Deed Books: Vol. R, p. 553; Vol. S, p. 288, 462; Vol. V, p. 147; Vol. Y, p. 451; Vol. AA, p. 605, Office of the Chancery Clerk, Adams County Courthouse, Natchez, Mississippi; Indentures, Washington County Deed Records, Deed Books: Vol. B, p. 145; Vol. F, p. 245; Vol. G, p. 376, Office of the Chancery Clerk, Washington County Courthouse, Greenville, Mississippi.

39. Indentures, Robert McCullough and Daniel Lippingcott and Stephen Duncan, January 1, 1828, Deed Book, Vol. Q, p. 38; Robert and Maria McCullough, Benjamin and Juliana Harmann, and Stephen Duncan, January 1, 1830, Deed Book, Vol. R, p. 553, Adams County Deed Records, Office of the Chancery Clerk, Adams County Courthouse, Natchez, Mississippi; Co-partnership Agreement, Robert McCullough and Stephen Duncan, 1831, Deed Book, Vol. B, p. 84, Wash-

ington County Deed Records, Office of the Chancery Clerk, Washington County Courthouse, Greenville, Mississippi.

40. Indenture, William C. Conner and Stephen Duncan, November 24, 1830, Adams County Deed Records, Deed Book, Vol. S, p. 288, Office of the Chancery Clerk, Adams County Courthouse, Natchez, Mississippi.

41. Indentures, all recorded in Adams County Deed Records: William M. and Sarah Hebron and Stephen Duncan, January 6, 1831, Deed Book, Vol. S, p. 462; Alfred and Eliza Cochran and Stephen Duncan, February 18, 1834, Deed Book, Vol. V, p. 147; John Watt and Stephen Duncan, February 23, 1839, Deed Book, Vol. AA, p. 605, Office of the Chancery Clerk, Adams County Courthouse, Natchez, Mississippi; Indentures, all recorded in Washington County Deed Records: Elijah Atcheson and Stephen Duncan, December 7, 1831, Deed Book, Vol. B, p. 145; William E. Hall and Stephen Duncan, January 30, 1837, Deed Book, Vol. F, p. 245, and August 29, 1839, Deed Book, Vol. G, p. 376, Office of the Chancery Clerk, Washington County Courthouse, Greenville, Mississippi.

42. James, 196.

43. John Hebron Moore, *Andrew Brown and Cypress Lumbering in the Old Southwest* (Baton Rouge: Louisiana State University Press, 1967), 24; Moore, *Emergence of the Cotton Kingdom in the Old Southwest*, 208–10.

44. Indenture between Stephen Duncan, President of the Natchez Rail Road Company, and Reuben M. Strother, November 14, 1838, Adams County Deed Records, Vol. AA, p. 416, Office of the Chancery Clerk, Adams County Courthouse, Natchez, Mississippi; Moore, *Andrew Brown and Cypress Lumbering in the Old Southwest*, 30–31. For more information on Mississippi's railroads, see Moore, *Emergence of the Cotton Kingdom in the Old Southwest*, 164–76, and Moore, "Railroads of Antebellum Mississippi," *Journal of Mississippi History* 41 (February 1979): 53–81.

6. PUBLIC DUTIES AND PRIVATE WORLDS

1. Diary Entry of William Johnson, December 12, 1837, in Hogan and Davis, eds., 210.

2. For a history of Trinity Episcopal Church, see Charles Stietenroth, *One Hundred Years with Old Trinity Church, Natchez, Mississippi* (Natchez: Natchez Printing and Stationery Company, 1922). See also Vestry Minutes, Trinity Episcopal Church, March 9, 1822, January 11, 1826, and April 3, 1837, Trinity Episcopal Church Records, MDAH.

3. Records of Trinity Episcopal indicate that the Duncan children were baptized at the church. As an adult, Catharine Bingaman Duncan was confirmed at the church. See Parish Register of Trinity Episcopal Church, Trinity Episcopal Church Records, MDAH. Vestry members who were intimately linked to Duncan through friendship, business, or family ties included Adam Bingaman, Gustavus Colhoun, James K. Cook, Samuel Davis, Richard G. Ellis, Benjamin Farrar, Levin R. Marshall, Dr. William Newton Mercer, Dr. Ayres P. Merrill, John Minor, William J. Minor, and Frederick Stanton. See Vestry Minutes of Trinity Episcopal Church, Trinity Episcopal Church Records, MDAH; Stietenroth, 67–69.

4. Stephen Duncan to Josiah S. Johnston, December 4, 1832, Josiah S. Johnston Papers, HSP

(quote); Aubrey Keith Lucas, "Education in Mississippi from Statehood to the Civil War," in McLemore, ed., 1:363.

5. Jefferson College began to enroll students in its preparatory program in 1811 and in its collegiate program in 1817. Minutes of the Trustees of Jefferson College, vol. 3, p. 13, January 10, 1831, Jefferson College Papers, MDAH; Stephen Duncan to Levin Wailes, December 30, 1830, Correspondence, Jefferson College Papers, MDAH. For a history of Jefferson College, see Lucas in McLemore, ed., 1:358–60.

6. Stephen Duncan to Levin Wailes, February 20, 1833, Correspondence, Jefferson College Papers, MDAH (quotes); Minutes of the Trustees of Jefferson College, vol. 3, p. 161, March 11, 1833, Jefferson College Papers, MDAH.

7. Levin Wailes to Stephen Duncan, March 14, 1833 (first and second quotes), and Stephen Duncan to Levin Wailes, March 15, 1833 (third quote), Correspondence, Jefferson College Papers, MDAH.

8. Stephen Duncan to Benjamin L. C. Wailes, October 2, 1833, Benjamin L. C. Wailes Papers, NTC, CAH, UT; Stephen Duncan to Levin Wailes, March 28, 1839, Levin Wailes Papers, NTC, CAH, UT; Stephen Duncan to President Pro Tem of Jefferson College, January 10, 1840, Correspondence, Jefferson College Papers, MDAH; Journal of the Board of Trustees of Jefferson College, vol. 4, p. 194, January 18, 1840, Jefferson College Papers, MDAH.

9. *Journal of the Convention of the State of Mississippi* (Jackson, Miss.: Peter Isler, 1832). For the state constitutional convention, see Robert E. May, *John A. Quitman: Old South Crusader* (Baton Rouge: Louisiana State University Press, 1985), 50–57; Miles, 32–43; Christopher J. Olsen, *Political Culture and Secession in Mississippi: Masculinity, Honor, and the Antiparty Tradition, 1830–1860* (New York: Oxford University Press, 2000), 30–32, 76.

10. Stephen Duncan to Levin Wailes, September 14, 1832, Benjamin L. C. Wailes Papers, MDAH.

11. Stephen Duncan to James C. Wilkins, May 10, 1830, James Campbell Wilkins Papers, Box 2E547, Folder 4, NTC, CAH, UT.

12. Stephen Duncan to John Ker, December 10 (first quote) and December 20 (second quote), 1828, John Ker and Family Papers, LLMVC, LSU.

13. Birth dates of the Duncan children are: Charlotte, 1821; Henry, August 1823; Maria, January 1, 1826; Samuel, 1830; Stephen Jr., 1836. The dates for Charlotte and Samuel were calculated from the ages given at the time of their internment at Laurel Hill Cemetery in Philadelphia, but may not be exact. See Cemetery Records, Laurel Hill Cemetery, Philadelphia, Pennsylvania. Stephen and Catharine had a sixth child whose year of death is given variously as 1833 (Wainwright, 36) and 1846 (Postlethwaite Genealogical Collection, MDAH). See also, Stephen Duncan to Emily Duncan, December 24, 1864, Newbold-Irvine Papers, Box 1, Folder 7, HSP. For Henry Duncan's dates, see his obituary in the *New York Times,* December 8, 1879. For Maria Duncan's dates, see Mary Pringle Fenhagen, "Descendants of Judge Robert Pringle," *South Carolina Historical Magazine* 62 (October 1961): 223–24. For Stephen Duncan Jr.'s birth date, see Catharine Bingaman Duncan to Mary Ann Gustine, February 10, 1857, Leverich Family Papers, 2B-1, Manuscript Department, NYHS. See also Smith, 47–48.

14. Stephen Duncan to Charles P. Leverich, September 5, 1834, and October 10, 1846 (first quote), Charles P. Leverich Papers, Box 1, Folder 1, and Box 2, Folder 24, MDAH; Stephen Dun-

can to Charles P. Leverich, Monday Evening, n.d. (second quote), Leverich Family Papers, Box 2B-1, Manuscript Department, NYHS.

15. See, for example, Stephen Duncan to Lemuel P. Conner, October 25, 1844, Lemuel P. Conner Papers, LLMVC, LSU.

16. On European travel, see Travel Diaries, Stephen Duncan and Stephen Duncan Jr. Papers, LLMVC, LSU. On New England travel, see Margarett Butler to Sarah Butler, August 4, 1838, Anna and Sarah Butler Correspondence, Box 1, Folder 1, LLMVC, LSU.

17. Layout of the Washington Square home can be deciphered from a carpeting invoice. See Invoice, John D. Haegar to Stephen Duncan, October 23, 1862, Bills 1855–1862, Leverich Family Papers, Box LB-4, Manuscript Department, NYHS.

18. Stephen Duncan to John Linton, June 2, 1831, Josiah S. Johnston Papers, HSP. Notations of other Natchez families who traveled to the North can be found throughout William Johnson's diary. For example, see entries for October 25, 1842, November 1, 1846, and October 25, 1847, in Hogan and Davis, eds., 411, 546, 589.

19. Stephen Duncan to Thomas Butler, November 28, 1833, Thomas Butler and Family Papers, Box 6, Folder 33, LLMVC, LSU.

20. Stephen Duncan to Sarah Duncan, October 10, 1833 (all quotes), Newbold-Irvine Papers, Box 2, Folder 6, HSP; William A. Irvine to Thomas Butler, October 16, 1833, Thomas Butler and Family Papers, Box 6, Folder 33, LLMVC, LSU. For a history of the Irvine family, see Wainwright.

21. Writing, Sarah Jane Duncan, September 13, 1833, Newbold-Irvine Papers, Box 2, Folder 4, HSP.

22. Wainwright, 37–43. According to Wainwright, the Irvines moved to Brokenstraw after Callender's birth. Letters from Sarah Jane to Emily Duncan written in January 1838 from Brokenstraw seem to indicate otherwise.

23. Sarah Jane Duncan Irvine to Emily Duncan, September 4, 1838, Newbold-Irvine Papers, Family Correspondence, Box 1, Folder 9, HSP. The voluminous correspondence between Sarah Jane and Emily can be found throughout the Newbold-Irvine Papers.

24. Sarah Jane Irvine to Emily Duncan, February 14, 1839, Newbold-Irvine Papers, Family Correspondence, Box 1, Folder 9, HSP.

25. Sarah Jane Irvine to Sarah Duncan Blaine, April 5, 1839, Newbold-Irvine Papers, Family Correspondence, Box 1, Folder 9, HSP.

26. Sarah Jane Irvine to Sarah Duncan Blaine, December 21, 1838, Newbold-Irvine Papers, Family Correspondence, Box 1, Folder 9, HSP.

27. Sarah Jane Irvine to Matilda Duncan, January 18, 1838 (all quotes), and Sarah Jane Irvine to Emily Duncan, December 28, 1838, Newbold-Irvine Papers, Family Correspondence, Box 1, Folder 9, HSP. For a description of all the servants on the Irvine property, see Wainwright, 40–41.

28. Sarah Jane Irvine to Emily Duncan, October 19, 1838, Newbold-Irvine Papers, Family Correspondence, Box 1, Folder 9, HSP.

29. Sarah Jane often made charitable contributions to the "assylum" and the "collection for the poor." She also made what appears to be spontaneous acts of charity, which are suggested by notations such as "Poor woman 3.00," "Beggar .25," "Groceries for a poor family 1.50." See

Sarah Duncan Irvine (Mrs.), Private Account Book, 1835, 1837, 1838, Newbold-Irvine Papers, Box 3, Folder 14, HSP.

30. Sarah Jane Irvine to Emily Duncan, February 28, 1839, and Sarah Jane Irvine to Sarah Duncan Blaine, April 16, 1839, Newbold-Irvine Papers, Family Correspondence, Box 1, Folder 9, HSP; Writings, Sarah Jane Duncan, September 13, 1833, Newbold-Irvine Papers, Box 2, Folder 4, HSP.

31. Sarah Jane Irvine to Emily Duncan, December 28, 1838 (first and second quotes), and April 19, 1839 (third quote), Newbold-Irvine Papers, Family Correspondence, Box 1, Folder 9, HSP.

32. Stephen Duncan to William A. Irvine, October 15, 1838, Newbold-Irvine Papers, Family Correspondence, Box 1, Folder 9, HSP.

33. Sarah Irvine to Sarah Duncan Blaine, April 16, 1839, Newbold-Irvine Papers, Family Correspondence, Box 1, Folder 9, HSP.

34. William A. Irvine to General Callender Irvine, June 28, 1839 (first four quotes), Box 4, Folder 11, and General Callender Irvine to William A. Irvine, July 6, 1839 (last quote), Newbold-Irvine Papers, Box 4, Folder 15, Newbold-Irvine Papers, HSP.

35. Stephen Duncan to Emily Duncan, July 4, 1839, Newbold-Irvine Papers, Box 1, Folder 7, HSP.

36. Stephen Duncan to William A. Irvine, July 12, 1839, Newbold-Irvine Papers, Box 1, Folder 8, HSP.

37. Mary B. Lewis to William A. Irvine, July 7, 1839, Newbold-Irvine Papers, Box 4, Folder 19, HSP.

38. Emily Duncan to William A. Irvine, July 17, 1839, and Emily Duncan to William A. Irvine, August 3, 1839, Newbold-Irvine Papers, Family Correspondence, Box 1, Folder 5, HSP.

39. Mary B. Leiper to William A. Irvine, August 14, 1839, Newbold-Irvine Papers, Box 4, Folder 12, HSP.

40. Emily Duncan to William A. Irvine, July 17, 1839, Newbold-Irvine Papers, Family Correspondence, Box 1, Folder 5, HSP. News of the death of James Ker can be found in Diary Entry of William Johnson, August 14, 1839, in Hogan and Davis, eds., 261.

41. Stephen Duncan to William A. Irvine, August 8, 1839, Newbold-Irvine Papers, Box 1, Folder 8, HSP.

42. Margaret Ellis Irvine to Emily Duncan, August 7, 1839, and Mary Lewis to Emily Duncan, August 7, 1839, Newbold-Irvine Papers, Family Correspondence, Box 1, Folder 9, HSP. Since Margaret was a young child, her correspondence was dictated and written by someone else, such as Mary Lewis or Emily Duncan.

43. Emily Duncan to William A. Irvine, August 18 (first quote) and 22 (second quote), 1839, Newbold-Irvine Papers, Family Correspondence, Box 1, Folder 6, HSP.

44. Emily Duncan to William A. Irvine, August 18 and 22 (quote), September 3, 1839, Newbold-Irvine Papers, Family Correspondence, Box 1, Folder 6, HSP.

45. Emily Duncan to William A. Irvine, September 3, 1839, Newbold-Irvine Papers, Family Correspondence, Box 1, Folder 6, HSP.

46. Stephen Duncan to William A. Irvine, October 5, 1830, Newbold-Irvine Papers, Box 1, Folder 8, HSP (first quote); William Irvine to Irvine Children, November 14, 1839, Newbold-Irvine Papers, Box 2, Folder 15, HSP (second quote).

47. Emily Duncan to William A. Irvine, April 26, 1841 (first quote), Newbold-Irvine Papers, Box 4, Folder 21, HSP; Emily Duncan to William A. Irvine, September 26, 1842 (second quote), Newbold-Irvine Papers, Family Correspondence, Box 1, Folder 4, HSP.

48. Margaret Ellis Irvine to William A. Irvine, May 10, 1841, Newbold-Irvine Papers, Box 4, Folder 21, HSP.

49. Emily Duncan to William A. Irvine, July 28, 1842, Newbold-Irvine Papers, Family Correspondence, Box 1, Folder 4, HSP.

50. William A. Irvine Account Book, 1835–1837, 1838, Newbold-Irvine Papers, Box 48, HSP.

51. Irvine operated the sawmills and owned the general store with his cousin, Galbraith Irvine. He also invested heavily in the proposed Sunbury and Erie Railroad, which was backed by Nicholas Biddle and capital from Philadelphia, and which would run adjacent to Brokenstraw. In an attempt to generate additional revenues out of his railroad investment, Irvine built a hotel to serve travelers near the proposed terminus, but plans for the railroad quickly dissipated, leaving him in debt. In 1834–1835, the value of Irvine's stock in various banks totaled almost $63,000. William A. Irvine Daily Account Book of Stock Bought and Sold, January 1, 1834, Newbold-Irvine Papers, Box 57, HSP. Also see Wainwright, 48–71.

52. Perhaps to fill the void left by his wife's death, Irvine ran for Congress on the Whig ticket. Adamantly opposed to this endeavor, Emily Duncan told him, "I am not politician enough to feel any thing but regret at your nomination; neither have I any Expectation that the Whigs will gain their election." Not only did Irvine lose, but his candidacy caused a bitter split with his cousin and business partner, Galbraith Irvine, who was a hardline Democrat. In a surprising attempt to comfort Irvine over the loss, Emily Duncan expressed her sympathy and acknowledged that the election had "made a division between you & your cousin, but it is over now." Weeks later, she begged him, "Do try to get through your business & come away from Irvine until this political excitement is over & your opponents will find who has been their best friend." In addition to the tactics used by the opposing political party, Emily Duncan held Catholics responsible for Irvine's loss. See Emily Duncan to William A. Irvine, September 3, October 26, and November 16, 1840, Newbold-Irvine Papers, Family Correspondence, Box 1, Folder 5, HSP.

53. Wainwright, 48–71.

54. Stephen Duncan to William A. Irvine, September 12 and 18 (all quotes), 1845, Newbold-Irvine Papers, Family Correspondence, Folder 2, HSP; William A. Irvine Wool Commission Book, Newbold-Irvine Papers, Box 41, HSP.

55. Stephen Duncan to William A. Irvine, September 18, 1845, Newbold-Irvine Papers, Family Correspondence, Folder 2, HSP (first quote); Stephen Duncan to William A. Irvine, November 16, 1848, Newbold-Irvine Papers, Box 1, Folder 2, HSP (second quote); Wainwright, 60–71.

56. Stephen Duncan to William A. Irvine, May 10, 1851, Newbold-Irvine Papers, Box 1, Folder 2, HSP; Wainwright, 60–61.

57. Irvine successfully persuaded Duncan to consider the purchase as an advance on his granddaughters' inheritance. They agreed that Irvine would become Duncan's agent and that he would operate the store and lumber business for Duncan, with the profits going to meet the interest on the purchase of the Irvine property. Duncan gave Irvine the authority to liquidate pieces of the property to eliminate the advance; after doing so, any remaining real estate would go back

to Irvine. It was a workable arrangement in theory, but Irvine refused to sell any property except what was necessary to pay the taxes on it. Duncan fumed at such a stance, which lessened the size of his granddaughters' inheritance. See Wainwright, 67.

58. Stephen Duncan to Emily Duncan, January 30 (first quote) and June 23 (second quote), 1860, Newbold-Irvine Papers, Box 1, Folder 7, HSP.

59. In 1861, Margaret and Sarah were adults, and they chose to keep and live on the land. Stephen Duncan to Margaret Irvine Biddle and Sarah Duncan Irvine, May 6, 1861, Newbold-Irvine Papers, Box 2, Folder 6, HSP; Stephen Duncan to Emily Duncan, 1862, Newbold-Irvine Papers, Box 1, Folder 7, HSP (quote).

60. In order to further solidify his granddaughters' futures, Duncan established a trust account for them. Stephen Duncan to Emily Duncan, January 30, 1860, Newbold-Irvine Papers, Box 1, Folder 7, HSP; Stephen Duncan to Margaret Irvine Biddle and Sarah Duncan Irvine, May 6, 1861, Newbold-Irvine Papers, Box 2, Folder 6, HSP; Wainwright, 68.

61. Another example of Duncan risking his reputation to help out family members was the case of his nephew-in-law, William J. Minor, who also fell upon hard times during the depression. Investing in horses and horse racing (along with Adam Bingaman), Minor ran into financial troubles. Duncan frowned upon Minor's spending habits and his preoccupation with racing, which caused him to neglect his plantation and business duties. Throughout the 1840s, Minor borrowed large amounts of money from Duncan and other members of the Natchez circle. Unlike Irvine, however, Minor pulled himself out of his financial difficulties. Rothstein, "Changing Social Networks," 83–84; J. Carlyle Sitterson, "The William J. Minor Plantations: A Study in Ante-Bellum Absentee Ownership," *Journal of Southern History* 9 (February 1943): 59–67.

7. SURVIVAL OF THE FITTEST

1. For the panic of 1837 in Mississippi, see Gonzales in McLemore, ed., 1:292–93; Miles, 130–34; North, 201–3; Schweikart, 48–90.

2. Moore, *Emergence of the Cotton Kingdom in the Old Southwest*, 18–21, 192–93. For the classic argument that Jackson's specie circular caused the economic collapse of the late 1830s, see Bray Hammond, *Banks and Politics in America from the Revolution to the Civil War* (Princeton: Princeton University Press, 1957); for an alternative interpretation, which privileges the role of British interest rates and the critical flow of specie to the United States, see Peter Temin, *The Jacksonian Economy* (New York: W. W. Norton, 1969). For cotton prices, see Weems, "Bank of the Mississippi," 773; Watkins, *King Cotton*, 29–30.

3. *Philadelphia Gazette and Commercial Intelligencer*, October 2, 1839.

4. Stephen Duncan to Charles P. Leverich, October 2 and 4, 1839, Charles P. Leverich Papers, Box 1, Folder 4, MDAH.

5. Stephen Duncan to Henry Clay, October 4, 1838, Henry Clay Papers, Thomas J. Clay Collection, Library of Congress, Washington, D.C. The Sub-Treasury Bill was passed by Congress in 1840.

6. Ibid.

7. Stephen Duncan to William A. Irvine, August 8, 1839, Newbold-Irvine Papers, Box 1, Folder 8, HSP.

8. Emily Duncan to William A. Irvine, December 19, 1839, Newbold-Irvine Papers, Family Correspondence, Box 1, Folder 6, HSP (first, second, and fourth quotes); Emily Duncan to William A. Irvine, February 6, 1841, Newbold-Irvine Papers, Box 4, Folder 21, HSP (third quote).

9. Stephen Duncan to Daniel W. Coxe, December 24, 1839, Leverich Company Correspondence, LLMVC, LSU.

10. As Emily Duncan wrote William Irvine, "The Agri-Bank brother thinks *good & safe,* but no dividend for some time." Emily Duncan to William A. Irvine, August 2, 1841, Newbold-Irvine Papers, Box 4, Folder 21, HSP.

11. In a letter to William J. Minor written in December 1839, Duncan discussed his stock situation. A few months later, he informed Daniel W. Coxe that he would "explain how my stock was disposed of. It was done a year ago." Stephen Duncan to William Minor, December 6, 1839, William J. Minor and Family Papers, LLMVC, LSU; Stephen Duncan to Daniel W. Coxe, February 4, 1840, Society Small Collections, HSP.

12. Stephen Duncan to William J. Minor, December 6, 1839, William J. Minor and Family Papers, LLMVC, LSU. As he instructed Minor: "Now I would buy no more cotton—sell no more postnotes—nor do any thing else in the way of financing beyond the sum of 200,000—Nor would I give more than 10 cts. for the best cotton, in payt. of debts—The sale of . . . cotton, ought to serve as a lesson to you! It will not net you 8 cts. and you give 12. And to convert the funds into specie will cost you 8 or 9 percent. So that you will lose 40 percent at that. It would be a desperate debt—indeed that would induce me to take cotton at 10 cts."

13. Ibid.

14. Moore, *Emergence of the Cotton Kingdom in the Old Southwest,* 238–41. Stanton recovered from his loss during the 1850s, becoming one of the wealthiest land- and slaveowners in Natchez. Rothstein, "Changing Social Networks," 83–84.

15. Stephen Duncan to William A. Irvine, August 8, 1839, Newbold-Irvine Papers, Box 1, Folder 8, HSP.

16. Diary Entries of William Johnson, September 8, 16, and 17, 1839, in Hogan and Davis, eds., 265–67; Moore, *Emergence of the Cotton Kingdom in the Old Southwest,* 192.

17. Diary Entry of William Johnson, May 8, 1840, in Hogan and Davis, eds., 280; R. Bruce Davis, "The Tornado of 1840 Hits Mississippi," *Journal of Mississippi History* 36 (February 1974): 43–51; James, 271–73; Moore, *Emergence of the Cotton Kingdom in the Old Southwest,* 192.

18. Emily Duncan to William A. Irvine, May 22 (quotes) and June 1, 1840, Newbold-Irvine Papers, Family Correspondence, Box 1, Folder 5, HSP.

19. Port Royal was located somewhere in western Pennsylvania, but its exact location is unknown. See Emily Duncan to William A. Irvine, June 1 (quote) and 10, 1840, Newbold-Irvine Papers, Family Correspondence, Box 1, Folder 5, HSP; William A. Irvine Account Book, 1835–1837, 1838, Newbold-Irvine Papers, Box 48, HSP.

20. Stephen Duncan to Daniel W. Coxe, December 24, 1839, Leverich Company Correspondence, LLMVC, LSU (first quote); Stephen Duncan to Daniel W. Coxe, February 4, 1840, Society Small Collections, HSP (all other quotes).

21. Emily Duncan to William A. Irvine, April 7 (first quote) and May 24, 1841 (second quote), Newbold-Irvine Papers, Box 4, Folder 21, HSP.

22. Stephen Duncan to Daniel W. Coxe, December 24, 1839, Leverich Company Correspondence, LLMVC, LSU.

23. Indenture, Elijah F. Atchison and Wife and Stephen Duncan, March 8, 1837, Washington County Deed Records, Deed Book, Vol. F, p. 343, Office of the Chancery Clerk, Washington County Courthouse, Greenville, Mississippi. Duncan sold Surget 1,280 acres in Monroe County, 79 acres in Noxubee County, 400 acres in Oktibbeha County, 328 acres in Chickasaw County, 326 acres in Pontotoc County, 82 acres in Winston County, and 81 acres in Attala County. Land Deed, Stephen and Catharine Duncan and Francis Surget, April 3, 1837, Oktibbeha County Deed Records, Deed Book, Vol. II, pp. 530–37, Office of the Chancery Clerk, Oktibbeha County Courthouse, Starkville, Mississippi.

24. Indentures, Washington County Deed Records, Deed Books, Vol. F, pp. 245, 343, and Vol. G, p. 90, Office of the Chancery Clerk, Washington County Courthouse, Greenville, Mississippi; Indentures, Adams County Deed Records, Deed Books, Vol. Y, p. 451, Vol. AA, p. 574, and Vol. BB, p. 60, Office of the Chancery Clerk, Adams County Courthouse, Natchez, Mississippi; Indenture, Oktibbeha County Deed Records, Deed Book, Vol. II, p. 535, Office of the Chancery Clerk, Oktibbeha County Courthouse, Starkville, Mississippi.

25. Henry Postlethwaite asked Duncan for a $24,389 loan, interest-free over a five-year period, on behalf of himself and his partner, Lineus Duprey. It was secured with only one Natchez city lot. Duncan, with the assistance of Alvarez Fisk, obliged. See Indentures, Washington County Deed Records, Deed Books, Vol. F, p. 245, and Vol. G, p. 376, Office of the Chancery Clerk, Washington County Courthouse, Greenville, Mississippi; Indentures, Adams County Deed Records, Deed Books, Vol. Y, p. 451, and Vol. AA, p. 605, Office of the Chancery Clerk, Adams County Courthouse, Natchez, Mississippi.

26. Richard H. Kilbourne Jr. *Debt, Investment, Slaves: Credit Relations in East Feliciana Parish, Louisiana, 1825–1885* (Tuscaloosa: University of Alabama Press, 1995), 11. William Scarborough notes that many of the Natchez elite did have diversified holdings. He concludes that this was probably standard among the very elite throughout the South, but that it might have been more prevalent in the Natchez region than in other regions. This may be due to the fact that many of the Natchez elite had northern connections, and there was less insularity among them than among the largest land- and slaveholders in South Carolina and Georgia. See William K. Scarborough, "Lords or Capitalists? The Natchez Nabobs in Comparative Perspective," *Journal of Mississippi History* 54 (August 1992): 239–67, and *Masters of the Big House: Elite Slaveholders of the Mid-Nineteenth-Century South* (Baton Rouge: Louisiana State University Press, 2003). Morton Rothstein also touches upon the Natchez elite's diversified economies in "Natchez Nabobs," 97–112, and "Changing Social Networks," 65–88.

27. The figure of $80,000 is a conservative estimate. See Indentures, Adams County Deed Records, Deed Books: Vol. DD, p. 70; Vol. EE, pp. 333, 341, 625; Vol. FF, pp. 266, 267, 432, 582; Vol. GG, pp. 597, Office of the Chancery Clerk, Adams County Courthouse, Natchez, Mississippi; Indenture, Alcorn County Deed Records, Deed Book, Vol. G, p. 417, Office of the Chancery Clerk, Alcorn County Courthouse, Corinth, Mississippi; Indenture, Issaquena County Deed Records, Deed Book, Vol. A, p. 225, Office of the Chancery Clerk, Issaquena County

Courthouse, Mayersville, Mississippi; Conveyance, St. Mary Conveyance Records, Conveyance Book, Vol. H, p. 405, Deed #7002, Office of the Clerk of Court, St. Mary Parish Courthouse, Franklin, Louisiana.

28. If Flowers had chosen the cotton option for all seven years, she would have delivered a total of 820,000 pounds of cotton. Even assuming that Duncan was only able to sell it for four cents a pound, which was below the average price, he would have received $32,800—a $12,800 profit on his $20,000 investment. Conveyance, William P. Smith, April 1, 1844, Tensas Parish Conveyance Records, Conveyance Book, Vol. A, p. 452; Indenture, William P. Smith and Stephen Duncan, April 15, 1844, Conveyance Book, Vol. A, p. 453; Conveyance, J. W. Montgomery, Parish Judge, to Stephen Duncan, February 15, 1845, Conveyance Book, Vol. A, p. 470; Conveyance, Stephen Duncan to Ann E. Flowers, Wife of David G. Michie, May 3, 1845, Conveyance Book, Vol. A, p. 537; Conveyance, Ann E. Flowers and David G. Michie to Stephen Duncan, October 21, 1850, Conveyance Book, Vol. C, p. 154, Office of the Clerk of Court, Tensas Parish Courthouse, St. Joseph, Louisiana.

29. Indentures in Adams County Deed Records: Land Deed, Sheriff of Adams County to Stephen Duncan, July 7, 1845, Deed Book, Vol. FF, p. 75; Land Deed, Stephen and Catharine Duncan to Phoebe Beaumont, February 26, 1846, Deed Book, Vol. FF, p. 266; Mortgage, February 2, 1846, Deed Book, Vol. FF, p. 267, Office of the Chancery Clerk, Adams County Courthouse, Natchez, Mississippi.

30. Duncan's first known legal transaction with a woman was with Lydia Dowell on April 10, 1839. For $5,000, Duncan sold Dowell two lots in downtown Natchez. Land Conveyance, Stephen and Catharine Duncan and Lydia Dowell, April 10, 1839, Adams County Deed Records, Deed Book, Vol. BB, p. 60, Office of the Chancery Clerk, Adams County Courthouse, Natchez, Mississippi. On the Mississippi Married Women's Property Act, see Sandra Moncrief, "The Mississippi Married Women's Property Act of 1839," *Journal of Mississippi History* 47 (May 1985): 110–25. A brief yet helpful discussion of the historical evolution of property rights can be found in Suzanne D. Lebsock, "Radical Reconstruction and the Property Rights of Southern Women" in *Half-Sisters of History: Southern Women and the American Past*, ed. Catherine Clinton (Durham, N.C.: Duke University Press, 1994), 110–12. Also see Lebsock's excellent *The Free Women of Petersburg: Status and Culture in a Southern Town, 1784–1860* (New York: W. W. Norton, 1984).

31. Of Duncan's six loans recorded in the Adams County chancery clerk's office in the 1840s, only one was extended to an individual who had previously borrowed from him—brother-in-law Adam Bingaman. Mortgage, Adam L. Bingaman and Stephen Duncan and Gustavus Colhoun, November 24, 1847, Adams County Deed Records, Deed Book, Vol. GG, p. 128; Indenture, Adam L. Bingaman and Adam L. Bingaman Jr. and Stephen Duncan and Gustavus Colhoun, November 24, 1847, Adams County Deed Records, Deed Book, Vol. GG, p. 130, Office of the Chancery Clerk, Adams County Courthouse, Natchez, Mississippi. Indentures, Adams County Deed Records, Deed Books: Vol. EE, pp. 362, 420, 473, 477; Vol. GG, pp. 128, 130; Vol. HH, p. 100, Office of the Chancery Clerk, Adams County Courthouse, Natchez, Mississippi.

32. Agreement, Stephen Duncan and Andrew Brown Jr., February 22, 1843, Adams County Deed Records, Deed Book, Vol. EE, p. 208, Office of the Chancery Clerk, Adams County Courthouse, Natchez, Mississippi; John C. Jenkins to his brother, July 28, 1849, in William Dunbar

Jenkins, "Early History of and Life at 'Elgin,' Adams County, Miss., as Narrated by Old Letters, Papers, and Family Records," vol. 1, 1897 (quotes). This manuscript was brought to my attention by Mimi Miller of the Historic Natchez Foundation; I would like to thank her for sharing it with me. It can be found in William Dunbar Jenkins Journals, Z/1885, microfilm roll #36577, MDAH.

33. Indentures, Adams County Deed Records, Deed Books: Vol. DD, pp. 629, 667, 668; Vol. EE, pp. 208, 342; Vol. FF, pp. 75, 266, 267, 525; Vol. GG, pp. 131, 213, 304; Vol. HH, p. 96, Office of the Chancery Clerk, Adams County Courthouse, Natchez, Mississippi; Conveyances, St. Mary Conveyance Records, Conveyance Books: Vol. G, p. 414, Deed # 6548, and p. 441, Deed # 6570; St. Mary General Mortgages, Mortgage Books: Vol. 10, p. 43, Mortgage #4737; Vol. 12, p. 176, Mortgage #5888, Office of the Clerk of Court, St. Mary Parish Courthouse, Franklin, Louisiana; Conveyances, Tensas Parish Conveyance Records, Conveyance Books, Vol. A, pp. 470, 537, Office of the Clerk of Court, Tensas Parish Courthouse, St. Joseph, Louisiana; Indenture, Tippah County Deed Records, Deed Book, Vol. E, p. 13, Office of the Chancery Clerk, Tippah County Courthouse, Ripley, Mississippi; Indentures, Washington County Deed Records, Deed Books: Vol. J, p. 2; Vol. K, pp. 113, 204, 206; Vol. L, p. 327, Office of the Chancery Clerk, Washington County Courthouse, Greenville, Mississippi. For Duncan's notes, see: Mortgage, John B. Murphy and Stephen Duncan, January 18, 1840, St. Mary Parish General Mortgage Records, Mortgage Book, Vol. 10, p. 43, Mortgage #4737, and Mortgage, Hiram Anderson to Stephen Duncan, January 16, 1846, Mortgage Book, Vol. 12, p. 176, Mortgage #5888, Office of the Clerk of Court, St. Mary Parish Courthouse, Franklin, Louisiana; Conveyance, John F. Harper, Sheriff of Tensas Parish, and Stephen Duncan, November 24, 1849, Tensas Parish Conveyance Records, Conveyance Book, Vol. C, p. 81, Office of the Clerk of Court, Tensas Parish Courthouse, St. Joseph, Louisiana.

34. Land Deeds, all found in Adams County Deed Records: Charles A. LaCoste, Trustee, and Stephen Duncan, April 5, 1843, Deed Book, Vol. DD, p. 629; Assignment, Robertson, Osgood, & Wells and Stephen Duncan, May 8, 1844, Adams County Deed Records, Deed Book, Vol. EE, p. 362, and Bill of Sale, Josephus Hewett, Commissioner, and Stephen Duncan, March 25, 1847, Adams County Deed Records, Deed Book, Vol. GG, p. 131, Office of the Chancery Clerk, Adams County Courthouse, Natchez, Mississippi.

35. Charles A. LaCoste, Assignee of Frederick Stanton, and Stephen Duncan, April 27, 1843, Deed Book, Vol. DD, pp. 667–68; Stephen and Catharine Duncan and Frederick Stanton and Henry Buckner, August 25, 1846, Deed Book, Vol. FF, p. 432, Office of the Chancery Clerk, Adams County Courthouse, Natchez, Mississippi.

36. Agreement, Robert and Elizabeth McCullough and Stephen Duncan, April 22, 1841, Washington County Deed Records, Deed Books, Vol. K, p. 113, and Agreement, Zenas and Martha Preston and Stephen Duncan, August 9, 1843, Washington County Deed Records, Deed Books, Vol. K, p. 113, and Vol. L, p. 327, Office of the Chancery Clerk, Washington County Courthouse, Greenville, Mississippi. I thank Richard H. Kilbourne Jr. for his extremely generous help in deciphering these documents, as well as conveying a greater understanding of their nature.

37. See Stephen Duncan to Charles P. Leverich, December 29, 1843, Charles P. Leverich Papers, Box 1, Folder 14, MDAH; Land Deed, Stephen and Catharine Duncan and Henry P. Dun-

can, April 7, 1847, Issaquena County Deed Records, Deed Book, Vol. A, p. 255, Office of the Chancery Clerk, Issaquena County Courthouse, Mayersville, Mississippi; U.S. Bureau of the Census, Manuscript Slave Schedules, Slave Schedule II, Adams and Issaquena Counties, Mississippi, 1850; U.S. Bureau of the Census, Manuscript Agriculture Schedules, Schedule IV, Adams and Issaquena Counties, Mississippi, 1850.

38. Landholdings have been determined through an examination of the U.S. census and should be considered a very conservative estimate, given that property owned by Duncan might have been listed under a manager's or agent's name and not all of Duncan's managers and/or agents are known. Furthermore, the census does not reflect holdings in which Duncan might have been a limited partner or have held a security interest. Duncan's largest holdings were in the Mississippi Delta, where he owned 7,700 acres of land and over 500 slaves. His next largest holdings were in Adams County, with 5,310 acres of land and 201 slaves. In total, he owned over 13,000 acres and 700 slaves in Mississippi. In Louisiana, he owned 1,300 acres of land, on which he enslaved 185 men, women, and children. See U.S. Bureau of the Census, Manuscript General Population Schedule, Schedule I, Adams County, Mississippi, 1850; U.S. Bureau of the Census, Manuscript Slave Schedules, Schedule II, Adams and Issaquena Counties, Mississippi, St. Mary and Tensas Parishes, Louisiana, 1850; U.S. Bureau of the Census, Manuscript Agricultural Schedules, Schedule IV, Adams and Issaquena Counties, Mississippi, St. Mary and Tensas Parishes, Louisiana, 1850.

39. U.S. Bureau of the Census, Manuscript Agricultural Schedules, Schedule IV, Adams and Issaquena Counties, Mississippi, St. Mary and Tensas Parishes, Louisiana, 1850.

40. U.S. Bureau of the Census, Manuscript Agricultural Schedules, Schedule IV, Adams and Issaquena Counties, Mississippi, St. Mary and Tensas Parishes, Louisiana, 1850. These calculations do not include the separate holdings of Emily or Matilda Duncan, Sarah Duncan Blaine, or William Irvine, or any holdings that Stephen's sons and sons-in-law independently acquired.

41. U.S. Bureau of the Census, Manuscript Slave Schedules, Schedule II, Adams and Issaquena Counties, Mississippi, St. Mary and Tensas Parishes, Louisiana, 1850.

42. Duncan's supporters believed that his "sound to the core, on great Whig principle" would serve the party well. See Henry Willliam Huntington to James G. Taliaferro, January 30, 1849, James G. Taliaferro and Family Papers, Box 2, Folder 10, LLMVC, LSU.

43. For the Leverich brothers, see Morton Rothstein, "Changing Social Networks," 80–83, and "Natchez Nabobs," 105–7. See also Henry W. Domett, *A History of the Bank of New York, 1784–1884* (Cambridge, Mass.: Riverside Press, 1884), 97–105. For Jane Ellis and George Rapalje, see Butler, 6–10. On Duncan's relationship with Jane Ellis Rapalje, see Stephen Duncan to Thomas Butler, May 30, 1818, Thomas Butler and Family Papers, Box 4, Folder 20; Stephen Duncan to Nancy Butler, August 29, 1815, Thomas Butler and Family Papers, Box 3, Folder 17, both in LLMVC, LSU. Will, Jane Rapalje, May 11, 1817, Ellis-Farar Family Papers, Box 1, LLMVC, LSU.

44. Rothstein, "Changing Social Networks," 80–82, and "Natchez Nabobs," 103–6; Domett, 97–105.

45. The dates of the marriages are not known; however, Matilda and Charles got married in 1839, most likely in September. For the many connections between the Duncan and Gustine families, see Leverich Family Papers, 1E, Box 3, Manuscript Department, NYHS; Smith, 48; Gus-

tine Courson Weaver, *The Gustine Compendium* (Cincinnati: Powell and White, 1929), 88–90; Rothstein, "Changing Social Networks," 76, and "Natchez Nabobs," 100. Emily Duncan to William A. Irvine, August 3, 1839, Newbold-Irvine Papers, Family Correspondence, Box 1, Folder 5, HSP (quote). For the role of kinship and economic power as well as kinship as an analytical category, see Carolyn Earle Billingsley, *Communities of Kinship: Antebellum Families and the Settlement of the Cotton Frontier* (Athens: University of Georgia Press, 2004), esp. chap. 4.

46. For example, Charles Leverich's involvement in the railroad industry gave Duncan an inside track into it. By the eve of the Civil War, Duncan owned over half a million dollars worth of railroad stock. Leverich was also president of the Bank of New York. For more information on the Duncan and Leverich family relationship, as well as the activities of the Leverich brothers, see Domett and Rothstein. For correspondence between members of the Duncan and Leverich families, see the Leverich Family Papers (NYHS) and the Charles P. Leverich Papers (MDAH). For a detailed examination of the cotton factoring business as well as credit relations, see Woodman, *King Cotton and His Retainers*, and Kilbourne Jr., *Debt, Investment, Slaves.*

47. Emily Duncan to Willliam A. Irvine, November 18, 1839, Newbold-Irvine Papers, Family Correspondence, Box 1, Folder 6, HSP.

48. For Maria Duncan's marriage to J. J. Pringle, see Fenhagen, 224. For Samuel M. Davis and the Davis family, see James, 154.

8. AN EMPIRE REALIZED

1. Diary Entry, March 18, 1853, Benjamin L. C. Wailes Diaries, Book 7, MDAH.

2. Stephen Duncan to Pierce Butler, August 25, 1847, Thomas Butler and Family Papers, Box 10, Folder 63, LLMVC, LSU (quote); Dawes, 84–85.

3. Duncan gave his portion of Matilda's estate to his sisters, Emily and Mary Ann. Document, February 8, 1848, Newbold-Irvine Papers, Box 1, Folder 7, HSP; Stephen Duncan to Charles P. Leverich, September 12, 1848, Charles P. Leverich Papers, Box 3, Folder 37, MDAH; Wainwright, 44.

4. Stephen Duncan to Charles P. Leverich, October 23 and December 15 (first quote), 1848, Box 3, Folders 38 and 39; Samuel M. Davis to Charles P. Leverich, January 6, 1849, Box 3, Folder 40; Stephen Duncan to Charles P. Leverich, May 22 (second and third quotes) and May 26 (fourth and fifth quotes), 1849, Box 3, Folder 46, all in Charles P. Leverich Papers, MDAH; John C. Jenkins to his brother, July 28, 1849, in Jenkins, "Early History of and Life at 'Elgin,'" MDAH (sixth quote).

5. Wainwright, 44–45. Sarah Duncan Blaine's estate was divided between Emily and Mary Ann with the stipulation that annual sums be paid to a variety of relatives and charities, including the Indigent Widows and Single Women's Society and the Infant School Society of Philadelphia for the "colored school." Will, Sarah Duncan Blaine, October 7, 1842, Newbold-Irvine Papers, Box 3, Folder 4, HSP, and the codicil to her will dated July 12, 1848, Newbold-Irvine Papers, Family Correspondence, Folder 3, HSP.

6. Message to be telegraphed, William A. Irvine to Galbraith Irvine, 1850, Irvine Family Papers, 1777–1869, Collection #1743A, HSP (first quote); C. I. Lewis to William A. Irvine, May 17, 1850, Newbold-Irvine Papers, Box 2, Folder 16, HSP (second quote); Mary B. Leiper to

William A. Irvine, June 10, 1850, Newbold-Irvine Papers, Box 2, Folder 4, HSP (third quote); Wainwright, 45-47. On the popularity of spiritualism in this period, see Ann Braude, *Radical Spirits: Spiritualism and Women's Rights in Nineteenth-Century America* (Boston: Beacon Press, 1989).

7. Diary Entry of William Johnson, January 5, 1850, in Hogan and Davis, eds., 688; Stephen Duncan to John Ker, February 2, 1830, John Ker and Family Papers, LLMVC, LSU (quote).

8. Rothstein, "Changing Social Networks," 84-85, and "Natchez Nabobs," 106-7; Indentures, Adams County Deed Records, Deed Books: Vol. II, p. 116; Vol. KK, pp. 374, 530, 361; Vol. LL, pp. 188, 222, 261, 487; Vol. MM, pp. 124, 472, Office of the Chancery Clerk, Adams County Courthouse, Natchez, Mississippi.

9. Stephen Duncan Account Statement with C. P. Leverich, July 13, 1861–June, 1862, Leverich Family Papers, Bills, 1855–1862, Manuscript Department, NYHS.

10. Emily Duncan Account Books and Financial Statements, 1848–1865, Newbold-Irvine Papers, Box 17, Folder 1, HSP; Henry S. Leverich to Emily Duncan, January 14 and 17, May 15 and 17, 1865, HSP; Stephen Duncan to Emily Duncan, February 28, 1860, Newbold-Irvine Papers, Box 1, Folder 7, HSP (quote).

11. Stephen Duncan to Emily Duncan, December 8, 1860, Newbold-Irvine Papers, Box 1, Folder 7, HSP.

12. Ibid.

13. Stephen Duncan to Emily Duncan, December 29, 1860, Newbold-Irvine Papers, Box 1, Folder 7, HSP. It is unclear whether Emily Duncan accepted this offer.

14. Catharine Bingaman Duncan to Mary Ann Duncan Gustine, February 10, 1857, Leverich Family Papers, Box 2B-1, Manuscript Department, NYHS.

15. Catharine Duncan to Mary Ann Duncan Gustine, February 10 (quotes) and 15, 1857, Leverich Family Papers, Box 2B-1, Manuscript Department, NYHS. For studies of plantation mistresses, slaveholding women, and planter families, see Anne Firor Scott, *The Southern Lady: From Pedestal to Politics, 1830–1930* (Chicago: University of Chicago Press, 1970); Catherine Clinton, *The Plantation Mistress: Woman's World in the Old South* (New York: Pantheon, 1982); Jane Turner Censer, *North Carolina Planters and Their Children, 1800–1860* (Baton Rouge: Louisiana State University Press, 1984); Orville Vernon Burton, *In My Father's House Are Many Mansions: Family and Community in Edgefield, South Carolina* (Chapel Hill: University of North Carolina Press, 1985); Elizabeth Fox-Genovese, *Within the Plantation Household: Black and White Women of the Old South* (Chapel Hill: University of North Carolina Press, 1988); Carol Bleser, ed., *In Joy and in Sorrow: Women, Family, and Marriage in the Victorian South, 1830–1900* (New York: Oxford University Press, 1991); Victoria Bynum, *Unruly Women: The Politics of Social and Sexual Control in the Old South* (Chapel Hill: University of North Carolina Press, 1992); Brenda E. Stevenson, *Life in Black and White: Family and Community in the Slave South* (New York: Oxford University Press, 1996); Marli F. Weiner, *Mistresses and Slaves: Plantation Women in South Carolina, 1830–1880* (Urbana: University of Illinois Press, 1998).

16. Catharine Duncan to Mary Ann Duncan Gustine, February 10, 1857, Leverich Family Papers, Box 2B-1, Manuscript Department, NYHS.

17. On courtship, notions of duty and honor, and marriage in southern white men's lives, see Steven M. Stowe, *Intimacy and Power in the Old South: Ritual in the Lives of the Planters* (Bal-

timore: Johns Hopkins University Press, 1987), particularly chaps. 2 and 3. See also Bertram Wyatt-Brown, *Southern Honor: Ethics and Behavior in the Old South* (New York: Oxford University Press, 1982).

18. Writings, Stephen Duncan Jr., January 1859, Duncan Family Papers, NTC, CAH, UT.

19. Catharine Duncan to Mary Ann Duncan Gustine, February 10, 1857, Leverich Family Papers, 2B-1, Manuscript Department, NYHS.

20. Ibid.

21. Conveyance, Stephen Duncan, Esq., to Stephen Duncan, M.D., March 26, 1850, St. Mary Parish Conveyance Records, Conveyance Book, Vol. G, Deed #6688, Office of the Clerk of Court, St. Mary Parish Courthouse, Franklin, Louisiana. Duncan's cousin, Stephen Duncan, Esq., was the son of Thomas Duncan. See Smith, *Thomas Duncan*, 46. Duncan's other St. Mary Parish land transactions are found in the following St. Mary Parish Conveyance Records: Alexander Fields to Stephen Duncan, June 12, 1855, Conveyance Book, Vol. K, p. 290, Deed #8067; Gabriel Fuselier to Stephen Duncan, August 8, 1855, Conveyance Book, Vol. K, pp. 1005, 1105, Deed #8145; John M. Foote to Stephen Duncan, February 5, 1858, Conveyance Book, Vol. M, p. 337, Deed #9453, Office of the Clerk of Court, St. Mary Parish Courthouse, Franklin, Louisiana.

22. The following deeds can be found in the Adams County Deed Records: Isaac and Pamela King to Hester Cummings, July 12, 1858, Deed Book, Vol. MM, p. 54; Hester Cummings to Stephen Duncan, December 13, 1858, Deed Book, Vol. MM, p. 141; Stephen Duncan to Nanette, January 30, 1863, Deed Book, Vol. NN, p. 388, Office of the Chancery Clerk, Adams County Courthouse, Natchez, Mississippi. References to Hester Cummings can be found throughout William Johnson's diary. See esp. 81, 81 n. 60, 97, 325, 360, 635, 636, 699, 728.

23. Stephen Duncan to Pierce Butler, December 29, 1849, Thomas Butler and Family Papers, Box 12, Folder 76, LLMVC, LSU. The following land conveyances can be found in the Pointe Coupee Parish Land Conveyance Records: Conveyance, Estate of Thomas Butler to Stephen Duncan, March 4, 1850, Conveyance Book, Vol. I, Deed #1366; Stephen Duncan to Maria Duncan Pringle, November 25, 1850, Conveyance Book, Vol. III, Deed #1623, Office of the Clerk of Court, Pointe Coupee Parish, New Roads, Louisiana. The Stump Lawn transaction included the two-story residence and its furniture, two double outhouses, a stable, a carriage house, carriages, a cab, and livestock. Land Deed, Henry P. Duncan to Stephen Duncan, December 31, 1851, Adams County Deed Records, Deed Book, Vol. II, p. 36, Office of the Chancery Clerk, Adams County Courthouse, Natchez, Mississippi.

24. Land Deeds, Adams County Deed Records, Deed Books: Vol. II, p. 36; Vol. MM, p. 148, Office of the Natchez Chancery Clerk, Adams County Courthouse, Natchez, Mississippi; Land Conveyance, Pointe Coupee Parish Conveyance Records, Conveyance Book, Vol. I, Deed #1366, Office of the Clerk of Court, Pointe Coupee Parish Courthouse, New Roads, Louisiana; Land Conveyances, St. Mary Parish Conveyance Records, Conveyance Books: Vol. G, Deed #6688; Vol. K, p. 290, Deed #8067; Vol. K, pp. 1005, 1105, Deed #8145; Vol. M, p. 335, Deed #9453, Office of the Clerk of Court, St. Mary Parish Courthouse, Franklin, Louisiana.

25. Stephen Duncan to Charles P. Leverich, February 29, 1848, Charles P. Leverich Papers, Box 2, Folder 32, MDAH (first quote); Stephen Duncan to Charles P. Leverich, February 7, 1858, Leverich Family Papers, Box 2B-1, Manuscript Department, NYHS (second quote).

26. Diary Entries, December 12, 15, and 19, 1856 (quotes), Benjamin L. C. Wailes Diaries, Book 16, Special Collections Library, Duke University, Durham, North Carolina. Duncan apparently sold Homochitto the following year to Susan Conner for $7,000. Adams County Deed Records, Stephen Duncan to Susan E. Conner, March 16, 1857, Deed Book, Vol. LL, p. 576, Office of the Chancery Clerk, Adams County Courthouse, Natchez, Mississippi.

27. Indenture, Stephen and Catharine Duncan and Charlotte B. Duncan Davis, June 6, 1850, Joseph Vidal and Family Papers, LLMVC, LSU (recorded in the Issaquena County Chancery Clerk's Office on December 27, 1862); U.S. Bureau of the Census, Manuscript Slave Schedules, Schedule II, Tensas Parish, Louisiana, 1850 and 1860; L'Argent Plantation Slave Lists, 1851, Stephen Duncan and Stephen Duncan Jr. Papers, LLMVC, LSU; Indenture, Stephen and Catharine Duncan and Stephen Duncan Jr., November 25, 1856, Josiah S. Winchester Papers, NTC, CAH, UT, also recorded in Issaquena County Deed Records, Deed Book: Vol. C, p. 288, Office of the Chancery Clerk, Issaquena County Courthouse, Mayersville, Mississippi. A partial listing of Duncan plantations can be found in Road Duty Book, Slaves Liable for Road Duty, Adams County, Mississippi, Duncan Family Papers, NTC, CAH, UT. The Homochitto and Ellislie plantations were listed as being in Adams County; however, evidence also suggests that Duncan also owned plantations with those names in Issaquena County.

28. Catharine Duncan to Mary Ann Duncan Gustine, February 10, 1857, Leverich Family Papers, Box 2B-1, Manuscript Department, NYHS (quote). For exact figures on the equal division of property and assets among the Duncan heirs, see the indenture between Stephen and Catharine Duncan and Stephen Duncan Jr., November 25, 1856, Josiah S. Winchester Papers, NTC, CAH, UT, also recorded in Issaquena County Deed Records, Deed Book: Vol. C, p. 288, Office of the Chancery Clerk, Issaquena County Courthouse, Mayersville, Mississippi.

29. Conveyance, Stephen Duncan to Andrew McWilliams, April 12, 1859, St. Mary Parish Conveyance Records, Conveyance Book, Vol. N, p. 72, Deed #9889, and p. 78, Deed #9890, Office of the Clerk of Court, St. Mary Parish Courthouse, Franklin, Louisiana; Andrew McWilliams to Charles P. Leverich, April 9, 1859, Leverich Family Papers, Box 2A-1, Manuscript Department, NYHS (quote).

30. Andrew McWilliams to Charles P. Leverich, November 16 (first and second quotes) and 25 (third–fifth quotes), 1859, Leverich Family Papers, Box 2A-1, Manuscript Department, NYHS.

31. Andrew McWilliams to Charles P. Leverich, November 25, 1859, Leverich Family Papers, Box 2A-1, Manuscript Department, NYHS.

32. Although McWilliams was able to make his payments on Duncan's note, natural forces beyond his control contributed to another short year in 1860, which might have contributed to his decision to leave the partnership. He noted to Charles Leverich that "I have done my part, & this failure is caused by the hand of providence over which I have no *power*. I hope for better luck next time." Andrew McWilliams to Charles P. Leverich, October 11, 1860 (quote), and December 29, 1859, Leverich Family Papers, Box 2A-1, Manuscript Department, NYHS. Sale of partnership can be found in Andrew McWilliams to Stephen Duncan, January 19, 1861, St. Mary Conveyance Records, Conveyance Book: Vol. N, p. 242, Deed #10606, Office of the Clerk of Court, St. Mary Parish Courthouse, Franklin, Louisiana.

33. Indenture, Stephen and Catharine Duncan to Charlotte B. Duncan Davis, June 6, 1850,

Joseph Vidal and Family Papers, LLMVC, LSU; Indenture, Stephen and Catharine Duncan to Stephen Duncan Jr., November 25, 1856, Josiah S. Winchester Papers, NTC, CAH, UT; Indentures, Adams County Deed Records, Deed Books: Vol. HH, pp. 179, 323, 324, 357, 427, 649; Vol. II, pp. 128, 158; Vol. KK, pp. 250, 292; Vol. LL, pp. 201, 278, 576; Vol. QQ, p. 108, Office of the Chancery Clerk, Adams County Courthouse, Natchez, Mississippi; Indenture, Issaquena County Deed Records, Deed Book, Vol. C, p. 288, Office of the Chancery Clerk, Issaquena County Courthouse, Mayersville, Mississippi; Conveyance, Pointe Coupee Parish Conveyance Records, Conveyance Book, Vol. III, Deed #1623, Office of the Clerk of Court, Pointe Coupee Parish Courthouse, New Roads, Louisiana; Conveyance, St. Mary Parish Conveyance Records, Conveyance Book, Vol. N, p. 72, Deed #9889, Office of the Clerk of Court, St. Mary Parish Courthouse, Franklin, Louisiana; Conveyance, Tensas Parish Conveyance Records, Conveyance Books, Vol. D, pp. 187, 315, Office of the Clerk of Court, Tensas Parish Courthouse, St. Joseph, Louisiana; Indenture, Wilkinson County Deed Records, Deed Book, Vol. P, p. 588, Office of the Chancery Clerk, Wilkinson County Courthouse, Woodville, Mississippi.

34. U.S. Bureau of the Census, Manuscript Agricultural Schedules, Schedule IV, Issaquena County, Mississippi, 1850 and 1860.

35. Overall, the family's assets increased 444 percent in value. This can be seen most dramatically in regard to individual plantations. Carlisle appreciated over 1,000 percent between 1850 and 1860; the combined value of its land, equipment, and livestock increased 837 percent. Similarly, Holly Ridge rose in value from $19,500 in 1850 to $234,120 in 1860—a 1,100.6 percent increase. U.S. Bureau of the Census, Manuscript Agricultural Schedules, Schedule IV, Issaquena County, Mississippi, and Pointe Coupee, St. Mary, and Tensas Parishes, Louisiana, 1850 and 1860 Tax Receipt, State of Mississippi, Adams County, 1860, Stephen Duncan and Stephen Duncan Jr. Papers, LLMVC, LSU.

36. U.S. Bureau of the Census, Manuscript Slave Schedules, Schedule II, Adams and Issaquena Counties, Mississippi, and Pointe Coupee, St. Mary, and Tensas Parishes, Louisiana, 1860; U.S. Bureau of the Census, *Population of the United States in 1860; Compiled from the Original Returns of the Eighth Census* (Washington, D.C.: Government Printing Office, 1864), 270; Plantation Slave Lists for 1861, Stephen Duncan and Stephen Duncan Jr. Papers, LLMVC, LSU.

9. UNDERGROUND NETWORKS

1. Stephen Duncan to Charles P. Leverich, May 7, 19, 22 (first quote), 26 (second quote), and 31, 1849, Charles P. Leverich Papers, Box 3, Folder 46, MDAH. For a discussion of cholera as well as general slave health, see Todd L. Savitt, *Medicine and Slavery: The Diseases and Health Care of Blacks in Antebellum Virginia* (Urbana: University of Illinois Press, 1978); Margaret Humphreys, *Yellow Fever and the South* (New Brunswick, N.J.: Rutgers University Press, 1992).

2. Carlisle Plantation Slave Lists, 1851, 1856, and 1862, Stephen Duncan and Stephen Duncan Jr. Papers, LLMVC, LSU.

3. U.S. Bureau of the Census, Manuscript Slave Schedules, Schedule II, Adams and Issaquena Counties, Mississippi, and Pointe Coupee and Tensas Parishes, Louisiana, 1860; Land

Conveyance, Stephen Duncan to Andrew McWilliams, April 12, 1859, St. Mary Parish Conveyance Records, Conveyance Book, Vol. N, p. 72, Deed #9889, Office of the Clerk of Court, St. Mary Parish Courthouse, Franklin, Louisiana; Auburn, Camperdown, Carlisle, Duncannon, Ellislie, Homochitto, L'Argent, Middlesex, Oakley, Oxford, and Reserve Plantation Slave Lists, 1851–1862, Stephen Duncan and Stephen Duncan Jr. Papers, LLMVC, LSU.

4. In 1860, the average number of slaves per large agricultural unit (50 or more slaves) in Pointe Coupee Parish was 99.48 slaves. One hogshead consists of 1,000 pounds of sugar. One cotton bale equals 400 pounds. U.S. Bureau of the Census, Manuscript Slave Schedule, Schedule II, and Manuscript Agricultural Schedule, Schedule IV, Pointe Coupee Parish, Louisiana, 1860; Joseph Karl Menn, *The Large Slaveholders of Louisiana, 1860* (New Orleans: Pelican, 1964), 314–23.

5. U.S. Bureau of the Census, Manuscript Agricultural Schedules, Schedule IV, Adams and Issaquena Counties, Mississippi, and Pointe Coupee, St. Mary, and Tensas Parishes, Louisiana, 1860. In 1860, cotton prices in New York averaged eleven cents per pound; the average price of a hogshead of sugar was $82 in New Orleans. That year, the Duncans produced 1,473 hogsheads of sugar worth $120,786 and 2,883,600 pounds of cotton worth $317,196. For prices see, Gray, 2:1027, 1033; Watkins, 30.

6. Eugene D. Genovese, *Roll, Jordan, Roll: The World the Slaves Made* (New York: Vintage, 1974), 5 (quote). For challenges to Genovese as well as reinterpretations of paternalism, see James Oakes, *The Ruling Race: A History of American Slaveholders* (New York: Alfred A. Knopf, 1982) and *Slavery and Freedom: An Interpretation of the Old South* (New York: Alfred A. Knopf, 1990); Laurence Shore, *Southern Capitalists: The Ideological Leadership of an Elite, 1832–1835* (Chapel Hill: University of North Carolina Press, 1986); Joan Cashin, *Family Venture: Men and Women on the Southern Frontier* (New York: Oxford University Press, 1991); Joseph P. Reidy, *From Slavery to Agrarian Capitalism in the Cotton Plantation South: Central Georgia, 1800–1880* (Chapel Hill: University of North Carolina Press, 1992); Scarborough, "Lords or Capitalists? The Natchez Nabobs in Comparative Perspective," 239–67, and *Masters of the Big House*, esp. chap. 11; Shearer Davis Bowman, *Masters and Lords: Mid-Nineteenth-Century U.S. Planters and Prussian Junkers* (New York: Oxford University Press, 1993); Morris, *Becoming Southern*; William Dusinberre, *Them Dark Days: Slavery in the American Rice Swamps* (New York: Oxford University Press, 1996); Jeffrey R. Young, *Domesticating Slavery: The Master Class in Georgia and South Carolina, 1670–1837* (Chapel Hill: University of North Carolina Press, 1999); Edward E. Baptist, *Creating an Old South: Middle Florida's Plantation Frontier before the Civil War* (Chapel Hill: University of North Carolina Press, 2002); Stephanie M. H. Camp, *Closer to Freedom: Enslaved Women and Everyday Resistance in the Plantation South* (Chapel Hill: University of North Carolina Press, 2004).

7. Even after Duncan conveyed certain plantations to his sons and sons-in-law, he maintained the slave lists for those plantations. Slaves were listed by their given names in what appears to be households or family groupings; in some instances, surnames and ages were also included. Plantation Slave Lists, 1851–1862, Stephen Duncan and Stephen Duncan Jr. Papers, LLMVC, LSU. Most (66.9 percent) of slave households contained children. U.S. Bureau of the Census, Manuscript Slave Schedule, Schedule II, Adams and Issaquena Counties, Mississippi, 1860.

8. Plantation Slave Lists, 1851–1862, Stephen Duncan and Stephen Duncan Jr. Papers, LLMVC, LSU.

9. Ibid.

10. Ibid.

11. Nine of the 25 new households created between 1851 and 1861 were made up of members who lived in different households in 1851. Carlisle Slave Lists, 1851, 1856, and 1861, Stephen Duncan and Stephen Duncan Jr. Papers, LLMVC, LSU.

12. Oakley Slave Lists, 1851 and 1862, Stephen Duncan and Stephen Duncan Jr. Papers, LLMVC, LSU.

13. Ibid.

14. Duncannon Slave Lists, 1851 and 1862, Stephen Duncan and Stephen Duncan Jr. Papers, LLMVC, LSU.

15. Households where the head of household is not known (3.3 percent) were eliminated from the sample.

16. Herbert G. Gutman, *The Black Family in Slavery and Freedom, 1750–1925* (New York: Vintage Books, 1976); Leslie H. Owens, *This Species of Property: Slave Life and Culture in the Old South* (New York: Oxford University Press, 1976); Jacqueline Jones, *Labor of Love, Labor of Sorrow: Black Women, Work, and the Family from Slavery to the Present* (New York: Basic Books, 1985); Deborah Gray White, *Ar'n't I A Woman? Female Slaves in the Plantation South*, rev. ed. (New York: W. W. Norton, 1999); Allan Kulikoff, *Tobacco and Slaves: The Development of Southern Cultures in the Chesapeake, 1680–1800* (Chapel Hill: University of North Carolina Press, 1986); Ann Patton Malone, *Sweet Chariot: Slave Family and Household Structure in Nineteenth-Century Louisiana* (Chapel Hill: University of North Carolina Press, 1992); Peter Kolchin, *American Slavery, 1619–1877* (New York: Hill & Wang, 1993); Wilma King, *Stolen Childhood: Slave Youth in Nineteenth-Century America* (Bloomington: Indiana University Press, 1995); Stevenson, *Life in Black and White*; Dusinberre, *Them Dark Days*; Hudson Jr., *To Have and To Hold*; Larry E. Rivers, *Slavery in Florida: Territorial Days to Emancipation* (Tallahassee: University of Florida Press, 2000); Marie Jenkins Schwarz, *Born in Bondage: Growing Up Enslaved in the Antebellum South* (Cambridge, Mass.: Harvard University Press, 2000); Baptist, *Creating an Old South*; Emily West, *Chains of Love: Slave Couples in Antebellum South Carolina* (Urbana: University of Illinois Press, 2004).

17. Stevenson, *Life in Black and White*, esp. xxii (first quote), 160 (second quote), 159–257. In *Them Dark Days*, Dusinberre also critically examines the effects of slavery on the slave family and its formation. See esp. 84–121.

18. Malone, esp. 13–19, 258.

19. Ibid., 13–19; Plantation Slave Lists, 1851–1862, Stephen Duncan and Stephen Duncan Jr. Papers, LLMVC, LSU.

20. The extant records do not indicate specific slave marriages.

21. Duncannon Slave Lists, 1851 and 1862, Stephen Duncan and Stephen Duncan Jr. Papers, LLMVC, LSU.

22. Reserve slave lists, 1851 and 1862, Stephen Duncan and Stephen Duncan Jr. Papers, LLMVC, LSU.

23. Carlisle Slave Lists, 1851, 1856, and 1861, Stephen Duncan and Stephen Duncan Jr. Papers, LLMVC, LSU.

24. Gutman, *Black Family*, 155–59, and charts 10, 11, and 12 (i-iv); Carlisle Slave Lists, 1851, 1856, and 1861, Stephen Duncan and Stephen Duncan Jr. Papers, LLMVC, LSU.

25. Gutman, *Black Family*, 158.

26. Testimony of Samuel B. Smith, Esq., before the American Freedmen's Inquiry Commission, November 19, 1863, in Ira Berlin et al., eds., *Freedom: A Documentary History of Emancipation, 1861–1867*, ser. 1, vol. 3, *The Wartime Genesis of Free Labor: The Lower South* (New York: Cambridge University Press, 1990), 749–54 (quote, 752).

27. In order to determine slave naming patterns, a sample of 223 families consisting of 675 children was examined across eight categories of naming patterns. These categories included children who were named after their 1) father, 2) mother, 3) other family member, such as grandparent, aunt, uncle, or sibling, 4) Biblical figure, 5) historical or classical figure, 6) African heritage, 7) a member of the Duncan family, or 8) none of the above.

28. Genovese, *Roll, Jordan, Roll*, 440–50; Gutman, *Black Family*, 185–201; Cheryll Ann Cody, "There Was No 'Absalom' on the Ball Plantations: Slave-Naming Practices in the South Carolina Low County, 1720–1865," *American Historical Review* 92 (June 1987): 563–96; Joyner, 217–22; Wood, 181–86.

29. Names can only be traced between 1851 and 1863, obscuring children who were named after relatives no longer living, or who might have been sold. Plantation Slave Lists, 1851–1862, Stephen Duncan and Stephen Duncan Jr. Papers, LLMVC, LSU.

30. Herbert Gutman's analysis of plantations in North Carolina and Louisiana reveal that over 40 percent of slave families named a child after the father and that, in some cases, half of slave families had named a child after a grandfather. See Gutman, *Black Family*, 185–201. In her study of the slaves on James Henry Hammond's South Carolina plantations, Drew Faust notes that 33.3 percent of slaves or slave families were named after the father. See Faust, 83–84, 392. According to Cheryll Ann Cody's exhaustive study of the Ball family plantations in South Carolina between 1800 and 1865, some 27.1 percent of slave families named a child after the father. See Cody, esp. 592. In a few instances, a father's name may have been given to a daughter, but in a feminine form. Plantation Slave Lists, 1851–1862, Stephen Duncan and Stephen Duncan Jr. Papers, LLMVC, LSU.

31. Gutman, *Black Family*, 190. Cody concluded that 15.3 percent of slave families named a daughter after a mother, while 37.5 percent of families named a daughter after a paternal grandmother and 20 percent after a paternal grandmother. Between 1720 and 1799, the frequency of naming a daughter after a maternal grandmother was as high as 70.6 percent. See Cody, 563–96, esp. 591–92. In *Stolen Childhood*, King also notes the high incidence of naming children after grandparents (pp. 6–7). Within the Duncan slave communities, the percentage of slaves naming children after a mother is closer to the pattern that Faust found on the Hammond plantations. Faust calculates that 5.9 percent of slaves or slave families were named in this manner. See Faust, 392. In a few instances within the Duncan slave communities, a boy was given a masculine form of his mother's name. Plantation Slave Lists, 1851–1862, Stephen Duncan and Stephen Duncan Jr. Papers, LLMVC, LSU.

32. Plantation Slave Lists, 1851–1862, Stephen Duncan and Stephen Duncan Jr. Papers, LLMVC, LSU.

33. Cody calculates that between 1840 and 1865, 39.5 percent of boys and 15.2 percent of girls

were given biblical names, compared to 6.4 percent of all children on the Duncan plantations. Cody, 581–82; Plantation Slave Lists, 1851–1862, Stephen Duncan and Stephen Duncan Jr. Papers, LLMVC, LSU.

34. This naming practice, which includes derivatives of traditional African names, was more prevalent in some slave communities than others. Gutman notes that African names were far less common by the mid-nineteenth century. See Gutman, *Black Family,* 186, 576 n. 4; Plantation Slave Lists, 1851–1862, Stephen Duncan and Stephen Duncan Jr. Papers, LLMVC, LSU.

35. Plantation Slave Lists, 1851–1862, Stephen Duncan and Stephen Duncan Jr. Papers, LLMVC, LSU. For a discussion of African names, see Gutman, *Black Family,* 186, chap. 5; Joyner, 217–24; Wood, 181–85.

36. Quote from Faust, 84. For the period 1840–1865, 0.4 percent of males and 5.8 percent of females had African names. Cody, 581–82.

37. On the master's influence on slave naming practices, see Joyner, 217; King, 7–8. Slave communities on the Duncan plantations were in alignment with Gutman's findings that less than 1 percent of slaves had classical names. Interestingly, Cody found that between 1840 and 1865, 10 percent of males and 10.8 percent of females on the Ball plantations had classical names—a much higher figure than on the Duncan plantations (2.7 percent). See Gutman, *Black Family,* 186; Cody, 580, 582.

38. Of the Duncan slaves who shared a name with a member of the Duncan family, 66.7 percent were male and 33.3 percent were female. Though these statistics are useful, the qualitative aspects of this naming practice should not be forgotten. As Drew Faust notes (p. 88), James Henry Hammond "gave names to slave offspring frequently enough to remind fathers and mothers that he, not they, owned new infants. Naming a child was not their right, he insisted, but a privilege the master could either grant or withhold." Plantation Slave Lists, 1851–1862, Stephen Duncan and Stephen Duncan Jr. Papers, LLMVC, LSU.

39. In 1850, St. Mary Parish contained 9,850 slaves, who comprised 72 percent of the parish population, of which Duncan owned 3.4 percent. Tensas Parish had one of Louisiana's highest planter absenteeism rates: in 1860, it had a population of 14,592 slaves, who outnumbered whites ten to one and comprised 91 percent of the parish population. In Issaquena County, blacks outnumbered whites twelve to one and comprised 92.5 percent of the county population. The Duncan family owned 14.6 percent of the 7,244 slaves in Issaquena County. See U.S. Bureau of the Census, *Seventh Census of the United States: 1850* (Washington, D.C.: Robert Armstrong, 1853), 473, 484, 486; U.S. Bureau of the Census, *Population of the United States in 1860; Compiled from the Original Returns of the Eighth Census* (Washington, D.C.: Government Printing Office, 1864), 194, 270.

40. Herbert G. Gutman, *Slavery and the Numbers Game: A Critique of* Time on the Cross (Urbana: University of Illinois Press, 1975), 140–47; Gutman, *Black Family;* Malone, 175–79, 232; Stevenson, 245–49; James Trussel and Richard Steckel, "The Age of Slaves at Menarche and Their First Birth," *Journal of Interdisciplinary History* 8 (Winter 1978): 477–505.

41. This average was computed from the data of 164 mothers on Reserve, Duncannon, Oakley, Carlisle, Ellislie, Middlesex, Homochitto, L'Argent, Oxford, and Camperdown plantations. The records only note children who survived and/or were recorded; therefore, the average does not reflect children who were sold, who died, or who were not recorded. Extremely old or young

ages for individual mothers were eliminated from the sample. See Plantation Slave Lists, 1851–1862, Stephen Duncan and Stephen Duncan Jr. Papers, LLMVC, LSU.

42. Ibid. For further discussion about female slave fertility and childbearing, see Jones, *Labor of Love, Labor of Sorrow,* 11–43, esp. 18–20; White, *Ar'n't I a Woman,* esp. chaps. 2 and 3; Jennifer L. Morgan, *Laboring Women: Reproduction and Gender in New World Slavery* (Philadelphia: University of Pennsylvania Press, 2004).

43. On the Good Hope plantation in South Carolina, half of the slave families had seven or more children. Gutman, *Black Family,* 50–51. The average for Virginia was 4.94 children; in Loudoun County, the average was between five and six children. Stevenson, 245–49. On Louisiana plantations, slave women had an average of between five and seven children. See Malone, 175–79. The overall and somewhat suspect average of 9.24 children per mother can be found in Robert W. Fogel, *Without Consent or Contract: The Rise and Fall of American Slavery* (New York: W. W. Norton, 1989), 149. For an in-depth examination of this issue through case studies of individual plantations in Georgia and South Carolina, see Dusinberre, esp. chap. 8.

44. On Reserve, 25 mothers gave birth to 102 live children for an average of 4.08 births per mother. Individual plantation averages, as well as aggregate averages, may not reflect children who were sold, who had died, or who were not recorded. Data compiled from a total sample of 211 mothers and 720 children on Reserve, Duncannon, Oakley, Carlisle, Ellislie, Middlesex, Homochitto, L'Argent, Oxford, and Camperdown plantations. See Plantation Slave Lists, 1851–1862, Stephen Duncan and Stephen Duncan Jr. Papers, LLMVC, LSU.

45. For general figures across the South, see Fogel, 147–49; Malone, 177–78; Stevenson, 245–49. The average number of years between slave children was computed from the Plantation Slave Lists, 1851–1862, Stephen Duncan and Stephen Duncan Jr. Papers, LLMVC, LSU. The totals given may not reflect children who were sold, who had died, or who were not recorded. Some mothers had extremely long intervals between births—five or six years. Extremely high child spacing ratios were eliminated from the sample.

46. Deborah White argues that the focus on "female labor in the fields superseded childbearing in importance" in the lower South states and therefore may account for the "lower black fertility rates in the lower and newer regions of the South (Alabama, Mississippi, Louisiana, and Texas)." See White, 69–70, 85–86 (quote, 69). William Dusinberre also notes the harshness of the work regime's affect on a woman's ability to bear children, writing, "One mother—who had two miscarriages, and all but one of whose children had died—suggested the causal connection between the women's work hours of field labor and the dreadful mortality rate among their infants." See Dusinberre, 243 (quote)–245. On abortion among slave women, see Davis, 3–15; Fox-Genovese, 324; White, 85–86; Morgan, *Laboring Women,* 113–14.

47. Plantation Slave List, 1851–1862, and Middlesex Slave List, 1862, Stephen Duncan and Stephen Duncan Jr. Papers, LLMVC, LSU.

48. For a complete discussion of slave housing, see John W. Blassingame, *The Slave Community: Plantation Life in the Antebellum South,* 2nd ed. (New York: Oxford University Press, 1979); Paul A. David et al., *Reckoning with Slavery: A Critical Study in the Quantitative History of American Negro Slavery* (New York: Oxford University Press, 1976); Dusinberre, *Them Dark Days;* Genovese, *Roll, Jordan, Roll;* Owens, *This Species of Property;* George P. Rawick, *From Sundown to Sunup: The Making of the Black Community* (Westport, Conn.: Greenwood Press, 1972);

George W. McDaniel, *Hearth and Home: Preserving a People's Culture* (Philadelphia: Temple University Press, 1982); John M. Vlach, *Back of the Big House: The Architecture of Plantation Slavery* (Chapel Hill: University of North Carolina Press, 1993).

49. U.S. Bureau of the Census, Manuscript Slave Schedules, Schedule II, Issaquena County, Mississippi, and Pointe Coupee and Tensas Parishes, Louisiana, 1860; Menn, 320-21; Carlisle, Duncannon, and Reserve Plantation Supply Lists, 1864, Stephen Duncan and Stephen Duncan Jr. Papers, LLMVC, LSU; Invoice to Stephen Duncan for 240 Blue Gray Blankets for Camperdown and Oxford, C. W. & J. T. Moore & Co., Bills, 1855-1862, Leverich Papers, Box LB-4, Manuscript Department, NYHS.

50. For more on slave rations and diet, see Blassingame, 251-54; David et al., 243; Fox-Genovese, 160-61, Genovese, *Roll, Jordan, Roll*, 62-63; 486; Owens, 50-51; Savitt, 86-98.

51. Plantation Supply Lists, 1861-1862; Carlisle, Duncannon, and Reserve Plantation Supply Lists, 1864, Stephen Duncan and Stephen Duncan Jr. Papers, LLMVC, LSU.

52. Camperdown Plantation Supply List, 1851; Carlisle Plantation Supply Lists, 1856, 1861 (first quote), and 1864; Carlisle and Reserve Plantation Supply Lists, 1864 (second quote); Duncannon and Reserve Plantation Supply Lists, 1864, Stephen Duncan and Stephen Duncan Jr. Papers, LLMVC, LSU. For a general discussion of slave clothing see, Blassingame, 251-54; Fox-Genovese, 120-28, 179-80, and passim; Genovese, *Roll, Jordan, Roll*, 550-61; Rawick, 73-74.

53. Stephen Duncan to Thomas Butler, May 30, 1818, Thomas Butler and Family Papers, Box 4, Folder 20, LLMVC, LSU (third quote); Stephen Duncan to William J. Minor, July 23, 1842, William J. Minor and Family Papers, LLMVC, LSU (second quote); Stephen Duncan to William A. Irvine, September 18, 1845, Newbold-Irvine Papers, Family Correspondence, Folder 2, HSP (first quote).

54. Stephen Duncan to Thomas Butler, July 1, 1823, Thomas Butler and Family Papers, Box 5, Folder 25, LLMVC, LSU.

55. Stephen Duncan to Leverich Company, January 29, 1859, Leverich Family Papers, Box 2A-1, Manuscript Department, NYHS.

56. Berlin et al., eds., *Freedom: A Documentary History of Emancipation, 1861-1867*, ser. 2, *The Black Military Experience* (New York: Cambridge University Press, 1982), 149.

57. In a letter written on December 21, 1853, and published the following April, Duncan noted that his slaves could complete their tasks when they "work[ed] with ordinary spirit," thus implying that he recognized that they did not always hold to his pace. Stephen Duncan, Letters to Editor, *American Cotton Planter* 2 (April 1854).

58. Andrew McWilliams to Charles P. Leverich, March 16, 1859, Leverich Family Papers, Box 2C, Manuscript Department, NYHS.

59. Andrew McWilliams to Charles P. Leverich, March 26 (first and second quotes) and April 10 (third quote), 1859, Leverich Family Papers, Box 2C, Manuscript Department, NYHS.

EPILOGUE

1. Stephen Duncan to Emily Duncan, December 15, 1860, Newbold-Irvine Papers, Box 1, Folder 7, HSP.

2. U.S. Bureau of the Census, Manuscript Agricultural Schedules, Schedule IV, Adams and

Issaquena Counties, Mississippi, and Pointe Coupee, St. Mary, and Tensas Parishes, Louisiana, 1860; Manifold of Duncan Securities, April 18, 1856, in James, 151; Stephen Duncan Securities List, May 1861, Leverich Family Papers, Bills, 1855–1862, Manuscript Department, NYHS; Stephen Duncan to Emily Duncan, December 15, 1860, Newbold-Irvine Papers, Box 1, Folder 7, HSP.

3. U.S. Bureau of the Census, Manuscript Slave Schedules, Schedule II, Adams and Issaquena Counties, Mississippi, and Pointe Coupee, St. Mary, and Tensas Parishes, Louisiana, 1860; Plantation Slave Lists, 1861, Stephen Duncan and Stephen Duncan Jr. Papers, LLMVC, LSU.

4. Stephen Duncan to Charles P. Leverich, December 22, 1859, Stephen Duncan Letters, MSS Collection #4641, LLMVC, LSU.

5. Stephen Duncan to Emily Duncan, December 15, 1860, Newbold-Irvine Papers, Box 1, Folder 7, HSP.

6. Stephen Duncan to Emily Duncan, December 29, 1860, Newbold-Irvine Papers, Box 1, Folder 7, HSP.

7. Stephen Duncan to Emily Duncan, May 13 (first, second, and sixth quotes) and 27 (seventh–eighth quotes), June 8 (third–fifth quotes), 1861, Newbold-Irvine Papers, Box 1, Folder 7, HSP.

8. Stephen Duncan to Emily Duncan, June 8, 1861, Newbold-Irvine Papers, Box 1, Folder 7, HSP.

9. Andrew McWilliams to Stephen Duncan, May 7, 1861, Leverich Family Papers, Box 2A-1, Manuscript Department, NYHS.

10. Wade Hampton III to Mary Fisher Hampton, January 14, 1864, in *Family Letters of the Three Wade Hamptons, 1782–1901*, ed. Charles E. Cauthen (Columbia: University of South Carolina Press, 1953), 101–2. On Hampton's indebtedness to Duncan, see Scarborough, *Masters of the Big House*, 391–92.

11. The estate of Stephen Duncan later filed claims for the stolen and destroyed property. Brief for Claimants, Executors of Stephen Duncan, Deceased, v. the United States, No. 2756, filed in the U.S. Court of Claims, December Term, 1874, MDAH; Estimate of Plantation Expenses (1864?), Stephen Duncan and Stephen Duncan Jr. Papers, LLMVC, LSU.

12. Mary Duncan to General Thomas, June 2, 1863, in Berlin et al., eds., *Freedom*, ser. 2, *Black Military Experience*, 147–48 (first quote); Mary Duncan to Abraham Lincoln, May 24, 1863, microfilm 23653, series 1, reel 53 Abraham Lincoln Papers, Library of Congress, Washington, D.C. (all other quotes); James, 152.

13. Stephen Duncan to Mary Lincoln, August 25, 1863, microfilm 25824, series 1, reel 57, Abraham Lincoln Papers, Library of Congress, Washington, D.C.

14. Stephen Duncan to Emily Duncan, December 24, 1864, Newbold-Irvine Papers, Box 1, Folder 7, HSP.

15. Stephen Duncan Jr. to Stephen Duncan, January 11, 1863 [1864?], Stephen Duncan Correspondence, Folder 1, LLMVC, LSU.

16. Henry P. Duncan to Stephen Duncan, July 21, 1865, Stephen Duncan Correspondence, Folder 1, LLMVC, LSU.

17. Mary Duncan to Abraham Lincoln, May 24, 1863, microfilm 23653, series 1, reel 53, Abraham Lincoln Papers, Library of Congress, Washington, D.C.; Stephen Duncan to Mary Lincoln,

August 25, 1863, microfilm 25824, series 1, reel 57, Abraham Lincoln Papers, Library of Congress, Washington, D.C.; F. Surget to Stephen Duncan, July 17 and August 3, 1865, Henry Duncan to Stephen Duncan, July 21, 1865, ? to Stephen Duncan, August 2, 1865, Henry P. Duncan to Dr. Stephen Duncan, August 5, 1865, Adam Badeau to Stephen Duncan, October 29, 1865, Charlotte Duncan Davis to Stephen Duncan, July and August 1, 1865, all in Stephen Duncan Correspondence, Folder 1, LLMVC, LSU.

18. Certificate of Death, Dr. Stephen Duncan, January 29, 1867, Department of Records, New York City Municipal Archives, New York, New York. For Duncan's funeral and burial wishes, see Stephen Duncan to Emily Duncan, December 24, 1864, Newbold-Irvine Papers, Box 1, Folder 7, HSP (quote).

+>-<+

BIBLIOGRAPHY

PRIMARY SOURCES

MANUSCRIPTS

Center for American History, University of Texas, Austin

Powhatan Ellis Papers

Natchez Trace Collection

Duncan Family Papers
Natchez Trace Steamboat Collection
Gabriel Tichenor Papers
Benjamin L. C. Wailes Papers
Levin Wailes Papers
James Campbell Wilkins Papers
Josiah S. Winchester Papers

Historical Society of Pennsylvania, Philadelphia

Chaloner and White Papers
Tench Coxe Papers
Irvine Family Papers, 1778–1843, Collection #1743 B
Josiah S. Johnston Papers
Newbold-Irvine Papers
Newbold-Irvine Papers, Family Correspondence
Society Miscellaneous Collection
Society Small Collections

Howard-Tilton Memorial Library, Tulane University, New Orleans

Benjamin Farar Papers, Collection #65

Library of Congress, Washington, D.C.

Henry Clay Papers in the Thomas J. Clay Collection
Papers of Abraham Lincoln

*Louisiana and Lower Mississippi Valley Collections, Hill Memorial Library,
Louisiana State University, Baton Rouge*

Anna and Sarah Butler Correspondence
Thomas Butler and Family Papers
Lemuel P. Conner Papers
Stephen Duncan Letters, Manuscript #4641
Stephen Duncan and Stephen Duncan Jr. Papers
William St. John Elliott Papers
Ellis-Farar Family Papers
John Ker and Family Papers
Leverich Company Correspondence
James G. Taliaferro and Family Papers
Joseph Vidal and Family Papers

Manuscript Department, New York Historical Society, New York City

Leverich Family Papers

Mississippi Department of Archives and History, Jackson

Jefferson College Papers
William Dunbar Jenkins Journals
Charles P. Leverich Papers
Natchez Steamboat Company Stock Certificate Book
Postlethwaite Genealogical Collection
Trinity Episcopal Church Records
Benjamin L. C. Wailes Diaries
Benjamin L. C. Wailes Papers
Works Progress Administration Historical Records Survey, Adams County, Mississippi, RG #60

Special Collections Library, Duke University, Durham, North Carolina

Benjamin L. C. Wailes Diaries

FEDERAL GOVERNMENT RECORDS

U.S. Bureau of the Census. Manuscript Agricultural Schedules, Schedule IV, Adams County and Issaquena County, Mississippi, 1850 and 1860

U.S. Bureau of the Census. Manuscript Agricultural Schedules, Schedule IV, Pointe Coupee Parish, St. Mary Parish, and Tensas Parish, Louisiana, 1850 and 1860

U.S. Bureau of the Census. Manuscript General Population Schedules, Schedule I, Adams County, Mississippi, 1820, 1830, 1840, 1850, and 1860

U.S. Bureau of the Census. Manuscript General Population Schedules, Schedule I, St. Mary Parish, Louisiana, 1840

U.S. Bureau of the Census. Manuscript Slave Schedules, Schedule II, Adams County, Issaquena County, and Tippah County, Mississippi, 1850 and 1860

U.S. Bureau of the Census. Manuscript Slave Schedules, Schedule II, St. Mary Parish and Tensas Parish, Louisiana, 1850 and 1860

COUNTY, PARISH, AND CITY RECORDS

Adams County Courthouse, Natchez, Mississippi

Adams County Deed Records, Office of the Chancery Clerk
Adams County Marriage Records

Alcorn County Courthouse, Corinth, Mississippi

Alcorn County Deed Records, Office of the Chancery Clerk

Assumption Parish Courthouse, Napoleonville, Louisiana

Assumption Parish Conveyance Records, Office of the Clerk of Court

Issaquena County Courthouse, Mayersville, Mississippi

Issaquena County Deed Records, Office of the Chancery Clerk

New York City Municipal Archives, New York

New York City Department of Records, Death Records

Oktibbeha County Courthouse, Starkville, Mississippi

Oktibbeha County Deed Records, Office of the Chancery Clerk

Pointe Coupee Parish Courthouse, New Roads, Louisiana

Pointe Coupee Parish Land Conveyance Records, Office of the Clerk of Court

St. Mary Parish Courthouse, Franklin, Louisiana

St. Mary Parish Conveyance Records, Office of the Clerk of Court
St. Mary Parish General Mortgage Records, Office of the Clerk of Court

Tensas Parish Courthouse, St. Joseph, Louisiana

Tensas Parish Conveyance Records, Office of the Clerk of Court

Tippah County Courthouse, Ripley, Mississippi

Tippah County Deed Records, Office of the Chancery Clerk

Washington County Courthouse, Greenville, Mississippi

Washington County Deed Records, Office of the Chancery Clerk

Wilkinson County Courthouse, Woodville, Mississippi

Wilkinson County Deed Records, Office of the Chancery Clerk

NEWSPAPERS AND PERIODICALS

American Cotton Planter
Natchez Ariel
Natchez Courier
New York Times
Philadelphia Gazette and Commercial Intelligencer

PUBLISHED GOVERNMENT RECORDS AND DOCUMENTS

Journal of the Convention of the State of Mississippi. Jackson, Miss.: Peter Isler, 1832.

U.S. Bureau of the Census. *Population of the United States in 1860, Compiled from the Original Returns of the Eighth Census.* Washington, D.C.: Government Printing Office, 1864.

————. *The Seventh Census of the United States: 1850.* Washington, D.C.: Robert Armstrong, 1853.

U.S. Court of Claims. Brief for Claimants. Executors of Stephen Duncan, Deceased, v. United States. No. 2756. December Term, 1874.

U.S. Department of State. *Census for 1820.* Washington, D.C.: Gales and Seaton, 1821.

————. *Fifth Census, or Enumeration of the Inhabitants of the United States.* Washington, D.C.: Duff Green, 1832.

————. *Sixth Census, or Enumeration of the Inhabitants of the United States as Corrected at the Department of State, in 1840.* Washington, D.C.: Blair and Rives, 1841.

PUBLISHED PRIMARY SOURCES

Annual Reports of the American Society for Colonizing the Free People of Colour of the United States. Vols. 20, 22–51. 1818–1910. Reprint, New York: Negro Universities Press, 1969.

Baldwin, Joseph G. *The Flush Times of Alabama and Mississippi: A Series of Sketches.* 1853. Reprint, Baton Rouge: Louisiana State University Press, 1987.

Berlin, Ira, et al., eds. *The Black Military Experience.* In *Freedom: A Documentary History of Emancipation, 1861–1867,* ser. 2. New York: Cambridge University Press, 1982.

———— et al., eds. *The Wartime Genesis of Free Labor: The Lower South.* Vol. 3 in *Freedom: A Documentary History of Emancipation, 1861–1867,* ser. 1. New York: Cambridge University Press, 1990.

Blaine, James G. *The Blaine Family: James Blaine, Emigrant, and His Children.* Cincinnati: Ebbert and Richardson, 1920.

Breeden, James O. *Advice among Masters: The Ideal in Slave Management in the Old South.* Westport, Conn.: Greenwood Press, 1980.

Butler, Pierce. *The Unhurried Years: Memories of the Old Natchez Region.* Baton Rouge: Louisiana State University Press, 1948.

Catterall, Helen Tunnicliff. *Judicial Cases Concerning American Slavery and the Negro.* 5 vols. Washington, D.C.: Carnegie Institute of Washington, 1926–1937.

Cauthen, Charles E., ed. *Family Letters of the Three Wade Hamptons, 1782–1901.* Columbia: University of South Carolina Press, 1953.

Claiborne, J. F. H. *Mississippi, as a Province, Territory, and State, with Biographical Notices of Eminent Citizens.* Jackson, Miss.: Power and Barksdale, 1880.

Donnan, Elizabeth, ed. *Documents Illustrative of the History of the Slave Trade to America.* 4 vols. Washington, D.C.: Carnegie Institution of Washington, 1953.

Fenhagen, Mary Pringle. "Descendants of Judge Robert Pringle." *South Carolina Historical Magazine* 62 (October 1962): 221–36.

General Catalogue of the Medical Graduates of the University of Pennsylvania, with an Historical Sketch of the Origins, Programs, and Present State of the Medical Department. 3rd ed. Philadelphia: Lydia R. Bailey, 1845.

Goodspeed's Biographical and Historical Memoirs of Mississippi, Embracing an Authentic and Comprehensive Account of the Chief Events in the History of the United States, and a Record of the Lives of Many of the Most Worthy and Illustrious Families and Individuals. 2 vols. Chicago: Goodspeed, 1891.

Gould, Virginia Meacham, ed. *Chained to the Rock of Adversity: To Be Free, Black, and Female in the Old South.* Athens: University of Georgia Press, 1998.

Gray, Thomas R., ed. *The Confessions of Nat Turner, the Leader of the Late Insurrection in Southampton, VA.* Baltimore: Lucas and Deafer, 1831.

————. *The Pursuit of a Dream*. New York: Oxford University Press, 1981.

History of Cumberland and Adams Counties, Pennsylvania. Chicago: Warner, Beers, 1886.

Hogan, William R., and Edwin A. Davis, eds. *William Johnson's Natchez: The Antebellum Diary of a Free Negro*. 3rd ed. Baton Rouge: Louisiana State University Press, 1993.

Maxwell, W. J., comp. *General Alumni Catalogue of the University of Pennsylvania*. Philadelphia: University of Pennsylvania General Alumni Society, 1917.

Parkinson, Sarah Woods. *Memories of Carlisle's Old Graveyard*. Carlisle: Mary Kirtley Lamberton, 1930.

Rowland, Dunbar, ed. *Mississippi, Comprising Sketches of Counties, Towns, Events, Institutions, and Persons, Arranged in Cyclopedic Form*. 3 vols. 1907. Reprint, Spartanburg, S.C.: The Reprint Company, 1976.

Reed, George L., ed. *Alumni Record, Dickinson College*. Carlisle, Pa.: Dickinson College, 1905.

Smith, Katherine Duncan. *The Story of Thomas Duncan and His Six Sons*. New York: Tobias A. Wright, 1928.

Weaver, Gustine Courson. *The Gustine Compendium*. Cincinnati: Powell and White, 1929.

Wiley, Bell I., ed. *Slaves No More: Letters from Liberia, 1833–1869*. Lexington: University of Kentucky Press, 1980.

SECONDARY SOURCES

Abrahams, Roger D. *Singing the Master: The Emergence of African American Culture in the Plantation South*. New York: Pantheon Books, 1992.

Anderson, Margo J. *The American Census: A Social History*. New Haven: Yale University Press, 1988.

Aptheker, Herbert. *American Negro Slave Revolts*. 5th ed. New York: International Publishers, 1987.

Arena, C. Richard. "Philadelphia—Mississippi Valley Trade and the Deposit Closure of 1802." *Pennsylvania History* 30 (January 1963): 28–45.

Bailyn, Bernard. *Voyagers to the West: A Passage in the Peopling of America on the Eve of Revolution*. New York: Alfred A. Knopf, 1986.

Bancroft, Frederic. *Slave Trading in the Old South*. 1931. Reprint, New York: Frederick Ungar, 1959.

Baptist, Edward E. *Creating an Old South: Middle Florida's Plantation Frontier before the Civil War*. Chapel Hill: University of North Carolina Press, 2002.

Bateman, Fred, James Foust, and Thomas Weiss. "The Participation of Planters in Manufacturing in the Antebellum South." *Agricultural History* 48 (April 1974): 277–97.

Beckles, Hilary McD. *Natural Rebels: A Social History of Enslaved Black Women in Barbados.* New Brunswick, N.J.: Rutgers University Press, 1989.

Berlin, Ira. *Slaves without Masters: The Free Negro in the Antebellum South.* New York: Oxford University Press, 1974.

Beyan, Amos J. *The American Colonization Society and the Creation of the Liberian State: A Historical Perspective, 1822–1900.* Lanham, Md.: University Press of America, 1991.

Billingsley, Carolyn Earle. *Communities of Kinship: Antebellum Families and the Settlement of the Cotton Frontier.* Athens: University of Georgia Press, 2004.

Billington, Ray A. *Westward Expansion: A History of the American Frontier.* 4th ed. New York: Macmillan, 1974.

Blassingame, John W. *The Slave Community: Plantation Life in the Antebellum South.* 2nd ed. New York: Oxford University Press, 1979.

Bleser, Carol, ed. *In Joy and in Sorrow: Women, Family, and Marriage in the Victorian South, 1830–1900.* New York: Oxford University Press, 1991.

Bolton, Charles C. *Poor Whites of the Antebellum South: Tenants and Laborers in Central North Carolina and Northeast Mississippi.* Durham, N.C.: Duke University Press, 1994.

Bond, Bradley. *Political Culture in the Nineteenth-Century South: Mississippi, 1830–1900.* Baton Rouge: Louisiana State University Press, 1995.

Bowman, Shearer Davis. *Masters and Lords: Mid-Nineteenth-Century U.S. Planters and Prussian Junkers.* New York: Oxford University Press, 1993.

Braude, Ann. *Radical Spirits: Spiritualism and Women's Rights in Nineteenth-Century America.* Boston: Beacon Press, 1989.

Brazy, Martha Jane. "An American Planter: Slavery, Entrepreneurship, and Identity in the Life of Stephen Duncan, 1787–1867." Ph.D. dissertation, Duke University, 1998.

———. "The World a Slaveholder Made: Stephen Duncan and Plantation Society." M.A. thesis, University of Wisconsin–Milwaukee, 1987.

Bridgeforth, Lucie Robertson. "Mississippi's Response to Nullification, 1833." *Journal of Mississippi History* 45 (February 1983): 1–21.

Burton, Orville Vernon. *In My Father's House Are Many Mansions: Family and Community in Edgefield, South Carolina.* Chapel Hill: University of North Carolina Press, 1985.

Bush, Barbara. *Slave Women in Caribbean Society, 1650–1838.* Bloomington: Indiana University Press, 1990.

Bynum, Victoria. *Unruly Women: The Politics of Social and Sexual Control in the Old South.* Chapel Hill: University of North Carolina Press, 1992.

Camp, Stephanie M. H. *Closer to Freedom: Enslaved Women and Everyday Resistance in the Plantation South.* Chapel Hill: University of North Carolina Press, 2004.

Cashin, Joan E. *Family Venture: Men and Women on the Southern Frontier.* Baltimore: Johns Hopkins University Press, 1991.

Cecelski, David S. *The Waterman's Song: Slavery and Freedom in Maritime North Carolina.* Chapel Hill: University of North Carolina Press, 2001.

Censer, Jane Turner. *North Carolina Planters and Their Children, 1800–1860.* Baton Rouge: Louisiana State University Press, 1984.

Civic Club of Carlisle. *Carlisle Old and New.* Harrisburg, Pa.: J. Horace McFarland, 1907.

Clinton, Catherine, ed. *Half Sisters of History: Southern Women and the American Past.* Durham, N.C.: Duke University Press, 1994.

————. *The Plantation Mistress: Woman's World in the Old South.* New York: Pantheon Books, 1982.

Cobb, James C. *The Most Southern Place on Earth: The Mississippi Delta and the Roots of Regional Identity.* New York: Oxford University Press, 1992.

Cody, Cheryll Ann. "There Was No 'Absalom' on the Ball Plantations: Slave-Naming Practices in the South Carolina Low Country, 1720–1865." *American Historical Review* 92 (June 1987): 563–96.

Cooper, William J., Jr. *Liberty and Slavery: Southern Politics to 1860.* New York: Alfred A. Knopf, 1983.

————. *The South and the Politics of Slavery, 1828–1856.* Baton Rouge: Louisiana State University Press, 1978.

Crocker, Mary Wallace. *Historic Architecture in Mississippi.* Jackson: University and College Press of Mississippi, 1973.

David, Paul A., et al. *Reckoning with Slavery: A Critical Study in the Quantitative History of American Negro Slavery.* New York: Oxford University Press, 1976.

Davis, Angela. "Reflections on the Black Woman's Role in the Community of Slaves." *The Black Scholar* 3 (December 1971): 2–15.

————. *Women, Race, and Class.* New York: Random House, 1981.

Davis, Edwin A., ed. *The Rivers and Bayous of Louisiana.* Baton Rouge: Louisiana Education and Research Association, 1968.

Davis, R. Bruce. "The Tornado of 1840 Hits Mississippi." *Journal of Mississippi History* 36 (February 1974): 43–51.

Davis, Thomas J. *A Rumor of Revolt: The "Great Negro Plot" in Colonial New York.* New York: Free Press, 1985.

Dawes, Emma Louise McGin. "Judge Thomas Butler of Louisiana: A Biographical Study of an Ante-Bellum Jurist and Planter." M.A. thesis, Louisiana State University, 1953.

de Grummond, Jewel Lynn. "A Social History of St. Mary Parish from 1845–1860." M.A. thesis, Louisiana State University, 1948.

DeRosier, Arthur H., Jr. *The Removal of the Choctaw Indians*. Knoxville: University of Tennessee Press, 1970.

Dick, Robert C. *Black Protest: Issues and Tactics*. Westport, Conn.: Greenwood Press, 1974.

Domett, Henry W. *A History of the Bank of New York, 1784–1884*. Cambridge, Mass.: Riverside Press, 1884.

Duft, John, and Peter Mitchell, eds. *The Nat Turner Rebellion: The Historical Event and the Modern Controversy*. New York: Harper and Row, 1971.

Dupre, Daniel. *Transforming the Cotton Frontier: Madison County, Alabama, 1800–1840*. Baton Rouge: Louisiana State University Press, 1997.

Dusinberre, William. *Them Dark Days: Slavery in the American Rice Swamps*. New York: Oxford University Press, 1996.

Eaton, Clement. *The Growth of Southern Civilization, 1790–1860*. New York: Harper and Brothers, 1961.

Egerton, Douglas R. *He Shall Go Out Free: The Lives of Denmark Vesey*. Madison, Wis.: Madison House, 1999.

Elkins, Stanley M. *Slavery: A Problem in American Institutional Life*. 3rd ed. Chicago: University of Chicago Press, 1976.

Faust, Drew Gilpin. *James Henry Hammond and the Old South: A Design for Mastery*. Baton Rouge: Louisiana State University Press, 1982.

Fields, Barbara Jeanne. *Slavery and Freedom on the Middle Ground: Maryland during the Nineteenth Century*. New Haven: Yale University Press, 1985.

Fogel, Robert W. *Without Consent or Contract: The Rise and Fall of American Slavery*. New York: W. W. Norton, 1989.

———, and Stanley L. Engerman. *Time on the Cross: The Economics of American Negro Slavery*. New York: Little, Brown, 1974.

Foner, Eric. *Reconstruction: America's Unfinished Revolution, 1863–1877*. New York: Harper and Row, 1988.

Foster, Charles I. "The Colonization of the Free Negroes in Liberia, 1816–1835." *Journal of Negro History* 38 (January 1953): 41–66.

Fox-Genovese, Elizabeth. *Within the Plantation Household: Black and White Women of the Old South*. Chapel Hill: University of North Carolina Press, 1988.

Frankel, Noralee. *Freedom's Women: Black Women and Families in Civil War Era Mississippi*. Bloomington: Indiana University Press, 1999.

Franklin, John Hope. *From Slavery to Freedom: A History of African Americans*. 7th ed. New York: Alfred A. Knopf, 1994.

Freehling, William W. *Prelude to Civil War: The Nullification Controversy in South Carolina, 1816–1836*. New York: Harper and Row, 1966.

Gates, Paul. *The Farmer's Age: Agriculture, 1815–1860*. New York: Holt, Rinehart, and Winston, 1960.

Genovese, Eugene D. *From Rebellion to Revolution: Afro-American Slave Revolts in the Making of the New World*. New York: Vintage Books, 1981.

———. *The Political Economy of Slavery: Studies in the Economy and Society of the Slave South*. New York: Pantheon Books, 1965.

———. *Roll, Jordan, Roll: The World the Slaves Made*. New York: Vintage Books, 1974.

———. *The World the Slaveholders Made: Two Essays in Interpretation*. New York: Pantheon Books, 1969.

———, and Elizabeth Fox-Genovese. *Fruits of Merchant Capital: Slavery and Bourgeois Property in the Rise and Expansion of Capitalism*. New York: Oxford University Press, 1983.

Goodman, Paul. *Towards a Christian Republic: Antimasonry and the Great Transition in New England, 1826–1836*. New York: Oxford University Press, 1988.

Gray, Lewis Cecil. *History of Agriculture in the Southern United States to 1860*. 2 vols. Washington, D.C.: Carnegie Institution of Washington, 1933.

Greenberg, Kenneth S. *Masters and Statesman: The Political Culture of American Slavery*. Baltimore: Johns Hopkins University Press, 1985.

Greenfield, Sydney, et al. *Entrepreneurs in Cultural Context*. Albuquerque: University of New Mexico Press, 1979.

Gutman, Herbert G. *The Black Family in Slavery and Freedom, 1750–1925*. New York: Vintage Books, 1976.

———. *Slavery and the Numbers Game: A Critique of "Time on the Cross."* Urbana: University of Illinois Press, 1975.

Hamilton, William Baskerville. "American Beginnings in the Old Southwest." Ph.D. dissertation, Duke University, 1937.

Hammond, Bray. *Banks and Politics in America from the Revolution to the Civil War*. Princeton: Princeton University Press, 1957.

Harding, Vincent. *There Is a River: The Black Struggle for Freedom in America*. 1981. Reprint, New York: Vintage Books, 1983.

Haynes, Robert V. *The Natchez District and the American Revolution*. Jackson: University Press of Mississippi, 1976.

Hermann, Janet Sharp. *Joseph E. Davis, Pioneer Patriarch*. Jackson: University Press of Mississippi, 1990.

Homer, Sidney, and Richard Sylla. *A History of Interest Rates*. 3rd ed. New Brunswick, N.J.: Rutgers University Press, 1991.

Horsman, Reginald. *The Frontier in the Formative Years, 1783–1815*. New York: Holt, Rinehart, and Winston, 1970.

———. *Race and Manifest Destiny: The Origins of American Racial Anglo-Saxonism*. Cambridge, Mass.: Harvard University Press, 1981.

Howe, Daniel Walker. *The Political Culture of the American Whigs*. Chicago: University of Chicago Press, 1979.

Hudson, Larry E., Jr. *To Have and To Hold: Slave Work and Family Life in Antebellum South Carolina*. Athens: University of Georgia Press, 1997.

Hulse, Thomas. "The Military Slave System and the Construction of Army Fortifications along the Antebellum Gulf Coast: Mobile Point and Pensacola, 1818–1854." M.A. thesis, University of South Alabama, 2003.

Humphreys, Margaret. *Yellow Fever and the South*. New Brunswick, N.J.: Rutgers University Press, 1992.

James, D. Clayton. *Antebellum Natchez*. Baton Rouge: Louisiana State University Press, 1968.

Johnson, Michael P. "Denmark Vesey and His Co-Conspirators." *William and Mary Quarterly*. 3rd ser., 58 (October 2001): 915–16.

Johnson, Walter. *Soul by Soul: Life inside the Antebellum Slave Market*. Cambridge, Mass.: Harvard University Press, 1999.

Jones, Jacqueline. *Labor of Love, Labor of Sorrow: Black Women, Work, and the Family from Slavery to the Present*. New York: Basic Books, 1985.

Jones, Norrece T., Jr. *Born a Child of Freedom, Yet a Slave: Mechanisms of Control and Strategies of Resistance in Antebellum South Carolina*. Middletown, Conn.: Wesleyan University Press, 1990.

Jordan, Winthrop D. *Tumult and Silence at Second Creek: An Inquiry into a Civil War Slave Conspiracy*. Baton Rouge: Louisiana State University Press, 1995.

———. *White over Black: American Attitudes towards the Negro, 1550–1812*. Chapel Hill: University of North Carolina Press, 1968.

Joyner, Charles. *Down by the Riverside: A South Carolina Slave Community*. Urbana: University of Illinois Press, 1984.

Kane, Harnett T. *Natchez on the Mississippi*. New York: Bonanza Books, 1947.

Kapsch, Robert J. "The Use of Numerical Taxonomy in the Study of Historical Buildings in the Natchez, Mississippi, Area." Ph.D. dissertation, Catholic University of America, 1982.

Kerr, Norwood Allen. "The Mississippi Colonization Society (1800–1860)." *Journal of Mississippi History* 43 (February 1981): 1–30.

Kilbourne, Richard H. *Debt, Investment, Slaves: Credit Relations in East Feliciana Parish, Louisiana, 1825–1885*. Tuscaloosa: University of Alabama Press, 1995.

Killens, John Oliver, ed. *The Trial of Denmark Vesey*. Boston: Beacon Press, 1970.

King, Wilma. *Stolen Childhood: Slave Youth in Nineteenth-Century America*. Bloomington: Indiana University Press, 1995.

Kolchin, Peter. *American Slavery, 1619–1877*. New York: Hill and Wang, 1993.

Kulikoff, Allan. *Tobacco and Slaves: The Development of Southern Cultures in the Chesapeake, 1680–1800*. Chapel Hill: University of North Carolina Press, 1986.

Lane, Mills. *Architecture of the Old South: Mississippi and Alabama*. New York: Beehive Press, 1989.

Lebsock, Suzanne. *The Free Women of Petersburg: Status and Culture in a Southern Town, 1784–1860*. New York: W. W. Norton, 1984.

Levine, Lawrence W. *Black Culture and Black Consciousness: Afro-American Folk Thought from Slavery to Freedom*. New York: Oxford University Press, 1977.

Litwack, Leon F. *North of Slavery: The Negro in the Free States, 1790–1860*. Chicago: University of Chicago Press, 1961.

Lofton, John. *Denmark Vesey's Revolt: The Slave Plot That Lit a Fuse to Fort Sumter*. Kent, Ohio: Kent State University Press, 1983.

Lowery, Charles D. "The Great Migration to the Mississippi Territory." *Journal of Mississippi History* 30 (August 1968): 173–92.

Malone, Ann Patton. *Sweet Chariot: Slave Family and Household Structure in Nineteenth-Century Louisiana*. Chapel Hill: University of North Carolina Press, 1992.

May, Robert E. *John A. Quitman: Old South Crusader*. Baton Rouge: Louisiana State University Press, 1985.

McCall, Edith. *Conquering the Rivers: Henry Miller Shreve and the Navigation of America's Inland Waterways*. Baton Rouge: Louisiana State University Press, 1984.

McClelland, Peter D., and Richard J. Zeckhauser. *Demographic Dimensions of the New Republic: American Interregional Migration, Vital Statistics, and Manumissions, 1800–1860*. Cambridge, Eng.: Cambridge University Press, 1982.

McDaniel, George W. *Hearth and Home: Preserving a People's Culture*. Philadelphia: Temple University Press, 1982.

McKee, Jesse O., and Jon A. Schlenker. *The Choctaws: Cultural Evolution of a Native American Tribe*. Jackson: University Press of Mississippi, 1980.

McKibben, Davidson Burns. "Negro Slave Insurrections in Mississippi, 1800–1835." *Journal of Negro History* 34 (January 1949): 73–94.

McLemore, Richard A., ed. *A History of Mississippi*. 2 vols. Jackson: University Press of Mississippi, 1973.

McWhiney, Grady. "Were the Southern Whigs a Class Party in Alabama?" *Journal of Southern History* 22 (November 1957): 510–17.

Mehlinger, Louis R. "The Attitude of the Free Negro toward African Colonization." *Journal of Negro History* 1 (July 1916): 276–301.

Meinig, Donald W. *The Shaping of America: A Geographical Perspective on Five Hundred Years of History*. Vol. 2 of *Continental America, 1800–1867*. New Haven: Yale University Press, 1993.

Menn, Joseph Karl. *The Large Slaveholders of Louisiana, 1860*. New Orleans: Pelican, 1964.

Miles, Edwin A. *Jacksonian Democracy in Mississippi*. Chapel Hill: University of North Carolina Press, 1960.

Moncrief, Sandra. "The Mississippi Married Women's Property Act of 1839." *Journal of Mississippi History* 47 (May 1985): 110–25.

Moore, John Hebron. *Andrew Brown and Cypress Lumbering in the Old Southwest.* Baton Rouge: Louisiana State University Press, 1967.

———. *The Emergence of the Cotton Kingdom in the Old Southwest: Mississippi, 1770–1860.* Baton Rouge: Louisiana State University Press, 1988.

———. "Mississippi's Ante-Bellum Textile Industry." *Journal of Mississippi History* 16 (April 1954): 81–98.

———. "Railroads of Antebellum Mississippi." *Journal of Mississippi History* 41 (February 1979): 53–81.

———. "Two Documents Relating to Plantation Overseers of the Vicksburg Region, 1831–1832." *Journal of Mississippi History* 16 (January 1954): 31–36.

Morgan, Edmund S. *American Slavery, American Freedom: The Ordeal of Colonial Virginia.* New York: W. W. Norton, 1975.

Morgan, Jennifer L. *Laboring Women: Reproduction and Gender in New World Slavery.* Philadelphia: University of Pennsylvania Press, 2004.

Morris, Christopher. *Becoming Southern: The Evolution of a Way of Life, Warren County and Vicksburg, Mississippi, 1770–1860.* New York: Oxford University Press, 1995.

———. "An Event in Community Organization: The Mississippi Slave Insurrection Scare of 1835." *Journal of Social History* 22 (Fall 1988): 93–111.

Mullin, Gerald W. *Flight and Rebellion: Slave Resistance in Eighteenth-Century Virginia.* New York: Oxford University Press, 1972.

Nash, Gary B., and Jean Soderlund. *Freedom by Degrees: Emancipation in Pennsylvania and Its Aftermath.* New York: Oxford University Press, 1991.

North, Douglass C. *The Economic Growth of the United States, 1790–1860.* Englewood Cliffs, N..J: Prentice-Hall, 1962.

Oakes, James. *The Ruling Race: A History of American Slaveholders.* New York: Alfred A. Knopf, 1982.

———. *Slavery and Freedom: An Interpretation of the Old South.* New York: Alfred A. Knopf, 1990.

Oates, Stephen B. *The Fires of Jubilee: Nat Turner's Fierce Rebellion.* New York: Harper and Row, 1975.

Okihiro, Gary Y., ed. *In Resistance: Studies in African, Caribbean, and Afro-America History.* Amherst: University of Massachusetts Press, 1986.

Olsen, Christoper J. *Political Culture and Secession in Mississippi: Masculinity, Honor, and the Antiparty Tradition, 1830–1860.* New York: Oxford University Press, 2000.

Owens, Leslie H. *This Species of Property: Slave Life in the Old South.* New York: Oxford University Press, 1976.

Pearson, Edward A., ed. *Designs against Charleston: The Trial Record of the Denmark Vesey Slave Conspiracy of 1822.* Chapel Hill: University of North Carolina Press, 1999.

Pearson, Edward, et al. "Forum: The Making of a Slave Conspiracy, Part 2." *William and Mary Quarterly*, 3rd ser., 59 (January 2002): 135–202.

Phillips, Ulrich B. *American Negro Slavery: A Survey of the Supply, Employment, and Control of Negro Labor as Determined by the Plantation Regime*. 1918. Reprint, Baton Rouge: Louisiana State University Press, 1966.

Polk, Noel, ed. *Natchez before 1830*. Jackson: University Press of Mississippi, 1989.

Powell, Lawrence N. *New Masters: Northern Planters during the Civil War and Reconstruction*. New Haven: Yale University Press, 1980.

Preyer, Norris W. "The Historian, the Slave, and the Ante-Bellum Textile Industry." *Journal of Negro History* 46 (April 1961): 67–82.

Raboteau, Albert J. *Slave Religion: The "Invisible Institution" in the Antebellum South*. New York: Oxford University Press, 1978.

Rawick, George P. *From Sunup to Sundown: The Making of the Black Community*. Westport, Conn.: Greenwood Press, 1972.

Rawley, James A. *The Transatlantic Slave Trade: A History*. New York: W. W. Norton, 1981.

Reidy, Joseph P. *From Slavery to Agrarian Capitalism in the Cotton Plantation South: Central Georgia, 1800–1880*. Chapel Hill: University of North Carolina Press, 1992.

Riley, Franklin L. "A Contribution to the History of the Colonization Movement in Mississippi." *Publications of the Mississippi Historical Society* 9 (1906): 331–414.

Rivers, Larry E. *Slavery in Florida: Territorial Days to Emancipation*. Tallahassee: University Press of Florida, 2000.

Roark, James L. *Masters without Slaves: Southern Planters in the Civil War and Reconstruction*. New York: W. W. Norton, 1977.

Robertson, David. *Denmark Vesey*. New York: Alfred A. Knopf, 1999.

Rohrbough, Malcolm J. *The Land Office Business: The Settlement and Administration of American Public Lands, 1789–1837*. New York: Oxford University Press, 1968.

———. *The Trans-Appalachian Frontier: People, Societies, and Institutions, 1775–1850*. New York: Oxford University Press, 1978.

Rosengarten, Theodore. *Tombee: Portrait of a Cotton Planter*. New York: William Morrow, 1986.

Rothstein, Morton. "The Changing Social Networks and Investment Behavior of a Slaveholding Elite in the Ante Bellum South: Some Natchez 'Nabobs,' 1800–1860." In *Entrepreneurs in Cultural Context*. Ed. Sydney M. Greenfield et al. Albuquerque: University of New Mexico Press, 1979.

———. "The Natchez Nabobs: Kinship and Friendship in an Economic Elite." In *Essays in Honor of Arthur C. Cole*. Ed. Hans L. Trefousse. New York: Burt Franklin, 1977.

———. "'The Remotest Corner': Natchez on the American Frontier." In *Natchez before 1830*. Ed. Noel Polk. Jackson: University Press of Mississippi, 1989.

Savitt, Todd L. *Medicine and Slavery: The Diseases and Health Care of Blacks in Antebellum Virginia.* Urbana: University of Illinois Press, 1978.

Scarborough, William K. "Lords or Capitalists? The Natchez Nabobs in Comparative Perspective." *Journal of Mississippi History* 54 (August 1992): 239–67.

———. *Masters of the Big House: Elite Slaveholders of the Mid-Nineteenth-Century South.* Baton Rouge: Louisiana State University Press, 2003.

———. *The Overseer: Plantation Management in the Old South.* Baton Rouge: Louisiana State University Press, 1966.

Schmitz, Mark. *Economic Analysis of Antebellum Sugar Plantations in Louisiana.* New York: Arno Press, 1977.

Schwartz, Marie Jenkins. *Born in Bondage: Growing Up Enslaved in the Antebellum South.* Cambridge, Mass.: Harvard University Press, 2000.

Schweikart, Larry. *Banking in the American South: From the Age of Jackson to Reconstruction.* Baton Rouge: Louisiana State University Press, 1987.

Scott, Anne Firor. *The Southern Lady: From Pedestal to Politics, 1830–1930.* Chicago: University of Chicago Press, 1970.

Sellers, Charles C. *Dickinson College: A History.* Middletown, Conn.: Wesleyan University Press, 1973.

Sellers, Charles G., Jr. "Who Were the Southern Whigs?" *American Historical Review* 59 (January 1954): 335–45.

Sherwood, Henry Noble. "The Formation of the American Colonization Society." *Journal of Negro History* 2 (July 1917): 209–28.

Shore, Laurence. *Southern Capitalists: The Ideological Leadership of an Elite, 1832–1885.* Chapel Hill: University of North Carolina Press, 1986.

Shryock, Richard H. *Medical Licensing in America, 1650–1965.* Baltimore: Johns Hopkins University Press, 1967.

Sinha, Manisha. *The Counterrevolution of Slavery: Politics and Ideology in Antebellum South Carolina.* Chapel Hill: University of North Carolina Press, 2000.

Sitterson, J. Carlyle. *Sugar Country: The Cane Sugar Industry in the South, 1753–1950.* Lexington: University of Kentucky Press, 1953.

———. "The William J. Minor Plantations: A Study in Ante-Bellum Absentee Ownership." *Journal of Southern History* 9 (February 1943): 59–67.

Smith, Joseph B. "A Frontier Experiment with Higher Education: Dickinson College, 1783–1800." *Pennsylvania History* 16 (January 1949): 1–19.

Soltow, Lee. *Men and Wealth in the United States, 1850–1870.* New Haven: Yale University Press, 1975.

Stampp, Kenneth M. *The Peculiar Institution: Slavery in the Ante-Bellum South.* New York: Vintage Books, 1956.

Starobin, Robert S. "Industrial Slavery in the Old South, 1790–1861: A Study in Political Economy." Ph.D. dissertation, University of California, Berkeley, 1968.

Steady, Filomina Chioma, ed. *The Black Woman Cross-Culturally.* Cambridge, Mass.: Schenkman, 1981.

Steckel, Richard H. "A Peculiar Population: The Nutrition, Health, and Mortality of American Slaves from Childhood to Maturity." *Journal of Economic History* 46 (September 1986): 721–41.

Stevenson, Brenda E. *Life in Black and White: Family and Community in the Slave South.* New York: Oxford University Press, 1996.

Stietenroth, Charles. *One Hundred Years with Old Trinity Church, Natchez, Mississippi.* Natchez: Natchez Printing and Stationery, 1922.

Stowe, Steven. *Intimacy and Power in the Old South: Ritual in the Lives of the Planters.* Baltimore: Johns Hopkins University Press, 1987.

Sydnor, Charles S. *The Development of Southern Sectionalism, 1819–1848.* Baton Rouge: Louisiana State University Press, 1948.

———. *Slavery in Mississippi.* New York: Appleton-Century, 1933.

Temin, Peter. *The Jacksonian Economy.* New York: W. W. Norton, 1969.

Thornton, J. Mills, III. *Politics and Power in a Slave Society: Alabama, 1800–1860.* Baton Rouge: Louisiana State University Press, 1978.

Tragle, Henry Irving, ed. *The Southampton Slave Revolt of 1831.* Amherst: University of Massachusetts Press, 1971.

Trefousse, Hans L., ed. *Essays in Honor of Arthur C. Cole.* New York: Burt Franklin, 1977.

Trussel, James, and Richard Steckel. "The Age of Slaves at Menarche and Their First Birth." *Journal of Interdisciplinary History* 8 (Winter 1978): 477–505.

Vaughn, William Preston. *The Antimasonic Party in the United States, 1826–1843.* Lexington: University of Kentucky Press, 1983.

Vlach, John M. *Back of the Big House: The Architecture of Plantation Slavery.* Chapel Hill: University of North Carolina Press, 1993.

Wade, Richard C. *Slavery in the Cities: The South, 1820–1860.* New York: Oxford University Press, 1964.

Wainwright, Nicholas. *The Irvine Story.* Philadelphia: Pennsylvania Historical Society, 1964.

Walston, Mark L. "'Uncle Tom's Cabin' Revisited: Origins and Interpretations of Slave Housing in the American South." *Southern Studies* 24 (1985): 357–73.

Watkins, James L. *King Cotton: A Historical and Statistical Review, 1790–1908.* New York: James L. Watkins and Sons, 1908.

Wayne, Michael. *The Reshaping of Plantation Society: The Natchez District, 1860–1880.* Baton Rouge: Louisiana State University Press, 1983.

Weaver, Herbert. *Mississippi Farmers, 1850–1860.* Nashville: Vanderbilt University Press, 1945.

Webber, Thomas L. *Deep Like the Rivers: Education in the Slave Quarter Community, 1831–1865.* New York: W. W. Norton, 1978.

Weems, Robert C., Jr. "The Bank of the Mississippi: A Pioneer Bank of the Old Southwest, 1809–1844." Ph.D. dissertation, Columbia University, 1951.

———. "The Makers of the Bank of the Mississippi." *Journal of Mississippi History* 15 (July 1953): 137–54.

———. "Mississippi's First Banking System." *Journal of Mississippi History* 29 (November 1967): 386–408.

Weiner, Marli F. *Mistresses and Slaves: Plantation Women in South Carolina, 1830–1880.* Urbana: University of Illinois Press, 1998.

White, Deborah Gray. *Ar'n't I a Woman: Female Slaves in the Plantation South.* New York: W. W. Norton, 1985.

Wiener, Jonathan M. *Social Origins of the New South: Alabama, 1860–1885.* Baton Rouge: Louisiana State University Press, 1978.

Williams, George Washington. *History of the Negro Race in America, 1619–1880.* New York: Arno Press, 1968.

Windley, Lathan. *A Profile of Runaway Slaves in Virginia and South Carolina from 1730 through 1787.* New York: Garland, 1995.

———. *Runaway Slave Advertisements: A Documentary History from the 1730s to 1790.* 4 vols. Westport, Conn.: Greenwood Press, 1983.

Wood, Peter H. *The Black Majority: Negroes in Colonial South Carolina from 1670 through the Stono Rebellion.* New York: W. W. Norton, 1975.

Woodman, Harold D. *King Cotton and His Retainers: Financing and Marketing the Cotton Crop of the South, 1800–1925.* Lexington: University of Kentucky Press, 1968.

Wright, Gavin. "'Economic Democracy' and the Concentration of Agricultural Wealth in the Cotton South, 1850–1860." *Agricultural History* 44 (January 1970): 63–85.

Wyatt-Brown, Bertram. *Southern Honor: Ethics and Behavior in the Old South.* New York: Oxford University Press, 1982.

Young, Amy L. "Archaeological Investigations of Slave Housing at Saragossa Plantation, Natchez, Mississippi." *Southeastern Archaeology* 18, Issue 1 (Summer 1999): 57–69.

Young, Jeffery R. *Domesticating Slavery: The Master Class in Georgia and South Carolina, 1670–1837.* Chapel Hill: University of North Carolina Press, 1999.

INDEX

Milton Keynes UK
Ingram Content Group UK Ltd.
UKHW012234050324
438739UK00018B/273